Epic Reinvented

Epic Reinvented

EZRA POUND AND
THE VICTORIANS

Mary Ellis Gibson

Cornell University Press

Ithaca and London

First published 1995 by Cornell University Press.

Library of Congress Cataloging-in-Publication Data

Gibson, Mary Ellis, 1952–
    Epic reinvented : Ezra Pound and the Victorians / Mary Ellis
Gibson.
        p. cm.
    Includes bibliographical references and index.
    ISBN 0-8014-3133-6 (cloth : alk. paper)
    1. Pound, Ezra, 1885–1972—Political and social views.   2. Pound,
Ezra, 1885–1972—Knowledge—Literature.   3. Pound, Ezra, 1885–1972.
Cantos.   4. English literature—19th century—History and criticism.
5. Politics and literature—United States—History—20th century.
6. Politics and literature—Great Britain—History—19th century.
7. Modernism (Literature)   8. Epic poetry, American—English
influences.   I. Title.
PS3531.082Z6345   1995
811'.52—dc20   95-19546

Printed in the United States of America

♾ The paper in this book meets the minimum requirements
of the American National Standard for Information Sciences—
Permanence of Paper for Printed Library Materials, ANSI Z39.48-1984.

For William Harmon

Contents

Preface

"You have no cosmos until you can order it," Ezra Pound declared in a draft of the early cantos. His warning anticipated the difficulties he was to face in inventing epic for modern readers. Pound assumed a cosmos that is disordered, fragmented, not properly speaking a cosmos at all. The poet's job, accordingly, is a struggle toward order. *The Cantos* remain a compelling poem because Pound's utopian project of creating cosmos was developed in the very difficulties that in many ways still form the cultural possibilities of art.

Many observers of modernism and modern culture have argued that radical right-wing politics, fascism particularly, often aestheticized the political; it is also commonly understood that one role of the avant-garde in creating modernism was overtly to politicize the aesthetic. My goal in this book is to examine how these tendencies connect. I believe, however, that such questions of art and politics when considered too abstractly lose their original claims on our attention. By focusing on Ezra Pound and on the particularity of his historical position I examine concretely a central example of how politics were aestheticized in the modernist moment; at the same time I examine in detail the ways construction of literary tradition and experiments with poetic form themselves entailed a politics.

My work places Pound's poetry in the context of nineteenth-century poetics and historiography and connects this context to modern politics; I argue that Pound's search for cosmos intensified contradictions already evident in Victorian culture. In the poetic tradition he inherited most immediately from Robert Browning, the belief in historical

order or aesthetic unity was countered by the skepticism and the ironies of existential historicism. The poet was as much a picker of historical bones as a prophet. Yet despite the marginal status of the
serious artist and the substantial attractions of historicist ironies,
Pound was, like his predecessors Carlyle, Ruskin, and Morris, per-
suaded that art and society were inextricably linked: greatness in either depended on greatness in both.

In tracing Pound's connections to his Victorian predecessors, I show
how the attempt at writing a postromantic epic engaged at once questions of art and social order and led directly to the problem of Pound's
politics. It is not simply that politics impinged thematically on poetry
but that, for Pound, problems of poetic form had political as well as
poetic consequences. These I explore as they are worked out in *The
Cantos*, examining both the formal problems of the poem's increasing
need for order and the politics of the poem's utopian vision. My concern is to show how the aesthetic Pound is the political Pound, how
Pound the visionary is Pound the historian.

Because my argument has formalist, historical, and political dimensions—and because I wish to demonstrate the connection of these elements in Pound's poetic practice—this book unites several theoretical
and methodological approaches. The first three chapters rely heavily
on archival research, citing unpublished materials in order to provide
a more complete picture of how Pound constructed his own nineteenth-century canon and developed his practice of imitation. These
materials provide a much fuller understanding than heretofore possible of Pound's complex appropriation of Browning and others as he
attempted to remake poetic diction and to conceive of a historicist
epic. The connections between Browning and Pound have significance
even beyond the purview of traditional influence study; for Pound
responded to his predecessors—and to Browning especially—in an
effort to make a case for poetry's importance in the modern world.
Accordingly, my approach attends to the stylistic and thematic connections commonly drawn in studies of poetic influence, but it is also
considerably broader; I understand Pound's connections to his predecessors not philologically or as a Bloomian family romance but in
terms of his cultural situation. Extrapolating from Walter Benjamin's
meditations on modern art and collecting, I consider Pound's relations
to the nineteenth century through two dominant metaphors that themselves imply both order and fragmentation: the poet as pedagogue or
canon builder and the poet as ragpicker.

Although I emphasize Pound's connections to his nineteenth-century English predecessors, I do not intend to minimize the significance for him of numerous other writers from Confucius to Propertius to Leopardi. Many important stories about such connections have been told elsewhere. Here, however, I seek to pull together the strands of criticism already developed by Christine Froula, George Bornstein, Carol Christ, James Longenbach, and others to contend that, however important even the troubadours, or Homer, or Dante may have been, Pound was situating himself as poet in the context of an American and British taste that notably derived from nineteenth-century models. To situate himself thus and to create a space for his own art, he created from among the works of his predecessors a personal canon about which he proselytized for the rest of his life.

Canon creation was for Pound the earliest attempt, indeed a paradigmatic one, to bring order from chaos; his canon and his imitation of earlier texts are characterized by dualism and contradiction. Chapters 1–3 examine his contradictions by attending to numerous early poems and drafts, to the material conditions of publishing, and to the ideological conditions of art, showing how these conditions persisted from the nineteenth century into the twentieth. They suggest that the project of epic itself developed in these contradictions.

In Chapters 4 and 5, I turn to questions of genre, history, and form in *The Cantos*. I bring the larger considerations of the first half of the book to bear on the problem of reading *The Cantos*. Accordingly, Chapters 4 and 5 differ methodologically from the rest in moving away, temporarily, from historical argument toward explicit theoretical debate about tropological reading. In critiquing earlier tropological theories and particular readings of *The Cantos*, I examine the value judgments implicit in them. On this basis, I engage directly the ongoing controversy that links modernism, fascism, and poststructuralist theory. The rhetorical tropology I develop resists the poststructuralist tendency to celebrate *The Cantos* as a metonymic epic. It resists as well both the early tendency in Pound scholarship to deny Pound's politics and the later tendency to divorce questions of politics and history from questions of form, genre, or diction. Though I have learned much from various arguments about Pound and tropes and much from Jean-Michel Rabaté's Lacanian reading of *The Cantos*, my own stance is closer to Jerome McGann's effort to read Pound under the sign of catastrophe and to work since the 1980s by Michael North and Lawrence Rainey; and though I have profited particularly by discussions of Pound's politics from William Chace's to Robert Casillo's and Tim Redman's, I have used such work in the service of an argument that attends to connections between politics and form, ideology and literary history. In attending simultaneously to poetics and politics, I assert in Chapters 4 and 5 that *The Cantos* proceed both metaphorically and metonymically. I show how particular metonymies and metaphors are caught up in the dualities of beauty and violence, order and chaos which the poem attempts to negotiate.

In Chapters 6 and 7, I return to the Victorian roots of Pound's poetic and political dualisms. Contending that he combined radical individualism with a radical desire for order, I argue that in consequence even the idealization of natural fecundity, even the Neoplatonic ideal of love in *The Cantos* are bound up with misogyny and other forms of violence. *The Cantos* are thus a doubled form where epic meets elegy and where an ideal order cannot, finally, be wrested from the fragments of modern culture.

My theoretical stance, then, moves from historical and cultural argument to tropological argument and back to explicit consideration of the ways Pound's historical situation formed his poetic practice. Whether we consider his work in its material and ideological contexts, or through a rhetorical tropology, or with attention to the cultural meanings of particular metonymies and metaphors, we see that Pound understood both literary and cultural history through a series of fundamental and unresolvable dualisms. He repeatedly sought to bring together aestheticist and realist practices of art, metaphorical and metonymic conceptualizations of history, epic and elegy, utopian vision and an almost overwhelming sense of cultural chaos. For Pound, the project of creating epic was therefore especially problematic. Epic becomes not so much rhetorical invention within common topoi as a form of cultural and historical *bricolage*. The makeshift epic is cobbled together on the fundamentally unstable premises of existential historicism, but his desire for order and the social and generic imperatives of epic defy the ironic equipoise of earlier historicism. The need for telos defies the antiteleological nature of the poetic or historical ragbag.

Despite the tensions in Pound's own work between telos and chaos, I have tried to render orderly a meditation on his contradictions, which can be understood in terms of literary history, genre, tropes, political thought, gender and sexuality, or in terms of his particular historical situation. My book moves dialectically among these understandings. At the same time, I treat Pound's poems for the most part in the order of their composition.

Chapter 1 examines how Pound constructed a nineteenth-century canon and why in that canon Browning had a central place. After a framing discussion of existential historicism, I analyze how Pound's celebration of the prose tradition in verse was his means of resisting fin-de-siècle aestheticism. The prose tradition is represented by James, Flaubert, Browning, and finally by Ford Madox Ford, who was for Pound a significant bridge between nineteenth- and twentieth-century letters. I examine both Ford's poetry and Browning's importance in Pound's responses to it. Despite Ford's and Pound's appropriation of Browning to an anti-aestheticist project, within Browning's own work was a complex relation to aestheticism, which Pound discovered also in the work of Walter Pater. Browning's and, still more, Pater's historicisms contained their own uneasy compromises with aestheticism, and thus both writers made ambiguous precedessors. An unpublished typescript, seven pages of prose and poetry called "In Praise of the Masters," found among Pound's college verse, demonstrates the ambiguities of his anti-aestheticist project. The work oscillates between Pateresque aestheticizing and a rough voice usually associated in Pound's early work with Browning's poetry. "In Praise of the Masters" exhibits the contradictions in the nineteenth-century canon Pound understood himself as inheriting.

Chapter 2 continues this exploration of Pound's early poetry, including several unpublished poems and drafts. These poems offer an extraordinary window on the young Pound at work; they reveal how crucial to him was the effort to come to terms with his nineteenth-century predecessors. What in the later work becomes a furious accumulation of detail in the service of coherence or order is in these early poems the happy ragpicking of a poet much given to imitation, translation, and parody. Indeed, translation and imitation were the means by which Pound assembled the fragments of tradition. In his appropriation of previous poetry, he had a marked tendency to alternate between what he perceived as contrary aesthetics—to write first one way and then another, to bring together in radical tension often-contrary impulses, and definitions or practices of poetry.

I continue to trace Pound's contradictions in a third chapter as I consider the various early drafts of the first cantos and the relationship between epic and historical conceptualization. In the early drafts of *The Cantos*, Browning's presence is crucial, and yet in subsequent drafts Pound moves away from Browning's stance. Browning's contextualist or existential historicist view, the ragpicker's journey through the archive, is incompatible with the task of creating or discovering coherence which Pound set himself in attempting a "poem of some length." The stance of the ragpicker was problematic enough for Browning's poem of great length, *The Ring and the Book*; yet that poem so ironizes its own attempts at epic that the demands of the genre are, to a large degree, deconstructed. Pound's *Cantos* propose no such self-ironizing despite their ironic moments. Avoiding irony, Pound faced a crisis of epic authorship, a crisis that became inseparable from the crisis of social authority. Thomas Carlyle, a century earlier, had been caught in the same web when he claimed that true history was the only possible epic. In this context we can see *The Cantos* as a poem of profound divisions, both formal and thematic, and we can understand the politics implicit even in its most visionary moments. For all the models of cause and effect or heroic historical activity they propose, *The Cantos* cannot make a coherent telos of modern capitalist culture or its past. The extraordinary accumulation of texts and materials in *The Cantos* itself testifies to the scene it attempts to explain.

Chapter 4 shows how the contradictions in Pound's appropriation of poetic tradition and in his search for historical coherence can be understood if one analyzes tropes in *The Cantos*. I argue here for a rhetoric, rather than an allegory, of tropes and for a model of tropological analysis that can account for contradiction as well as coherence. I critique the poststructuralist tendency to read all tropes toward an ironic aporia and to celebrate *The Cantos* in particular as a metonymic examination of their own undoing. My rhetorical reading of Pound's tropes attends both to their structural role and to their cultural meanings. Specifically, Pound's *Cantos* operate with competing modes of historical conceptualization. A close examination of *The Fifth Decad of Cantos* shows that the poem works at once metaphorically and metonymically.

The very tropological doubling of *The Cantos* and the ideological work of specific metaphors and metonymies are the subjects of Chapters 5 and 6. Focusing on *The Pisan Cantos* in Chapter 5, I examine how Pound transforms tropes appearing earlier in the poem, and I call attention to the way the poem, after the collapse of Italian fascism, oscillates between epic and elegy. In Chapter 6, I show how even in *The Pisan Cantos*, where many critics have thought Pound somehow transcends his political errors, the visionary claim guaranteeing the poem's utopian political hopes is based in a radically dualist understanding of the feminine that itself had nineteenth-century roots. Tracing these roots, I examine the idealization and anathematization of the feminine in Pre-Raphaelite art and fin-de-siècle culture and the persistence of these attitudes in the making of modernism—in "Hugh Selwyn Mauberley," in Pound's editing of *The Waste Land*, and in his vorticist manifestos. The Italian cantos, 72 and 73, and his notes for *The Pisan Cantos* reveal the complex political dimensions of the visionary order Pound so persistently opposed to the chaos of modern culture.

Pound's hope of a new world order, in politics and in art, cannot escape the limitations of its past. *The Pisan Cantos* are implicated in the past of the whole project of *The Cantos* and in the wider historical past as well. My brief concluding chapter returns Pound's contradictions to their nineteenth-century context. Exploring his dualism and what Jerome McGann might call his "romantic illusions," I read his mythical method not as a modernist invention ex nihilo but as a modernist transformation of the romantic desire to heal a gap between word and thing, between the poet and society. The poet who works in this gap is an exile, who in Pound's understanding must make cosmos from chaos. He must become, if he can, the hero as poet. The poet who must imagine cosmos ends by aestheticizing order and power and by guaranteeing their congruence in his poem's visionary claims.

The ambiguous, and sometimes forlorn, hope of Pound's epic is based on a vision we might grasp by imagining the sorts of monuments *The Cantos* themselves put before us. Atop a pedestal, bronzed, horsed, and armed, rides an Italian condotierre, Sigismundo Malatesta or another like him; facing him, stands Aphrodite restored to her pedestal at Terracina, looking at him with blind marble eyes. In these monuments and in their historical, material, and literary contexts we come to the heart of Pound's created world; we are caught between violence and love, between power and art.

I am grateful for the assistance of many colleagues and friends who have contributed significantly to this book. I would like especially to thank James Longenbach and Gail McDonald, who read the work in manuscript, saved me from errors, and asked provocative questions. My editors, Janet Mais and Kay Scheuer, have been extraordinarily helpful. Many other colleagues, friends, and students have responded to portions of this work, and I am indebted to them for support and for many useful suggestions: Fran Arndt, Walter Beale, Jeutonne Brewer, James Chandler, Leigh Anne Couch, Keith Cushman, Mary Elder, John D'Emilio, William Harmon, Marilyn May Lombardi, Sharon Snider Ringwalt, Patricia Roberts, and Alan Shapiro. I am grateful for the helpful suggestions of the rhetoric reading group at the University of North Carolina at Greensboro, particularly to Marsha Holmes and Hephzibah Roskelly, and for the assistance of the women's studies colloquium. Like all scholars who study Ezra Pound, I have found my own work made immeasurably easier thanks to Donald Gallup's bibliography, and I have relied incalculably often on Carroll Terrell's *Companion to the Cantos*. As always, I am indebted to the editorial judgment and personal encouragement of Charles Orzech.

In the course of my research I received valuable aid from several institutions. I am grateful for a research assignment provided by the University of North Carolina at Greensboro and for the continuing assistance of the librarians at Jackson Library. This book would not have been possible without the assistance of librarians at the Poetry Magazine Collection in Regenstein Library, University of Chicago; the Southern Historical Collection at University of North Carolina at Chapel Hill; and the Beinecke Rare Book and Manuscript Library, Yale University. I am most indebted to the editors of New Directions Publishing Corporation and the trustees of the Ezra Pound Literary Property Trust for granting permission to quote both published and unpublished materials.

For permission to quote unpublished materials by Ezra Pound, grateful acknowledgment is made to the following:

Previously unpublished material by Ezra Pound, Copyright © 1995 by the Trustees of the Ezra Pound Literary Property Trust; used by permission of New Directions Publishing Corporation, agents.

Excerpts from the unpublished letters of Ezra Pound to Charleen Whisnant Swansea by permission of the Southern Historical Collection, Wilson Library, University of North Carolina at Chapel Hill and of Charleen Whisnant Swansea.

Excerpts from the unpublished letters of Ezra Pound to Harriet Monroe, from *Poetry* Magazine Papers, 1912–36, by permission of the Department of Special Collections, the University of Chicago Library.

Excerpts from the unpublished writings of Ezra Pound by permission of the Yale Collection of American Literature, Beinecke Rare Book and Manuscript Library, Yale University.

Grateful acknowledgment is also given to New Directions Publishing Corporation and Faber and Faber Ltd. for permission to quote from the following copyrighted works of Ezra Pound: *The Cantos* (Copyright © 1934, 1937, 1940, 1948, 1956, 1959, 1962, 1963, 1966, and 1968 by Ezra Pound); *Collected Early Poems* (Copyright © 1976 by the Trustees of the Ezra Pound Literary Property Trust); *Pound/Ford*

MARY ELLIS GIBSON

Greensboro, North Carolina

A Note on Texts

For the detailed and complex publishing history of Ezra Pound's early poetry, see Donald Gallup, *Ezra Pound: A Bibliography*. All published early poems are here cited as published in *Collected Early Poems* (New Directions, 1976) or in *Personae: The Shorter Poems of Ezra Pound* (New Directions, 1990, rev. ed., edited by Lea Baechler and A. Walton Litz). *Collected Early Poems* reprints Pound's early books including *A Lume Spento, A Quinzaine for This Yule, Personae, Exultations, Canzoni,* and *Ripostes,* along with withdrawn and unpublished poems. Pound republished some of these poems in the collected volume he also titled *Personae,* which forms the basis for the Baechler and Litz edition; this later version of *Personae* (1926) includes many poems written and published after the earlier volume of the same name, which was first published in 1906. In their edition of the later *Personae,* Baechler and Litz also include as an appendix the early version of ''Three Cantos'' and other uncollected poems.

Abbreviations for Works of Ezra Pound

C	*The Cantos*
CEP	*Collected Early Poems of Ezra Pound*
GB	*Gaudier-Brzeska: A Memoir*
GK	*Guide to Kulchur*
LE	*Literary Essays of Ezra Pound*
PD	*Pavannes and Divagations*
P/F	*Pound/Ford: The Story of a Literary Friendship*
P/J	*Pound/Joyce: The Letters of Ezra Pound to James Joyce*
PPC	*Ezra Pound's Poetry and Prose Contributions to Periodicals*
PSP	*Personae: The Shorter Poems of Ezra Pound*
SL	*Selected Letters of Ezra Pound, 1907–1941*
SP	*Selected Prose, 1909–1965*
SR	*The Spirit of Romance*

Epic Reinvented

Chapter 1

Pound's Nineteenth-Century Canon: Historicism, Aestheticism, and the Prose Tradition in Verse

Having discovered his own virtue the artist will be more likely to discern and allow for a peculiar *virtù* in others. The erection of the microcosmos consists in discriminating these other powers and in holding them in orderly arrangement about one's own.

> —Pound, "I Gather the Limbs of Osiris"

The historicist act revives the dead and reenacts the essential mystery of the cultural past, which, like Tiresias drinking the blood, is momentarily returned to life and warmth and allowed once more to speak its mortal speech and to deliver its long-forgotten message in surroundings unfamiliar to it.

> —Fredric Jameson, "Marxism and Historicism"

Seldom has a poet been so enthusiastic and active a pedagogue as Ezra Pound. Forever lecturing, hectoring, providing reading lists, Pound promulgated his economic and social ideas and his own version of literary history. He clearly shared the Ruskinian sense that art, economic relations, and political structures are mutually intertwined and that art is the measure of a culture's health. Hence the attractiveness for Pound of the Confucian command *cheng ming*, rectify the terminology. Such rectification, for Pound, inevitably involved hierarchy; making hierarchies in turn required an aesthetic judgment that was simultaneously a political and historical judgment. Pound claimed, in an early draft of "Three Cantos," "You have no cosmos

till you can order it" (Beinecke Library, at Yale); even earlier, in "I
Gather the Limbs of Osiris," he suggested that new art is made possible by assembling a tradition—by joining separate limbs or by uniting and ordering elements in a "microcosmos"[1] (SP, 29). Making a
literary canon was for him the earliest and paradigmatic instance of
a larger impulse toward order in art and society.

Pound's greatness and his catastrophe lay in this effort toward order as he negotiated the relationship of theory and practice in both
poetry and politics. In matters of poetic form, theory and practice were
inextricably intertwined. Through constructing a literary canon Pound
developed his own sense of what art might look like in the modern
world, a sense foundational to modernist poetics; at the same time,
and equally, the practice of poetic imitation and experimentation
formed his poetic theory. Canon creation was vital to and developed
from poetic experimentation. Political experimentation was much less
in Pound's line than linguistic experimentation, and the gap between
the theory and practice of politics explains, in significant part, the
disasters of his poetry.[2] If ultimately Pound's poetics was not a sufficient model for his politics and if his politics, conversely, could not
bring coherence to his poetics, he nevertheless persisted in the struggle
to create a cosmos sufficiently ordered for a poem of epic ambition.
Even before and certainly after this epic ambition took shape, canon
creation both enabled him to write his own poetry and was an effort
to create a culture and a history adequate to such poetry.

Both Pound's poetics and his politics are linked in complex ways
to nineteenth-century historicism. A careful examination of these connections suggests why Robert Browning was the most important immediate forebear in Pound's canon; Browning's historicism was, for
Pound, both an antidote to and a link with fin-de-siècle aestheticism.
Browning's work enabled Pound to envision a poetry that reached
into history and politics in the cultural context of fin-de-siècle art. As
he imitated and distanced himself from the Pre-Raphaelites and the
Georgian aesthetes, Pound encountered the problematic aestheticism
already implicit in nineteenth- and early twentieth-century historicism
and already resisted in Browning's poetry. But despite the difficulties

---

1. Consult the list of abbreviations for full titles of the frequently cited works of Pound.
2. Tim Redman thinks "Pound had a deficient sense of practical politics. Although this
   did not prevent him from successfully treating politics in his poetry, he lacked dis-
   cernment about the meaning of contemporary political events" (*Ezra Pound and Italian
   Fascism*, 173). I argue in subsequent chapters, as I think Redman means to imply,
   that Pound had varying degrees of success in treating contemporary political events.

within historicist thinking, Pound's essential need to write was grounded in the affective dimension of historicism, the imaginative impulse awakened by encountering figures from the past. This impulse served as an alternative to a present that Pound by 1909 was criticizing as "crepuscular" (CEP, 96).

I argue here that existential historicism furnished for Pound, as it did for his predecessors, only a precarious equipoise; it involved a balance between aestheticism and empiricism, between skepticism and utopian hopes. Ultimately he found this balance impossible and even undesirable to maintain; in his early poetry, however, he attempted to renegotiate its terms. His early efforts at canon formation were similarly driven in large part by an anti-aestheticism to which historicism could only provide ambiguous alternatives. The ambiguities of existential historicism, moreover, are given concrete form in Pound's poetic canon as well as in his poetic practice. To trace his relationship to Browning, then, is to examine Pound's attraction to historicist ways of thinking, to see why and how he constructed a nineteenth-century canon, and to define the initial contradictions within which his poetry was made.

In examining these issues I begin here by reconsidering the ambiguities in existential historicism itself. Basing my work on suggestions by Fredric Jameson and James Longenbach, I go beyond their argument that historicism threatened to devolve into aestheticism or empiricism and maintain that a utopian invocation of authority provided yet a third alternative to historicist contemplation of the past, an alternative Pound found increasingly attractive. In his early poetry, however, existential historicism functions as a tentative equipoise, one intimately tied to resisting aestheticism. In his early prose, his creation of a nineteenth-century canon was the ideological form of this resistance to aestheticism. Though his notions of art came to be profoundly influenced by his Confucianism, Pound's lifelong proselytizing for such a canon was initially and powerfully rooted in nineteenth-century attempts to value art in the face of industrial capitalism. The second half of this chapter examines how Pound read Browning's poetry differentially, as mediated through aestheticist and anti-aestheticist discourses, and it shows how this reading shaped Pound's poetic practice. If we examine his response to Ford Madox Ford's version of Browning and the Victorians and then examine Pound's complex response to Walter Pater's version of Browning, we can triangulate the ambivalences of Pound's early poetry. Both Pater's historicist aestheticism and Ford's response to his predecessors shaped the way Pound developed his own discourse of modernism and his own poetic diction. In concluding this chapter and in Chapter 2, I examine the doubled and uneasy poetics of Pound's early work. A discussion of Pound's early unpublished poem "In Praise of the Masters" exemplifies concretely the ambivalences of his response to the past.

Historicism as Precarious Equipoise

New readers of Pound's poetry are likely to start from "Hugh Selwyn Mauberley," *Cathay*, or the early cantos. In each case they find either the resuscitation of the past or reflection on that effort. Translation in *Cathay* resuscitates a culture foreign in time and place for most English and American readers; "Hugh Selwyn Mauberley" greets the reader immediately with complex ironies concerning the poet's role and the ordinary understanding of history as a "march of events"; *The Cantos* begin with a supposedly mythical encounter with spirits of the dead, an encounter complexly mediated by history. In each case, and for most of Pound's poetry, the impulse to write is deeply connected to the imaginative encounter with the past; where affective impulse meets the more properly logical dimension of poetry it is often in reflection on history or on literary history. The resuscitation of the dead, through translation or historical imagination, answers the poet's own need for a subject; it allows him to claim—without also directly claiming divine inspiration—that he tells the truth; and it serves, for Pound, as a commentary on the present.

If Keats described a kind of self-annihilation before sparrows in the gravel or a room full of people, Pound—instructed by his imitations of Browning, as well as by his reading of Keats—claims self-annihilation in the face of history. In the early poem "Histrion," he declares, modifying Browning's metaphor from *The Ring and the Book*, "'Tis as in midmost us there glows a sphere / Translucent, molten gold, that is the 'I' / And into this some form projects itself" (1908; CEP, 71). This affective process is specified even more clearly and concretely in "Provincia Deserta" (1916). Here Pound's paratactic language is itself designed to emphasize the affective power of the encounter with history or even of its recollection[3]:

3. James Longenbach discusses parataxis in the Malatesta cantos and demonstrates that it is connected to Yeats's presentation of Pater's description of the Mona Lisa at the beginning of the *Oxford Book of Modern Verse*. Such a technique avoids "the idea of linear causation in time and [stresses] the idea that all history is contemporaneous"

I have looked south from Hautefort,
           thinking of Montaignac, southward.
I have lain in Rocafixada,
           level with sunset,
Have seen the copper come down
           tingeing the mountains,
I have seen the fields, pale, clear as an emerald.
                                   (PSP, 126)

There are both immediacy and an elegiac tinge to this encounter, but Pound's emphasis is on the affective power of thinking about history: "I have walked over these roads; / I have thought of them living" (PSP, 127).

Such affective power is the poet's own impetus to write; his encounter with the past in turn furnishes commentary on the present. As early as "Revolt: Against the Crepuscular Spirit in Modern Poetry" (in the 1909 edition of *Personae*) Pound prays at least for mighty dreams to set against the thin and impoverished present, for a god to "grapple chaos and beget / Some new titanic spawn" (CEP, 97). He would prefer "men" to dreams and "shapes of power" to "shadows." In practice the "titanic spawn" become Pound's own recreations of heroic figures from the past. These, implicitly, are both colorful and powerful, as distinguished from the pale historical pageantry he associates with Georgian aestheticism and ultimately with Victorian medievalizing. In these typical moments from Pound's early poetry and in his early Browningesque monologues, such as "Cino" (1908) and "Marvoil" (1909), we can see both the attitudes crucial to existential historicism and something of the tension within historicist understandings of history (CEP, 9–12, 94–96).

In characterizing Pound as an existential historicist I am largely following Fredric Jameson's typology of historicisms and its application to Pound's poetry by James Longenbach, though my discussion has also been influenced by Hayden White's definition of contextualism (*Metahistory*, 17–21) and Maurice Mandelbaum's understanding of cultural history. Like Jameson and Longenbach, I see existential historicism as a historical view with its own built-in tensions, including the problem of aestheticism and the tendency to collapse into empiricism. Existential historicism is not uniquely a tension-ridden stance toward history, but it is more precariously balanced than providential, tragic,

---

(*Modernist Poetics*, 40). In addition to its Pateresque parataxis "Provincia Deserta" reflects the 1890s tendency to describe landscape in the language of jewels.

or cyclic understandings of history, all of which involve a powerful teleological imperative to recuperate contradictions.

Pound's historicism can best be understood in the context of historical speculation that begins with Ranke and Carlyle and finds a moment of relative coherence in the poetry of Browning, the history of Burckhardt, and the poetic history of Pater and is later theorized in the work of Dilthey, Croce, Collingwood, and Ortega.[4] The central feature of this variety of historicism is the affective encounter with history. As in Pound's "Provincia Deserta," the historian, or subject, confronts the historical object, thereby confirming both the historian's own historicity and the significance of the past to the present. As Jameson puts it, "*Historicity* as such is manifested, by means of the contact between the historian's mind in the present and a given synchronic cultural complex from the past" ("Marxism and Historicism," 157). Existential historicism begins in the romantic historiography that emphasizes the spirit of the age, in the Rankean dictum that every age is immediate to God, and in the practice of cultural history. Exploration of synchronic connections is more important than teleology or stories of development. The historian gives rapt attention to the particulars of a historical moment and so makes history a matter of vital urgency. As Jameson argues, such urgency is fundamental to any history that does not leave the past merely a dead letter. The process of historical reflection charges both past and present with significance.

The affective power of the encounter with the past is notable in existential historicist writing from Browning's introduction to *The Ring and the Book*, to Pater's conclusion to *The Renaissance*, to Dilthey's notion of *Verstehen* (Dilthey, *Pattern and Meaning*, 111–32, and Makkreel, *Dilthey*, 322–31). In this emphasis we see a profound continuity with earlier forms of romanticism, despite the fact that teleological and progressivist beliefs in the unfolding of history are abandoned or muted. In *Force and Freedom*, Jacob Burckhardt describes the historian's encounter with the past in a metaphor very like that Coleridge had used years earlier to describe imagination. The student of history, Burckhardt says, must allow the mind to "enter into a real, chemical combination, in the full sense of the word, with the original source" (98). This process transforms both the source and the historian. As in Pound's "Histrion," history and the histrionic are closely related; the

---

4. For discussion of Carlyle's early historicism and for an argument that both Ranke and Carlyle contribute to the shape of historicism in England and to the nature of Browning's historicism, see Gibson, *History and the Prism of Art*, chap. 2.

poet or historian, through contemplation of the past, is at once filled with its malleable spirit and becomes a curiously malleable mold though which the past projects itself into the present. If in the process of the historical encounter the subject is pliant, so the object becomes a focus for aesthetic contemplation. In "Provincia Deserta," Pound's object is the landscape itself, spread before the poet's mind's eye like a map of its own significance.

Such rapt contemplation of the past is necessarily antiteleological and tends to make existential historicism a kind of aestheticism.[5] The fundamental premise of any aestheticism is the difference between the object aesthetically perceived and the ordinary even when, or especially when, the ordinary becomes the object. The aesthetic impulse in existential historicism is predicated on the perceived difference or distance between the historian and the historical object. The poet contemplates history not as a march of events but as a cultural pattern different from the present.

To capture this difference without too thoroughly compromising the synchronic principle on which historicist investigation is built, Pater, Burckhardt, and Browning all evoke the image of the web in a stream. Browning, through his dubious philosopher Cleon, and Burckhardt, in his reflections on history, also use the metaphor of the mosaic to describe the contemplation of history. All these figures indicate both pattern and tenuousness, as do Browning's and Pound's description of the poet as ragpicker, which I discuss at length in the next chapter. Such figures reveal the historicist writer constituting history not in terms of telos or mechanisms of cause and effect but in terms of an aesthetically pleasing but often fleeting pattern. In the process, even scraps and detritus, the mingling of past and present, are made objects of aesthetic reflection. As Burckhardt describes the ideal history, "Beside the mutable there appears the multitudinous, the mosaic of peoples and civilizations, which we see mainly as mutual contrasts or complements. We should like to conceive a vast spiritual map on the projection of an immense ethnography, embracing both the spiritual and the material world."[6]

---

5. Jameson calls the "methodological spirit of existential historicism" a "historical and cultural aestheticism" in which all "praxis" is suspended and the historian's attitude toward the historical past is one of "aesthetic appreciation and recreation, and the diversity of cultures and historical moments becomes thereby . . . a source of immense aesthetic excitement and gratification" ("Marxism and Historicism," 157).

6. Burckhardt, *Force and Freedom*, 83–84. For a more extended treatment of these matters see Gibson, *History and the Prism of Art*, chaps. 1 and 2.

Burckhardt uses such words as "detachment," "disinterestedness," "contemplation," and "skepticism" to describe the attitude necessary to the aesthetic dimension of historicism. This attitude has self-evident tensions. The rapt attention, the "chemistry" of existential historicism is to be transmuted into "detachment." Such detachment can only imply for the historian, eventually, either the detachment from the moral consequences of one's own actions or the detachment of the present from the past.

As a kind of aestheticism, existential historicism requires paradox-ically the detached contemplation of the past and the fusion of the historian with the historical source. It demands a skeptical equipoise, particularly as it refuses to construct providential historical schemes. But inherent in this balance are the difficulties of specifying the rela-tionship of past, present, and a possible future and the perplexities of assigning significance or value to the "multitudinous" details the his-torian brings into view. Jameson identifies the political disengage-ment of sheer aestheticism as one problematic outcome of existential historicism; the other, in his view, is the devolution of history into the "meaningless succession of facts of empiricist historiography" ("Marxism and Historicism," 157). Aestheticist history makes only in-direct claims on its own historical moment; empiricist history, of the kind Thomas Carlyle derided as Dryasdust history, makes still fewer claims (*Cromwell*, *Works*, 6:8). For a poet like Browning who negotiated a complex relationship with his readers, and still more for a poet like Pound who harbored epic ambitions, aestheticism and empiricism were equally troublesome. We can see both poets resisting aestheti-cism and empiricism even as they attempted to maintain the signifi-cance of the history they chose to write about.

Browning's ironies allowed him to resist empiricism and aestheti-cism, for instance in his ironic critique of his monologuist Cleon's ironic detachment. Yet this skeptical poise had its own difficulties, reflected in the comments in Browning's own time about his relativ-ism and "multitudinousness" (see James). For Browning, moreover, skepticism and irony were consistently brought up against the prov-idential model of Christian history. Browning's monologues, *Sordello*, and to a lesser extent *The Ring and the Book* decline to sketch a prov-idential history; nevertheless, the skeptical equilibrium of Browning's irony was always tipping into a defense of skepticism itself as em-bedded in a larger providence. Such a move is most clearly evident in the Pope's monologue in *The Ring and the Book* and the "Epilogue" to *Dramatis Personae*. It entails what Elinor Shaffer has called the notion of progressive revelation ("*Kubla Khan*," 218). Browning's equipoise is in spirit very like Ranke's claims that every age is "immediate to God" and that history represents a teleology without a telos (Stern, *Varieties*, 55; Krieger, *Ranke*). Browning's multitudinousness never quite dissolves into an empiricism; his skepticism is rarely subsumed entirely into a teleology; the judgments implicit in his ironies lie somewhere between absolutist moral codes and sheer relativism. But Browning's poetry, like Burckhardt's and Pater's histories, leaves uncomfortably open the question of how the past has meaning for an imaginable historical future.

This is precisely the problem Jameson proposes to negotiate in his desire to claim the affective power of existential historicism for a properly Marxist project, and it is the juncture where Pound's poetry moves away from existential historicism. Jameson cites Jules Michelet's history of the French Revolution as a paradigmatic example of the existential historicist account in which passionate engagements with past, present, and future meet. In Michelet, Jameson argues, existential historicism becomes not bourgeois aestheticism but revolutionary commitment. Michelet is a prototype in his own time of a "hermeneutic relationship to the past which is able to grasp its own present as history only on condition it manages to keep the ideal of the future, and of radical and utopian transformation, alive" ("Marxism and Historicism," 177). Michelet's commitment to the future clearly leads us beyond the equipoise of existential historicism and into a project of social transformation; there the past gains part of its affective force from the desire to specify a "utopian" future. This utopian project represents a third possible end to the difficulties of existential historicism, and one ultimately more attractive to a poet of epic ambitions than either empiricism or aestheticism.[7]

It also raises the further problem of utopian thinking. Jameson's example of Michelet calls to mind another historian of the French Revolution, whose work began in the equipoise of existential historicism and ended in the celebration of authoritarian power. Thomas Carlyle's move to a more teleological and utopian idea of the future raised questions of authority—questions about how historical argu-

---

7. Here my reading of Pound's existential historicism diverges from Longenbach's in *Modernist Poetics*; as I contend in Chapters 5 and 6, Pound's existential historicism eventually becomes a utopianism of a particularly dubious kind rather than devolving, as Longenbach argues, into empiricism. As Longenbach shows, however, Pound's allegiance to multitudinous facts significantly shapes our process of reading *The Cantos*.

ment connects past, present, and future and how historical visionaries can claim authority on behalf of themselves or others. These questions took on particular urgency as Carlyle came increasingly to see the historical field not as a web of multitudinous detail or a "vast" spiritual map but as true chaos resistant to all but the most powerful human attempts at order, as in *Latter-Day Pamphlets*.

Pound's poetics and his practice of relentlessly espousing a canon were from the first caught in this problem of existential historicism. His work was torn not between empiricism and pure aestheticism but between the aestheticist potential of existential historicism and a utopian, and eventually an authoritarian, alternative. First in poetic style and then in the historical past, Pound sought "shapes of power" to oppose a crepuscular age. His endless proselytizing for his version of a literary canon and in particular, his construction of a nineteenth-century canon were ways of resisting aestheticism. He resisted both the aestheticism intrinsic to the practice of existential historicism and the potential aestheticism within the postromantic poetry which Browning's own historicist poetry had itself set out to oppose. Thus any discussion of Pound's response to aestheticism is complicated by the varying meanings and contexts of aestheticist claims; Browning's own critique of the aestheticism he recognized within the historicist project was ambivalent enough that Pater, for example, could characterize Browning's work as a "poetry of situations" (*Renaissance*, 171). Pater's own writing in turn was for Pound both deeply attractive and seriously limited.

The conception of art as a separate aesthetic realm and of history as subsumable into such art was problematic for Browning, finessed by Pater, and adopted or ironically flaunted by late nineteenth-century aesthetes. Pound's early poetry is an unstable mix of resistance to all these positions. As is often the case in one's deepest resistances, his opposition to aestheticism was only just equal to its complex attractions. Both Pound's early poetic practice and his later utopian vision attested to this tension.

Pound's nineteenth-century canon can best be understood, then, as the ideological form of his resistance to aestheticism. He celebrated Browning's historicism and other elements of what he and Ford Madox Ford called the realist prose tradition; these notions of art were antidotes to gentility and to decadence. But Browning's poetry could be understood in terms of the prose tradition and in terms of a Pateresque poetry of situations. Pound's poetic practice was forged in these dichotomies; his canonical pronouncements articulated them.

Canons and Culture

I begin here by sketching the nineteenth-century canon as Pound came to conceive and propagate it as part of his personal pedagogy. My examples range over his career; for though eccentric, his vision of his Victorian antecedents was remarkably stable—perhaps a reflection of his reading habits and certainly reflective of his practice of assimilating new discoveries without discarding contradictory elements.[8] Pound's creation of canonical hierarchies depended heavily and explicitly on his sense of the needs of his own time.[9] Whereas T. S. Eliot, in "Tradition and the Individual Talent," was interested in the way a contemporary work changes the works that come before it, Pound explored the other side of the same process. His letters and essays reveal a fascination with the way the past can be remade in order to enable a particular future to come after it.

The very urgency of Pound's canonical pronouncements was rooted in his need to make way for his own poetics and in the larger project of making society hospitable to art. He was embarked on a course, anti-aestheticist at the outset, which had as its goal a renovation of both art and society. Such a vision itself was deeply rooted in nineteenth-century thought and in the Victorian response to industrial capitalism. It was crucial for William Morris and before him for Ruskin. Indeed the combination of canonical, pedagogic, and social concerns in Ruskin's later essays prefigures Pound's urgent efforts to propagate a canon. Ruskin's "Of King's Treasuries," the first essay in *Sesame and Lilies*, was, as I show in the next chapter, the text out of which came Pound's unpublished poem "Rex." The essay, subtitled "How and What to Read," is almost uncannily Poundian. It suggests connections among precise language, the discrimination of good and bad (or merely entertaining) books, and good government. Ruskin proposes an aristocracy of reading; in reading books by great leaders and thinkers, he asserts, one enters a true aristocracy, not to teach but to be taught, not to imbibe the opinions of great writers but to acquire precision of thought. His definition of the educated man prefigures Pound's assertion that his prescriptions in his own essay "How to Read" will require one to read fewer rather than more books.[10] It hints

8. Humphrey Carpenter, in *A Serious Character*, details Pound's reading habits, particularly his tendency to read in snippets and his statement in old age that he had read too little and too slowly (42–44).
9. For the most thorough treatment of this issue and a broad discussion of Pound, Eliot, and education, see McDonald, *Learning to Be Modern*.
10. "How to Read," LE, 16. Redman argues that in "How to Read" we see the ways

as well at the sources for the modernist's uncomfortable relationship with the reading audience.

In a striking passage Ruskin compares good reading to true gold mining, chiseling, and fusing and declares:

> And, therefore, first of all, I tell you, earnestly and authoritatively, (I *know* I am right in this), you must get into the habit of looking intensely at words, and assuring yourself of their meaning, syllable by syllable— nay letter by letter. For though it is only by reason of the opposition of letters in the function of signs, to sounds in function of signs, that the study of books is called "literature," and that a man versed in it is called, by the consent of nations, a man of letters instead of a man of books, or of words, you may yet connect with that accidental nomen- clature the real principle;—that you might read all the books in the British Museum (if you could live long enough), and remain an utterly "illiterate," uneducated person; but that if you read ten pages of a good book, letter by letter,—that is to say with real accuracy,—you are for evermore in some measure an educated person.... A well-educated gentleman may not know many languages ... but whatever language he knows, he knows precisely; whatever word he pronounces he pro- nounces rightly; above all he is learned in the *peerage* of words.... a few words well chosen, and distinguished, will do work that a thousand cannot, when every one is acting, equivocally, in the function of another. ("Of King's Treasuries," 64–66)

Finally, he contends that the situation of England, particularly its ec- onomic corruption (which in Ruskin's footnotes extends especially to banking and credit), is so abysmal that the English cannot read. "No reading is possible for a people with its mind in this state," he de- clares. "No sentence of any great writer is intelligible to them. It is simply and sternly impossible for the English public, at this moment, to understand any thoughtful writing,—so incapable of thought has it become in its insanity of avarice" (83). Happily Ruskin believes England's "disease" is not yet incurable.

Pound moves from canon creation to politics. He claims that "by transferring his canons of judgment from art to politics, Pound was able to move confidently into an entirely new field" (*Ezra Pound and Italian Fascism*, 89). Redman, like Leon Surette in "Ezra Pound and British Radicalism," valuably indicates Ruskin's importance for Pound in linking art and politics. As will be evident, I agree only partially with Redman's argument that in the 1910s, Pound made a "passage from aesthete to politically engaged poet" (120). Certainly this is an accurate description of Pound's increasing concern with politics; but I show below that he can be said to have taken his aestheticism with him into politics.

With less restraint and more epithets Pound's "How to Read" is a similar exercise. He too attacks English avarice, primarily in the form of British publishers' reluctance to challenge or discard Palgrave's *Golden Treasury* (the economic metaphors of the anthology, the "treasury," provide both Ruskin and Pound with a significant instance of material language for discussing the value of art). Just as Ruskin hopes to cure the "disease" of England by exhorting his audience to read and read properly and precisely, so Pound provides a "vaccine" for the situation he describes as a "bog, a marasmus." He invokes what he believes to be the positive social consequences of truly learning how to read. Literature does have a function in the state, he asserts, but not that of coercing the acceptance of "any one set . . . of opinions." Literature "has to do with the clarity and vigour of 'any and every' thought and opinion." The poet pedagogue's role is crucial:

> It has to do with maintaining the very cleanliness of the tools, the health of the very matter of thought itself. Save in the rare and limited instances of invention in the plastic arts, or in mathematics, the individual cannot think and communicate his thought, the governor and legislator cannot act effectively or frame his laws, without words, and the solidity and validity of these words is in the care of the damned and despised *litterati*. When their work goes rotten—by that I do not mean when they express indecorous thoughts—but when their very medium, the very essence of their work, the application of word to thing goes rotten, i.e. becomes lushy and inexact, or excessive or bloated, the whole machinery of social and of individual thought and order goes to pot. This is a lesson of history, and a lesson not yet half learned. (LE, 21)

Just as Ruskin evokes the scene of bad Latin quantities and false uses of words in Parliament and in European governments generally, so Pound connects reading, right naming, and law. Pound's own notion of canon and its social importance has its Victorian as well as its Confucian antecedents.

Like Confucian right naming or Ruskinian correct words, a literary canon for Pound takes on the flavor of a necessary hierarchy; at the same time, it is made, explicitly, with the need of another renaissance, a literary utopia, in mind. So, for example, Pound's editorial efforts for *Poetry* magazine can be understood as an exercise in creating a canon from the present. As he writes Harriet Monroe, the editor of *Poetry*, in 1916, he complains of strained literary relations between the United States and England. No one "worth anything" in England will "submit stuff for editorial selection," and the situation is made worse

by the "political degradation of our country" (SL, 5 March 1916, 71).
Political "degradation" is clearly congruent with lack of editorial selectivity in America—thus for *Poetry*, being "the best magazine in
American is NOT good enough." In such matters of judgment, Pound
writes, "There is also an absolute standard." This letter, like much of
his editorial correspondence, exhibits the sense that "absolute" stan-
dards and the political/aesthetic needs of the current situation make
selectivity both crucial and of immediate use. The process of canon
creation, then, is not an aestheticist project, though it responds as fin-
de-siècle aestheticism did to the marginalization of the artist and
though it shares with aestheticism an implicit cultural critique.
Pound's canonical efforts were an attempt at reorganizing both art
and society.

The Propagation of a Canon

In Pound's letters to aspiring writers one sees the genial and pedagogic face of this understanding of art. The significance of Homer,
Dante, Confucius, and the Provençal poets in his canon is well known.
In his letters to younger writers Pound-as-pedagogue clearly believes
that any relationship to these literary monuments must also be mediated by a proper relation to the recent past. Two instances of his
"instruction," one from 1916 and one from the 1950s, show the remarkable stability of his nineteenth-century canon and the way in
which it was the ideological form of resistance to fin-de-siècle poetry.
This resistance was extended to encompass certain Victorian predecessors, notably Tennyson and the Pre-Raphaelites.

As D. D. Paige has noted, Pound's early letters to Iris Barry
recommend a "formidable regimen," the nature of which became the
basis of "How to Read" (SL, xxi). Pound puts Barry through a course
of reading in Greek, Latin, and French. Extolling the French prose
tradition and finally commenting on English poetry, he insists that
Barry be grounded in classics first, particularly the *Greek Anthology*,
the *Odyssey* if a translation could be found, and Catullus, Propertius,
and Ovid. Virgil is dismissed as a "second-rater, a Tennysonianized
version of Homer" (July 1916, SL, 87). Next in the pantheon come
Provence, Dante, and Cavalcanti, followed by Villon—but Swinburne's translations, though "very fine in themselves," are too luxu-
rious, not "hard enough" for someone learning to write. Gautier,
Flaubert, and Stendhal are next recommended, and this brings Pound
finally to English poetry. "Perhaps," he exclaims, "one shouldn't read

it at all." But he forces himself to admit Chaucer has everything, though he himself has been led to archaizing by him. His pantheon at this point also includes Crabbe, Landor, and Browning—all of whom he implicitly sets in the context of a prose tradition. Crabbe tried to "put things down as they were," and Landor is a "whole culture," though not technically accomplished. The Elizabethans and Yeats share the fate of being too often imitated—here as elsewhere Pound connected Elizabethan poetry with what he thinks of as a sloppy and overly ornamental strain. Wordsworth as usual comes in for ambiguous criticism: he is a "dull sheep" but can describe nature. The poet that Pound himself confesses he has too often imitated is Browning, and thus he suspects Browning and Chaucer both as over-powering models: "The hell is that one catches Browning's manner and mannerisms" (27 July 1916, SL, 90).

If she wishes to write English poetry then, Barry is counseled to view her English predecessors in a curious light, valuing among nine-teenth-century predecessors Crabbe and Landor and warily approach-ing Browning. English poetry is mediated first by the prose tradition, Stendhal and Flaubert, which provides a canonical standard. Second, the late Latin poets become a medium through whom the poetry of the immediate past is read; for they share the historical situation Pound identified as his own. The Roman poets were living with "the same problems as we have." They had "the metropolis, the imperial posts to all corners of the known world" (SL, 90).[11] As Pound defines it, the modern poet's response to the situation of the late Roman poets might be either to take an ironic position in the metropolis as the voice of urban late imperialism or to create a historical poetry whose inclu-sive sweep encompasses "all the corners of the known world," or at least outlines its monuments. Landor's work accordingly encompasses a "whole culture." Browning's history and Swinburne's translations might be said to do the same, though both Swinburne's and Brown-ing's "coin has been debased" by modern imitation.

Pound's letters to Barry, especially those of canonical instruction, are equally concerned with language, history, and economics partic-ularly in the sense of poem as coinage/currency. The contemporary historical situation and language of poetry are then to be judged and

11. In this as in many of his attitudes Pound shares the premises of the 1890s, the Georgian poets, and Victorian historians and theorists of language. On similar anal-ogies to Rome, see Dowling, *Language and Decadence*, 84–103. Of course Pound's position as an American expatriate significantly complicated the meaning of this analogy.

remade in the context of canonical hierarchies. The poet reading re-
stores or recognizes proper value in poetry.

Forty years later Pound was still instructing the young through a
similar canon, though the prose tradition held a perhaps less crucial
place. The importance of reconstructing a nineteenth-century canon is
evident in his repeated attention to the work of his Victorian predecessors as translators. Translation is integral to the construction both
of canons and of a viable poetic language for the modern world. I
suggest in the next chapter how Pound viewed translation and imitation not as stages the poet must simply pass beyond but as integral
to the very nature of his poetics. His letters are proof that his attempt
to create a canon from all the "corners of the known world" led him
to understand the canon of Victorian poetry in terms of translation.
D. G. Rossetti, Swinburne, Landor, and Browning—all of them translators—continue to appear in Pound's letters as he seeks to instruct
younger poets in the nature of the craft.

Pound's unpublished letters to Charleen Whisnant Swansea are an
interesting expression of the continuity of these concerns. In 1955,
Swansea wrote Pound asking his advice about her own poetry and
translations, and in the context of a discussion of her translations of
Catullus, the persistence of Pound's Victorian canon becomes clear.
He tells her she has gotten, "in a couple of spots, up to the late
Mr. Bwowning" (*sic*). But he advises revision, citing Ford's dictum
" '40 ways to write Anything, and the first one you use probably
wrong.' " The contours of a translator's canon appear clearly:

> Try 'em in Browningese. Lets see what happens.
>
> And D.G. R. allus: "only thing is NOT to make bad
> poEm out of a good one."
> The sound of the orig / the grade A. max / cum laude
> teething ring.
> and don't let me give way to temptation and make
> POSitive suggestion. . . .
> Swinburne DID know some gk / R. B. made the WORST
> single line in the Agamemnon / a peachereenaaaaaaa.
> a BEEyEUTEE.
> But when R.B. makes fer to sing. he is the best after???
> Campion (or whatever the dates are) Waller and co/
>
> available idioms / R.B. and Ez (as in TRAX choroi).[12]

12. Pound, typescript letter to Swansea, 8 February 1955, Charleen Whisnant Swansea
Papers, #4027, Ezra Pound Sub-group.

In later letters Pound advises Swansea on Golding's Ovid, Binyon's translation of the *Commedia*, and D. G. Rossetti's translation of the *Vita Nuova*. And he declares that Browning and Gautier "did not voluntarily stultify themselves and retire to the backe room of a arty shoppe." Presumably in this they resemble Homer, Dante, and Shakespeare, who "did NOT try to dodge problem of keeping alive in their eras" (Swansea, n.d.). Moreover, Pound applauds Swansea's study of Victorian literature, implying that unlike her boring professor, she has a firm sense of true literary values; presumably she could "flunk" that "dam Prof" on Beddoes and Landor. The act of translation, the creation of a canon of Victorian translators and a canon of Victorian poetry commensurate with it, are part of the effort to remake the past so that poetry may be about the "problem of keeping alive" in the modern world.

As Pound's pedagogic letters make clear, the modern poet must come to terms with various ways of appropriating the past—via history, translation, or poetic tradition. Pound's nineteenth-century canon was designed to champion an existential historicist approach to history and an inclusive analytic intelligence he associated with Flaubert's *l'histoire morale contemporaine*. It set out to oppose what Pound derided, inaccurately but sweepingly, as the Macaulay-Tennyson approach to history. This odd pair I take to represent for Pound bourgeois self-satisfaction (Whiggish history) and the fashionable melancholy and medieval trappings of Victorian aestheticism.

As Pound comes to terms with the nineteenth century, Flaubert's *l'histoire morale contemporaine* becomes a measure of value for the historians and for the Victorian poets who constitute his canon of immediate predecessors. The Victorian poets Pound praises share with Flaubert and certain historians a "perception of paucity." Typical historians and Macaulay-Tennyson interpreters of history are guilty of shallow "analyses of motivation" and "inadequate measurement of causality." Flaubert fought against abstraction, and Pound admires him along with Michelet, Stendhal, and the Goncourts because they "all wanted to set down an intelligible record of life in which things happened" ("Jefferson-Adams Letters," SP, 149). Like Flaubert and like the translators who make other realms available, "Balzac, Trollope and Henry James extended the subject. EXTENDED the subject, they as Dante before them and as every real writer before them or since, extended the domain of their treatment" (153). In this realm of social/historical treatment Browning and certain other Victorian poets share with the novelists and historians a kind of "realism."

In discussing his own treatment of Provence, Pound describes himself as extending the subject. In a letter to Felix Schelling of July 1922 he says explicitly that he has used Provence as subject matter, "trying to do as R. B. had with Renaissance Italy" (SL, 179). Pound associates himself and Browning with a "realistic" tradition in historical or fictional prose, as opposed to a romanticized one. He declares in the same letter: "About Provence. The Wm. Morris tapestry treatment of the Middle Ages is unsatisfactory. The originals are more vital, more realist. De Born wrote songs to provoke real war, and they were effective. This is very different from Romantic or Macaulay-Tennyson praise of past battles" (SL, 178–79).

In rewriting the canon of nineteenth-century poetry, then, Pound praises a group of poets who achieve the standard presented by a Flaubert or a Michelet. Central among them of course is Browning; when Pound described his literary genealogy to René Taupin he declared Browning "son père" and attributed his own "réforme" equally to Browning "denué des paroles superflus" and to Flaubert—"mot juste, presentation ou constatation" (May 1928, SL, 218). Pound has good words for D. G. Rossetti, Swinburne, and Edward Fitzgerald's *Rubaiyat* but reserves his greatest praise for Crabbe, Browning, Landor, Hardy, and less emphatically, Beddoes (SL, 217).[13] He readily judges the poets he admires: "All right. It, Hardy's verse is full of Browning. Browning being 'the only poet younger than himself' who aroused Beddoes' interest. And Beddoes' editor omits Landor from the list of poets writing english after the death of Shelley. My god what an England" (GK, 286). Pound finally concludes that Beddoes is of limited effectiveness because of his archaic diction, but he praises Landor for the ability to see out of his own age without becoming archaic, or perhaps "romantic" in the Tennyson-Macaulay fashion. In an early essay on Landor, he compares Landor's achievement with what seems to him a model interpretation of another age: "Indubitably Landor never gave so complete a verse interpretation as *The Ring and the Book*. There are, indeed, too many absolutely unanswerable questions around by any attempt to compare these two writers. Browning in verse is presumably the better poet; largely perhaps because Landor never learned to write a long passage of verse without

13. Pound may have been unaware of the curious coincidence that Browning actually became Beddoes's literary executor and looked after Landor's affairs in the poet's old age. Landor's treatment of Italy, especially his imaginary conversation between Filippi Lippi and Pope Eugenius IV, had interested Browning many years before Yeats and Pound read Landor at Stone Cottage. On Beddoes and Browning see Donner, *Browning Box*; on Pound, Yeats, and Landor see Longenbach, *Stone Cottage*.

in some way clogging and blocking the reader's attention" (SP, 387). Almost twenty years later, Landor and Hardy still have a place in the Pound pantheon along with Browning, certain novelists, and various historians because they all strive toward what Pound conceives as realistic presentation. Flaubert and Stendhal attempt "to set down things as they are"; Crabbe writes a history of England in 1800; Browning creates a complete interpretation of another age in *The Ring and the Book* ("Landor," SP, 387).

Browning and Flaubert thus form for Pound a pair of crucial hinges between his own present and the literary past. Each is understood to further a realist project; each avoids archaism, solipsism, the tendency to regard the past as pageantry or the present as "crepuscular." Whatever the aestheticist potential of Browning's poetry, Michelet's history, or Flaubert's fiction, Pound values their resistance to stylish vagueness, historical pageantry, and bourgeois complacency. He believes Browning and Flaubert particularly extend the subject into the corners of the known world, both past and present. In his anti-aestheticist canon Pound explicitly values Browning's diction and implicitly admires his realist tendency to critique both overt didacticism in art (as in "Fra Lippo Lippi") and aestheticist withdrawal (as in "Pictor Ignotus"). Similarly, he values Flaubert's ironic scrutiny of bourgeois values and, in *Bouvard and Pécuchet*, his dissection of the potentially endless romance of learning itself.

Pound, Ford, and the Prose Tradition in Verse

A crucial impetus in Pound's development of his nineteenth-century canon was his relationship with Ford Madox Ford. Not only did Ford, famously, ridicule Pound's early poetic diction; he was a living link to Victorian poets and artists. Ford's friendship encouraged Pound in the articulation of anti-aestheticist principles. It allowed him to situate himself against and to align himself with various predecessors even as it provided the ideological backbone of these canonical pronouncements.[14] In Ford's own understanding of nineteenth-century English literature, Browning was the most important single presence—and a

14. For a useful discussion of Pound, Ford, and realism see Bush, *Genesis of Ezra Pound's Cantos*. Yeats's friendship and experiments with diction were also crucial and probably more important to the shape of Pound's poetry, whereas Ford's strictures and friendship contributed to Pound's ability to articulate his critical positions. For a thorough discussion of Yeats and Pound see Longenbach, *Modernist Poetics* and *Stone Cottage*.

living one. As Ford recounted, with his characteristic approximation of accuracy, he "was born, suckled, weaned, and cradled amongst poets—poets who made great noises. . . . I had to listen to numbers of people like the Rossettis and Browning and Tennyson reading verse aloud . . . they held their heads at unnatural angles and appeared to be suffering the tortures of agonising souls. It was their voices that did that. They were doing what Tennyson calls, with admiration: 'Mouthing out their hollow O's and A's' " (*Critical Writings*, 156–57). That Ford actually heard Browning in such a fashion is unclear; his comments make it plain that he recognized Browning as out after something other than sonority. In fact Ford and, following him, Pound habitually linked Browning with Flaubert and opposed both to Tennysonian sonority.

In their correspondence and reviews of each other's work, Ford and Pound engaged in an anti-aestheticist campaign that—though it elided their various debts to Pater, the Pre-Raphaelites, and their successors—allowed them to claim a "New Tradition." We can see the contours of this canon by attending to Ford's pronouncements on Pound and Pound's responses to Ford's poetry.

Ford draws a direct link between Pound's modernist project and a nineteenth-century canon in his review of Pound's "How to Read." In this review, which can stand as Ford's own version of "How to Read," he singles out Browning and Pound as major innovators:

> Browning and Ezra are the two great major poets of our and the immediately preceding Age. That Ezra reveals. I use the word "major" to designate verse-poets who can hold your attention with their verses during extended periods of time. There have been a great many—*atque ego in Arcadia vixi!*—who can hold it, say, as 'gilders'. Up against the strong wind of an emotion or an excitement, we can make our flights. It is only Browning and Ezra since Bugbear Shakespeare who have been able to make a non-stop flight from, say, Philadelphia to, say, Cathay, revictualling, as it were in the air above Casa Guidi. (Quoted in P/F, 103)

The clue to the greatness of Pound, Browning, and Shakespeare is found in the prose tradition; it is the "simple one" of making a poem interesting, of making it move. Ford contends that Homer, Dante, and all "writers of hexameters, terza rime, rhymed Alexandrines, blank verse [Browning?] are in effect *prosateurs*" who seek through versification to make their poems move; by the time of Stendhal, Ford claims, "as Ezra adumbrates," the writer sensed these forms of versification as slackening speed; for "in the end—low be it uttered—a reader has to be held by the subject" (P/F, 105). The desiderata of the prose tradition in verse are movement and speed, equally dependent on subject matter, style, and form; and the greatest exemplars of this tradition are certain epic poets before Stendhal, Browning, and certain novelists since Stendhal. In this tradition Browning provides a pivot between Stendhal, who preceded him by a generation, and Pound who succeeded him by as many years. The pivotal figure in prose is of course Flaubert.

If Browning and Pound have extended the subject, they have also extended the language. These connections are particularly clear in Ford's memoir *Thus to Revisit* (1921); in which he cites poets who early interested him, two living—Walter De la Mare and Robert Bridges—and two dead—Christina Rossetti and Robert Browning. Of all four, he asserts, "It was the prose quality of those passages, not the metrical values, to which I attached importance. . . . Christina Rossetti was an infinitely great master of words, but the emotions her work always gave me were those of reading prose—and so it was with Browning." Ford goes on to recount how he recently surprised himself by saying to Pound, "The only English poet that matters twopence is Browning! I don't know what Mr. Pound answered . . . but he did not knock me down, so that I dare say he was substantially in agreement with myself" (130–31). Later, in his discussion of the early days of imagism, Ford pairs Browning with Hardy, contending first for the importance of prose values in forming the language of poetry: "In the matter of language at least, first Browning and then Mr. Hardy, showed the way for the Imagiste group—Browning dragging in any old word from an immense, and Mr. Hardy doing the same thing from a rather limited, vocabulary. . . . Browning, an immense and buoyant personality, simply threw his immense ranges of syllogisms about as a lusty child splashes in the water of his bath" (*Thus to Revisit*, 153). At the end of his career Ford characterized Browning as getting words to do their work by using them "with the violence of a horse-breaker, giving out the scent of a he-goat" (*March of Literature*, 774). Browning's language along with Hardy's and Christina Rossetti's provided the modern poet with a living possibility for the use of language. In contrast, Tennyson, D. G. Rossetti, and Swinburne were, as inheritors of the used up language of Keats and Shelley, dead "before they were even born" (*Thus*

to Revisit, 152).[15] Thus Ford positions Pound and Browning against
"poetical" poetry. Despite his own imitations of Shelley, Browning
becomes the key figure in Ford's and Pound's antiromantic, anti-
aestheticist ideology.

Ford makes his own argument for the origins of what we now call
modernism by identifying Browning with the New Tradition. According to Ford, Browning and Christina Rossetti began the New Tradition: "Browning was almost the first amongst poets to invent a new
verse form—or at any rate to attempt to invent a new verse form—
for each of his varying mental phases. In that he was trying to get
nearer to an expression of his immense personality. For her smaller
personality Christina attempted to do the same thing. . . . This New
Tradition was carried much further by Mr. Hardy." He goes on to
characterize the evolution of Hardy's poetry as a movement toward
more "intimate self-expression" in which the "versification became,
not so much more irregular, but more rough" (*Thus to Revisit*, 155).

Browning's place as founder of the New Tradition is based on characteristics his Victorian contemporaries remarked—characteristics integral to his historicism but troubling to his contemporaries. Ford's
comments recast in a positive way Arnold's complaint about Browning's multitudinousness (letter to Clough, 1848–49, 97). Ford's attitude
toward Browning's diction and form resembles Swinburne's description of the "diabolical versatility of violence" Browning inflicted upon
the mother tongue ("Chaotic School," 41). The terms of Ford's, Arnold's, and Swinburne's discussions are not dissimilar; yet the valuation of Browning's multitudinousness and his formal and stylistic
innovation has changed. This positive valuation is directly linked to
Ford's understanding of Browning's historicism.

Like Pound, Ford constructs his canon by contrasting the Macaulay–
Tennyson–Pre-Raphaelite approach to the past with the approach of
the "realist" practitioners of fiction and history. In his *March of Literature*, Ford contrasts three kinds of artists: those who take political
sides in their work (and at worst falsify reality, at best write "The
Marseillaise"); those who "paint attractive pictures of other days or
of imaginary golden ages"; and those who observe the characteristics
of their times and render them precisely. Dante and Villon belong to
the last category; the "Georgian-Victorian" poets to the second. In the

15. Pound never shared Ford's dismissal of Swinburne, but his admiration was obvi-
    ously tempered by his conviction that Swinburne's verse was "soft." Pound praised
    Swinburne's metrical facility and his translations, though his imitations of Swin-
    burne were confined to the early poetry.

hundred years of poetry preceding him, Ford finds only two poets who arrive at precise historical rendering: whereas most poets "stitched tapestries of a middle ages that never existed," Wordsworth did pay some attention to his own age, and Browning conducted "an archaeology when paying attention to medieval villains." Finally, Ford argues, "it is almost impossible to read today" the *Idylls of the King*, "because one can get cheap editions of the *Morte d'Arthur* and Browning or read Mr. Pound's projections of medievally incestuous, murdering mercenary princes who built the most beautiful palaces and collected Greek manuscripts" (765–66).

Ford situates Browning and Pound together, then, in manner and in matter. Their approaches to the past, to language, and to innovation separate them from Tennysonian tapestry and ally them with the virtues of the prose tradition, with antiromanticism, with (masculine) hardness.[16] Browning's immersion in Italian history, Ford concludes, gave him a critical perspective on his own culture. In Ford's view, Browning "became a tougher Englishman by living in Florence" (*March of Literature*, 765).

It is in this latter sense of prose tradition as antiromanticism and antinostalgia that Ford considers Pound as a historian and Browning as an "archaeologist." In his 1927 review of Pound's *Personae*, Ford defends Pound's use of historical matter and declares his delight and amazement that Pound more and more "assumes the aspect of a poet who is the historian of the world and who is far more truly the historian of the world than any compiler of any outline of history" (P/F, 85–86). That Pound can with equal ease write about Voltaire, the troubadours, "Les Millwin," and "Mr. Nixon" is for Ford a basis for the highest praise. Getting inside history and diagnosing the present are complementary abilities, but the "compiler" of outlines can accom-

---

16. Longenbach discusses Pound's dismissal in *The Spirit of Romance* of the archaeological approach to history; here "archaeology" is Pound's term for philology and for positivist history. Pound defends his own "artistic" approach to the past. Ford uses the notion of archaeology approvingly to describe Pound's work, and in this instance archaeology is antipositivist and, like Pound's "artistic" history, stands against mere chronicles. See Longenbach, *Modernist Poetics*, 50. I return to this gendering of poetry in Chapter 6. It is notable that despite Ford's celebration of masculine "hardness" he persistently defends Christina Rossetti's work in the face of Pound's obvious indifference, and the reading lists and discussion in his *March of Literature* are remarkable for the significant place they accord to women writers in English. He does, however, resort to a gendered language of evaluation both in this passage and in accusing Tennyson of "sub-nauseating sissiness" (*March of Literature*, 766).

plish neither task any better than the Tennysonian poet of the romanticized past. Browning's and Pound's historical practice is neither
pageantry nor empiricism.[17] As Ford sees it, Browning, Flaubert, and
Pound extend the historical subject by avoiding both nostalgia and
scientific history.

Pound's contributions to this critical program are evident both in
the canonical pronouncements I have examined and in his responses
to Ford's poetry. Pound's first review of Ford's work is a discussion,
in March 1912, of Ford's *High Germany*. This review specifies a number
of poems Pound also singles out for praise in later reviews, especially
in the important one he titled "The Prose Tradition in Verse" (P/F).
Pound's choices among Ford's poems and the terms of his praise indicate that Pound indeed viewed Ford as a transitional figure between
the best of Victorian poetry—namely Browning's—and the modern
moment. In the 1912 review of *High Germany* he praises those poems
in the volume that owe most to Browning and explicitly discusses this
connection:

> Thus in Mr. Hueffer there is a fecundity of poetic idea and of im-
> pression, but the rendering, as in "All the Dead," first offends a little,
> then, as we see the relation of the conversational passages to those more
> intense, it impresses us. Here, we say, is life articulated; things in re-
> lation. It is Browning's method brought up to date. Yet on the third or
> fourth reading, the jokes are stale. We believe that which is really poetic
> in the poem could have been—with much more labor, to be sure, on
> the author's part—conveyed without them. Yet this poem, very
> strongly, and "The Starling," and "In the Little Old Market-Place," do
> convey the author's mood, a mood grown of his own life, his own belief,
> not second-hand, or culled from books. They are true music. (P/F, 10)

The whole of the book Pound characterizes as an experiment in modernity.

17. Ford similarly yokes analysis of past and present in the prefatory remarks to his
Women and Men, a volume Pound repeatedly singled out for praise and which owes
its title, if not part of its treatment of subject, to Browning. Ford declares that he
has been attempting an analysis of the differences between women and men in
contemporary Europe, but he remarks, "I do not profess to have studied the matter
historically. History is an excellent thing and when it is treated by scientific historians it becomes infinitely more misleading than anything I could hope to write"
(14). Clearly, then, to Ford's mind the Tennysonian approach to the past and the
"outlines" of scientific historians are equally inadequate. What is needed is the
precise language and the precision of observation provided by the prose tradition
and by its equivalent practitioners in poetry.

If Ford's poems are seen as up-to-date Browning, Pound's singling out "To All the Dead" makes a great deal of sense. Ford's poem evokes the central moment of historicist encounter with the past: resuscitation of the dead. And it owes much to Browning's technique. "To All the Dead" involves a dramatis persona who may mean more or less than he says and on whom various ironies are not lost. In its presentation of persona, its conversational language, interpolated dialogues, ellipses, and metrical experimentation against a blank verse norm, "To All the Dead" is in the line of Browning's blank verse monologues. Its satire on the banalities of contemporary life is reminiscent of "Bishop Blougram's Apology," though its pattern is closer to the associative meditation of *Sordello* or to some of Browning's dramatic lyrics than to Blougram's casuistry.

In "To All the Dead" the speaker retreats from the university town of the volume's title poem, "High Germany," and seeks the upland heather, a burial barrow as it turns out; he seeks the dead for relief when his "mind's all reeling with Modern Movements" (*Collected Poems*, 101), and he encounters speaking ghosts, lovers divided who are working a revolution against death and seeking to be reunited even in the grave. The ghosts move about him, drinking cold dew from each others' lips. When this vision fades, the speaker comes back to the present. He encounters a fingerpost that symbolizes the power of Germanic philology to overcome the living encounter with the past:

> And in the moonlight a wan fingerpost
> (I could not read the lower row of words.)
> Proclaimed: *'Forbidden'* That's High Germany.
> Take up your glasses. 'Prosit!' to the past,
> To all the Dead!
>
> (108)

The lower row of words perhaps represents the footnotes of Dryasdust historiography. In calling up the dead, Ford's poem becomes a critique of modern life. Uneven as it is, it stands between the third book of Browning's *Sordello* and the early cantos as "Browning's method brought up to date." In the context of his historical concerns and his canonical project, Pound's overgenerous praise of "To All the Dead" has its own logic.

It is harder at first to see why Pound is enough taken with "The Starling" and with "In the Little Old Market-Place" to comment on them, repeatedly, with favor. But these poems, too, renovate a nineteenth-century canon. In his review of Ford's *Collected Poems* in the *New Freewoman* (15 December 1913) Pound praises "The Starling" for its "naturalness of language and the suavity with which the rhyme-sounds lose themselves in the flow of the reading" (P/F, 15). He attributes this naturalness of speech to the French writers from whom Ford has learned. "The Starling" may also appeal as a rewriting of George Meredith's "The Lark Ascending." "In the Little Old Market-Place" is more certainly a rewriting of Browning's "The Statue and the Bust" for the modern temper. The speaker of "In the Little Old Market-Place" declares himself "sadly defective" in his knowledge of "olden / Sacred and misty stories" and shows us a marketplace statue, a nameless saint, who becomes the bored knight before a maiden, equally bored. Browning's critique of misplaced morality and chivalry in "The Statue and the Bust" is transmuted into an understated explication of ennui in the contemporary sexual marketplace.

Still more than these poems, Pound apparently liked Ford's "On Heaven," which he urged Harriet Monroe to publish and which he nominated for the *Poetry* award for 1913–14. Again, this poem is an inversion of its Victorian predecessor, this time of D. G. Rossetti's heaven in "The Blessed Damozel." Its light ironies, its undoing of sublimities, deflates the union of the earthly lovers reunited in heaven—Ford's heaven becomes a café in the south of France. Like almost any of Browning's monologuists, Ford's speaker imagines heaven in earth's image, though he exploits more than Browning would have done the utter ordinariness of this imagining.

Although Pound does not explicitly articulate Ford's debts to Browning, the poems he singles out for praise are, as he declares, Browning's method "brought up to date." For Pound as for subsequent readers, Ford's poetry is more important in its contribution to modernist arguments than in itself.

Pound's and Ford's discussions about poetry, history, and style clearly extended to—and grew from—detailed considerations of language. The best example we have occurs in their exchange of letters about Canto 8 (later Canto 2) before its publication in *The Dial* in May 1922. The desired end of reforming language is both the mot juste and "roughness" of speech.[18] In his letter of 21 March 1922, Ford makes

18. The writings of Pound and Ford in the 1910s and 1920s show the two writers seeking in common a revaluation of tradition and a reformation of language, sometimes by divergent means. Many critics have cited Pound's longer review of Ford's *Collected Poems*, "The Prose Tradition in Verse," for its remarks on Words-

several "zoological" suggestions about Pound's draft canto, criticizing his naming of animals and the imprecision of his descriptive language. "Do *waves*," Ford asks, "wirling or billowy things run in the valleys between hillocks of beach— *beach-grooves*? I don't think they do" (P/F, 64). Pound replies to this criticism and, probably, to Ford's penciled criticisms on the manuscript: "Surely one speaks of 'receding wave'. It may be technical looseness of phrase, but it is certainly 'English'. . . . English simply hasn't the mot juste in the french meaning. And french is abs. paralyzed and dying from a too strict logicality" (21 March 1922, P/F, 66). Precise description, then, is at issue. But Ford also reacts to the texture of the language. He questions whether Pound's Anglo-Saxon compounds weaken precision, but he is unwilling to suggest omitting them: "My dislike for them may be my merely personal distaste for Anglo-Saxon locutions which always affect me with nausea & yr. purpose in using them may be the purely aesthetic one of roughening up yr. surface. I mean that, if you shd. cut them out you might well get too slick an effect" (3 March 1922, P/F, 64). It is of course Browning's roughness that Ford admired; here he seems to fear that Pound's roughness may slide into archaism. In response Pound concurred about the necessity of rough texture and rhythm: "I tried a smoother presentation and lost the metamorphosis" (21 March 1922, P/F, 65). The historicized diction of Anglo-Saxon–style compounds, though it risks archaism, creates what Ford praised as roughness and what Pound, in this case, called "metamorphosis."

Pound's Anglo-Saxon compounds are a special problem for Ford because he believes the poet's or novelist's task is to escape the medievalizing tapestry of history and seek something altogether tougher. Although the legacy of the nineteenth century was too complex to contain in this dichotomy between the Macaulay-Tennyson approach to history and Browning's tougher one, Pound and Ford required such a dichotomy. Its necessary simplification was based in an ideological

worth, the mot juste, and prose. There Pound differentiates his own evaluation of poetic tradition from Ford's, agreeing in principle with Ford while disagreeing about the relative merits of Christina Rossetti: "I would be the last to deny that a certain limpidity and precision are the ultimate qualities of style; yet I cannot accept his opinion. Christina had these qualities, it is true—in places, but they are to be found also in Browning and even in Swinburne at rare moments . . . others have found them elsewhere, notably in Arnaut Daniel and in Guido, and in Dante, where Christina herself would have found them" (P/F, 17–18). "The Prose Tradition in Verse" shows Pound's and Ford's essential agreement, and occasional divergences, in evaluating poetic language and tradition.

anti-aestheticism that allowed Pound to clear the ground for his own work. But such canonical argument, as the example of Anglo-Saxon compounds demonstrates, could not simplify the actual process of making poems. His Anglo-Saxonisms could be understood to unite roughness and archaism.

For Pound, an escape from a romanticized tapestry of history was not easily accomplished even with the aid of Flaubert or of the Browning who was "toughened" by living in Florence. Despite Browning's toughness and because of his historicism, Browning's legacy—to say nothing of Flaubert's—was in itself more complex than Ford and Pound could allow themselves to make it in their canonical strictures. The ambivalence within Browning's historicism—the aestheticist possibilities he articulated and resisted—are writ large in Walter Pater's versions of existential historicism and of Browning. An examination of Pater's historicism and Pound's responses to it can help us to see how the characteristics opposed in Pound's and Ford's ideological strictures meet in Pound's early poetic practice.

Pater and the Instabilities of Historicism

Pater both fits and resists Pound's version of the Victorian canon, the version he designed as medicine for his time. Insofar as Pound's Victorian canon was ideologically anti-aestheticist, Pater's vocabulary—of delicacy, sweetness, and charm—would have been unwelcome; for it seemed to detach art from the world. Yet this very stance also appealed to Pound in his early poetry, and Pater's solution to the problem of aesthetic detachment, his insistence on recurrence, provided an equipoise that had a lasting impact on Pound's work. Just as Ford rejected both scientific history and pageantry in praising Browning's and Pound's history, so Pater, too, presented Pound with the possibility of a historicism that was neither empiricist nor antiquarian. Ford found in Browning's and Pound's poetry both realism and intimate self-expression; though Pater's aestheticism assured that he would be refused admission to Ford's New Tradition, he sought a similar combination in historicist presentation of the past.[19] Though Pater's language is significant only in Pound's early poetry, his response to the historicist dilemma of attachment and detachment had a lasting impact on Pound's method in *The Cantos*.

19. Carolyn Williams demonstrates the connection between Pater's historicism and forms of realism in art; see *Transfigured World*, 52.

In Pater's aesthetic historicism, as in Burckhardt's historiography and Browning's ironic monologues, we can see the balance between attachment and detachment so crucial to the existential historicist understanding of history. This balance can also be read as a historicist recasting of the subjective/objective issues at the heart of romantic poetics; such issues had been worried too by Victorian poets, notably in Browning's "Essay on Shelley." Carol Christ has pointed out the importance of this tension in Pater's thought for both Pound and Yeats. As she succinctly puts it, "In many ways Pater embodies the heritage of Victorian poetry and poses the problems that modern poetry seeks to solve. He refines experience to a number of fugitive impressions upon the acute sensibility, while he holds forth the dream that these impressions could contain within themselves objectivity and universal resonance without intervening discourse" (*Victorian and Modern Poetics*, 73). In this combination of subjectivity and objectivity Pater can claim to redefine an objectivity more significant than that of impersonal scientific history. As Carolyn Williams puts it, Pater's aestheticism "appears as an ironic transvaluation of the stance of scientific objectivity" (*Transfigured World*, 32).

Pater's transvaluation of "scientific objectivity" depends not only on aesthetic distance but also on the persistence of the past in the present. What Pater calls in *Greek Studies* the "resemblance" of the past to the thought of the present is a variation on the romantic notion of the spirit of the age; it assumes the persistence of the past and the necessity of living in the present via an understanding of the past. This centrality of history James Longenbach has connected to Pater's notion of "general consciousness" (*Modernist Poetics*, 38). He quotes Pater's evocation of Wordsworth:

> For in truth we come into the world, each one of us, 'not in nakedness,' but by the natural course of organic development clothed far more completely than even Pythagoras supposed in a vesture of the past, nay, fatally shrouded, it might seem, in those laws or tricks of heredity which we mistake for our volitions; in the language which is more than one half of our thoughts; in the moral and mental habits, the customs, the literature, the very houses which we did not make for ourselves; in the vesture of a past, which is (so science would assure us) not ours, but of the race, the species: that *Zeitgeist* or abstract secular process, in which, as we could have had no direct consciousness of it, so we can pretend to no future personal interest. (Pater, *Plato*, 72–73; quoted in Longenbach, *Modernist Poetics*, 37)

Here Pater engages in his familiar parenthetic and clausal ironies. We are "fatally shrouded, it might seem," and we cannot claim these "vestures" as our own, or so "science would assure us." Like Ford, Pater ironically dismisses these scientific assurances that the past is an abstract process without individual or "personal" implications. For him the objective realm of history must have "personal" significance.

Pater's project, if anything, is to make the "abstract secular processes" of history, the "vestures" of the past, a matter of immediate and intense perception. Such a process can be understood as a form of impersonality, but only when impersonality is compatible with intense individual perception. He wishes to transmute the possibly "fatal" shroudings of history into "an instinct of the human mind itself, and therefore also a constant tradition in its history, which *will* recur; fortifying this or that soul here or there in a part at least of that old sanguine assurance about itself" (*Plato*, 73). His metaphors of previous existence evoke Wordsworth, even as his metaphor of history as "vesture" evokes Carlyle, whose own discussion of language, customs, and habits as historical clothes was a basis for the intellectual tradition of existential historicism in England. In Pater's view, to claim the vestures of history requires Diltheyan sympathetic penetration of the lived experience of the past, an assurance at the same time of difference and recurrence.

For Pater this process is "secular" and a substitute for other forms of belief, and his secular solution to the historicist dilemma of connecting present and past is crucial in Pound's poetics. As Carolyn Williams has maintained, Pater's process of Christianizing the classics and classicizing Christianity, of layering time as recurrence in this way, creates a *"frisson* of irony," which is a "signal of aesthetic effect, but also creates that effect *as aesthetic* in the first place. The shift in context frees content or belief into form" (*Transfigured World*, 63). It also makes for the romantic recuperation of loss, for what Williams calls the "Shelleyan prophetic strain" in Pater's work. Secularization becomes recurrence, which by the very intensity of its perception, may guarantee meaning.

Pater's aesthetic effect yokes claims to reality (historical recurrence) and to personal interest; it yokes affect and detachment; and it grounds his curious equipoise—his oxymoronic protest that "illusions" of recurrence are real. Take for example a passage in "Demeter and Persephone" in *Greek Studies*, an essay close to Pound's own concerns in *The Cantos*. There Pater wishes to emphasize the persistence of "the mood of the age in which the story of Demeter and Persephone was first created." The traces of this mood or temper persist, he says, into his own time; and the age in which the story was created, when "it talked of the return of Kore to Demeter," was "not using rhetorical language, but yielding to a real illusion" (100).

Pater thus achieves in discussing the origins of myth an equivalent to his own historicist equilibrium. What is the force of Pater's history itself but the yielding to "a real illusion"? In such an oxymoron we see precisely the odd valence of Pound's later claim that metamorphoses are real, both in an early poem like "The Tree" (CEP, 35) and in *The Cantos*. Real, yes, but real as aesthetic experience.[20] Though for Pound as for Pater such reality can never entirely escape irony, yet these "real illusions" ground the eventual prophetic strain of *The Cantos*.

In Pater's oxymoron "real illusion" we see the defense of both particularity and recurrent pattern. Like Pound after him and like Browning, Pater sought to contain the multitudinousness of existential historicism. Carolyn Williams argues that Pater attempted to balance the multiple details of history and the potential "atomism of epiphanic moments" with notions of repetition and continuity (*Transfigured World*, 4–5). Fragmentation is an ever-present danger, as is the potential that the reader will find not "real illusion" but mere illusion.

The antidotes to fragmentation and to mere illusion are form and intensity. Pater's process of secularization and the aesthetic irony it implies free "content into form." And it is precisely at this juncture that Pater's historicist aestheticism is linked to Pound's modernism. Pound invokes Pater's defense of form in defending Jacob Epstein, Gaudier-Brzeska, and Wyndham Lewis when he cites Pater for the dictum that all art approaches the condition of music (GB, 120). In the same defense of new art, Pound refers equally to Pater's belief that

20. Here I take the view that Pound's invocation of "pagan" stories, and eventually his "mythical method," have much more to do with aestheticism as a secularized and historicized reply to religious belief than with "mysticism." In "The Tree," he becomes a "tree" precisely in order to reconstitute or to elaborate myths of metamorphosis. Compare Carolyn Williams's argument that *"only* in the final analysis [is] the mythopoeic element predominant over the historical, but it is generated in the first place *by* the historical sense, which must not be overlooked" (*Transfigured World*, 82). In short, Pound's myths and metamorphoses are, in my view, a substitution of historicist affective encounters with the past for religious meditative practices or "occult" proceedings like Yeats's. If we wish to attribute "mysticism" to Pound, as Longenbach and others do, we must still remark the differences between Yeats and, say, Blake on the one hand and Pound and Pater on the other. This is not, of course, to discount Yeats's considerable influence on Pound, which has been discussed in detail by Nagy and Longenbach, among others.

the excellence of an art is in its intensity. His defense of Pater's intensity continues the strain of thought he developed in "I Gather the Limbs of Osiris," where Pateresque intensity underlies the notion of luminous detail.[21] "Arts work on life as history works on the development of civilization and literature," he declared. "The artist seeks out the luminous detail and presents it." The live detail will retain its luminosity while "ideas" about the detail change (SP, 23). The detail, for Pound and for Pater, is a form of condensation. As Pater puts it in the essay on the school of Giorgione, the "highest sort of dramatic poetry . . . presents us with a kind of profoundly significant and animated instants [*sic*], a mere gesture, a look, a smile, perhaps—some brief and wholly concrete moment—into which, however, all the motives, all the interests and effects of a long history have condensed themselves" (*Renaissance*, 118). His emphasis on recurrence is directed at the historicist difficulty of connecting present and past, and it has, equally, nostalgic and utopian potential. Pater's and Pound's emphases on intensity are directed at the atomistic tendency of historicism; and the "freeing of content into form" makes conceptual room for aestheticizing politics. Pater avoids anti-aesthetic irony, utopian thinking, and aestheticizing politics. He balances in what he himself might have called a "delicate pause" (171).

Pound was to find that epics are not made in such delicate pauses. The equipoise of existential historicism could not last when invoked in such a project as *The Cantos*. In his early poetry, however, he works within the difficulties of historicism as both Pater and Browning presented them. He can be said to have negotiated between what became Ford's version of Browning on the one hand and Pater's more openly aestheticist version on the other, alternating between the two as he made his own poems.

Pater's Browning of course has something in common with Ford's. Pound, Ford, and Pater all appreciated Browning's ability to make poems of what Pater called "a character in itself not poetical." In his essay on Winkelmann, he describes Browning's poems through an optical metaphor to which Browning himself was partial:

> To realise this situation, to define, in a chill and empty atmosphere the
> focus where rays, in themselves pale and impotent, unite and begin to

21. Longenbach also implicitly connects Pater to "I Gather the Limbs of Osiris," and he cites Burckhardt as the most significant historicist forebear to Pound's defense of luminous detail and his belief in the ability to resuscitate the past. See *Modernist Poetics*, chap. 2.

burn, the artist may have, indeed, to employ the most cunning detail, to complicate and refine upon thought and passion a thousandfold. Let us take a brilliant example from the poems of Robert Browning. His poetry is pre-eminently the poetry of situations. The characters are always of secondary importance; often they are characters in themselves of little interest; they seem to come to him by strange accidents from the ends of the world. His gift is shown by the way in which he accepts such a character, and throws it into some situation, or apprehends it in some delicate pause of life, in which for a moment it becomes ideal. (*Renaissance*, 171)

Browning, then, is credited with a "poetry of situations." He finds the "cunning detail"; he pieces his art together out of "accidents from the ends of the world." And, crucially for Pater, he transfigures such accidents. Pound's luminous detail and Pater's "cunning detail" are close cousins. Both Pater and Pound find such detail in Browning's "poetry of situations." Ford too attributes precise detail to Browning.

Yet Pater's Browning and Ford's Browning are also strikingly different. Pater's idealization and Ford's emphasis on "he-goat" language (in Pound's earlier phrase "Hippity-hop o' the accents") represent different readings of Browning's historicism, though both Pater and Ford are attracted by the very vividness of it.[22] Pater understands Browning's historicism as isolating character in a "delicate pause of life." This approach emphasizes the poet's aesthetic detachment from the historical object and at the same time stresses the intensity of the poet's art. Ford, in contrast, emphasizes Browning's detachment (his exile in Italy) as lending him a critical edge against England and fueling his poetry for its struggle with language. For Pater, Browning's poetry is magnificent for its range; its "magic" is to achieve intricacy and clarity. Browning's "Dis Aliter Visum; or, Le Byron de Nos Jours," Pater says, is a cobweb of allusions and refracted light "balanced on a needle" (*Renaissance*, 171). For Ford and for Pound in their effort to create a new canon, Browning's strength is his historical range and his struggle with making heterogeneous language into poetry.

In Pound's poetic practice, however, Browning's historicism and Pater's details can be assimilated either to aestheticist distancing or to a realism at least ostensibly anti-aestheticist.[23] In his early poetry Pater

22. See Pound's "Mesmerism" (1908), CEP, 17–18.
23. As he develops his anti-aestheticist canon, Pound never entirely relinquishes his

and Browning appear side by side; for Pound is reading Browning's Renaissance to some extent through Pater. At the same time, Pound is imitating those aspects of aestheticist and even decadent poetry which owed much to Pater's criticism as well as to French poetry.[24] Yet because he assimilates both Browning's rough diction and, to some extent, his ironic critique of aestheticism, Pound resists assimilating Browning entirely to Pater's reading of him. The presentation of the troubadours in Pound's early monologues "Cino" and "Marvoil" and the exclamatory optimism of "Fifine Answers" make for a Browningesque "poetry of situations"; historicist these poems are, but they avoid the Pateresque "delicate pause" (CEP, 9–10, 94–96, 18–19).

The intensity of Pound's proselytizing for his canon takes him— and at the same time takes his poetry—beyond even Browning's resistances to aestheticism. His eventual attempt at epic, too, makes urgent the question of how the poem responds to immediate social and political realities. Of course Pater's and Browning's historicism variously engaged these questions as well. Pater's historicism suggested that the present could be, implicitly, criticized as "the meaner world of our common days" (*Renaissance*, 170). Browning's historicist ironies had a less nostalgic and often a more politically pointed application than Pater's historicist recurrences.[25] But Pound's own proselytizing for his canon reveals a more urgent need than either Pater's or Browning's to engage with the social and political realities of his day. Pound's proselytizing more closely resembles Ruskin's insistence that the very forms and language of art have immediate connections to political and economic power.

Browning and Pater were content to analyze the Renaissance and to draw comparisons to their own time; Pound eventually attempted to make a renaissance, initially at least with the very tools he acquired

---

admiration for Pater, as is evident in Pater's place in *Gaudier-Brzeska*. But he comes to value Browning's and Burckhardt's historicism more highly than Pater's. In *Guide to Kulchur*, for example, Pound forgives Pater's treatment of Pico della Mirandola and cites him along with Browning and Burckhardt. Pater, like Browning, achieves intensity; whatever his faults, Pound says, he is not "DULL. . . . The supreme crime in a critic is dullness." But Pound declares (possibly thinking of his own beginnings) that Pater is "adolescent reading, and very excellent bait" (160).

24. For a detailed reading of Pound's specific debts to the poetry of the 1890s and to D. G. Rossetti and Swinburne see Nagy, *Poetry of Ezra Pound*, chaps. 2–4.

25. For example, Browning's treatments of sexuality and power in numerous poems; his engagement with the Higher Criticism in *Christmas-Eve and Easter Day*, "Karshish," and the "Epilogue" to *Dramatis Personae*; his treatment of Napoleon III in "Prince Hohenstiel-Schwangau."

from a historicist understanding of the past. Thus in *Gaudier-Brzeska* (1916), Pound specifies the daring of Wadsworth, Gaudier-Brzeska, Lewis, and Fenollosa as the making of a renaissance: "The interest and perhaps a good deal of the force of the group I mention lie in the fact that they have perfectly definite intentions; that they are, if you like, 'arrogant' enough to dare to intend 'to wake the dead' . . . that they dare to put forward specifications for a new art, quite as distinct as that of the Renaissance, and that they do not believe it impossible to achieve these results. . . . The Renaissance sought a realism and attained it. It rose in a search for precision and declined through rhetoric and rhetorical thinking, through a habit of defining things in terms of something else" (GB, 117). Content may here, as in Pater's work, become form, but form is assumed to have consequences beyond the work of art or of history itself. A new art can make a new renaissance, which eventually, comes for Pound to imply new economic relations and forms of power. Such new art begins in the historicist daring to "wake the dead."

The beginning of Pound's own poetry some ten years before the publication of *Gaudier-Brzeska* shows us the roots of his eventual canonical pronouncements from about 1912 on. Within the historicist approach to the past, he develops both the language of Pater's delicacy and charm and the kind of realism that he and Ford later ascribed to Browning. Pound tries on, like the vestures of his own literary past, the clothes of Pater and Browning. The result in this apprentice work is a curious stance—part aesthetic poseur and part anti-aestheticist posturing. Pound's rather precarious combination of voices reveals the instabilities of the historicism he inherited; it foreshadows the more profound contradictions of his later work. The most obviously doubled of Pound's early efforts is an unpublished manuscript called "In Praise of the Masters."

The Victorian Canon in the Poet's Workshop

"In Praise of the Masters" is a seven-page typescript with pencil emendations (Beinecke Library). It consists of a cover sheet with prose introduction, a two-page dramatic monologue spoken by Rembrandt, and two half sheets and two full sheets of prose conclusion taking the form of a letter to an editor meant to accompany the poem and ten reproductions of paintings. It is found among Pound's college verse and probably dates from 1906–7.

This early poem is a curious example of poetry trying to be realistic

or "tough" in the manner of Browning and of prose tending to be
poetic in a style reminiscent of Pater's impressionism. The text is given
in full in the appendix, but I should note here that Pound's prose
exordium begins with a triple reference to Shelley, Browning, and
Dante. "Oh yes, I have studied Browning, but one does not imitate
by using a sonnet of Dantesque form." He notes Shelley "has written
no poem for painting" and Browning none "for the masters." Unlike
Browning, who investigates characters "from the end of the world"
in Pater's phrase, Pound makes the master speak directly. The poem
is a dramatic monologue with Rembrandt speaking something like
Browning's knottiest language. He owes a reasonable amount to Fra
Lippo Lippi and perhaps even something to Kipling. Rembrandt begins:

> No I don't cotton to your squirks and spirals.
> Beauty be dagged sir. My work (life).
>   My own mug sir, so please you, yes sir,
> three on one wall here. Vain?
> Bless your simplicity, were I a vain man
> would I tell all time coming that my nose was
> blunt as a sack stein? Vain sir, God please you
> . . . .
>   Yes I know your thin Botticelli's, your vainly cute sunspangles
> and tumble down roses. Thin as a web sir.
>   But we're a cold land sir, none o that ruction.

The speaker goes on to insist that he paints himself and his mistress
in "just our day's toggery." He asks incredulously "This like Mona
Lisa?" And he deflates all talk of beauty:

>   But beauty? what in hell's eggs are you
> grumbling and mumbling o beauty for?
> I paint what I see sir. Damme. Lights and no lights,
> folk as they come to me. Your spindle shanked
> goddesses, where do you find em?
> I see no such a running o our ways.

Rembrandt concludes, defending his art, "Egad tis the truth sir. An't
sticks." As if to excuse the metrical sloppiness of this attempt, the poet
adds in explanatory fashion at the page's bottom: "Being a blunt man,
he hath small care o metrics and luted enwebments." As the poet
creates him via Browning, Rembrandt clearly is no Pater.

One wonders, however, about the poet. He follows the poem both with a note exhibiting his impatience with editors and with his pedagogic suggestion that the poem be published along with "ten old masters." This voice, the impatient pedagogic voice of "How to Read" or many of the later prose pieces, rapidly modulates into something infinitely more Pateresque. Clearly Pound knew whereof he spoke when he called Pater "adolescent reading." For Pound, reading and writing were never separate undertakings, and Pater here provides both adolescent reading and writing.

In the prose continuation accompanying the dramatic monologue, Pound speaks of two poems; the first clearly is the monologue "wherein he [Rembrandt] speaketh." Pound then speaks of a second poem as a "deeper thing," though no second poem is attached and I have as yet found none. The prose itself, however, becomes its own poem in a Pateresque fashion, though without Pater's skill at punctuating appended phrases and clauses. It begins: "I have read my Rembrandt, I have pondered on the Mona Lisa as men have and will till canvas be a name and paint is forgotten. But most of all 'The Annunciation' had come as a new thing to me. . . . I had said Rembrandt is the Shaxpeare of paint. But the Mona Lisa tainted the Third of Saskia; twas as if one should compare Anne Hathaway and Beatrice, the earthly Beatrice. And then faint and above them all wonderfully like one that shall be nameless, Angelico's maiden." Pound goes on in this vein, invoking the Annunciation in Latin and English and describing himself as "rapt into ecstasy". He concludes by returning to the prints he intends to enclose for the editor, not now berating some imagined editor but evoking him as an inspired fellow art lover: "That I send you only ten of the signets is my weakness, but oh, you have memories. You must have understood and borne with you some of spell and lure that dwelleth in the shadows of their limning. And the lost lyrics of their tone, the strange faint shades that dwelt there ere time half hid them in forgetfulness. And left their whispers for only him that will watch the lights change upon their surfaces." By the conclusion of this piece, both paint and prose are aspiring to music. The harsh reality of Rembrandt's northern climate is submerged in the aqueous light of Pater's Italy. And the voice of the pedagogue like the tough voice of the monologuist has diminished to a whisper.

By the time he comes to revise the early cantos, Pound has found, through translation, quotation, and the combination of voices, through the direct evocation of Homeric myth, a way of approaching "strange faint shades that dwelt there" until time "half hid them in forgetfulness." In other early poems, he addressed, much more directly than here, Browning, Shakespeare, Dante, even Anne Hathaway. Through these efforts he arrived at a way of turning the various voices of canonical instruction, of Pateresque vision, and of Ford's prose tradition to good account. The "king's treasury" that is *The Cantos* is radically inclusive and makes radical appeals to hierarchy. It is enmeshed in the contingencies of existential historicism and attempts to go beyond such contingency.

As I show in the next two chapters, one significant way Pound transmuted the need for canon making into the very texture of art was through his repeated imitation of Browning. In much of Pound's early poetry, as in "In Praise of the Masters," construction of canons, imitation, and poetic self-creation were one.

"In Praise of the Masters" exemplifies early on Pound's propensity to imitate in order to grapple with the complexities of his historical position. The poet is by turns a pedagogue and an aesthete, a hard-nosed historicist excavator of the past with all its blemishes and one who cultivates beauty with something like an appreciative detachment. This poem, like many from Pound's early years, is made amid conflicted notions of the poet's cultural situation and among the ambivalences of historicism. The contradictions given concrete form in this early effort and in others like it are expressed in the urgency of Pound's later canonical pronouncements, in his prolonged and complex practice of imitation, and in more accomplished experiments with diction and form. The poet eventually becomes a defiant thief of culture who would—sometimes brilliantly, sometimes obscurely—remake the language from his multifarious borrowings. "In Praise of the Masters" can scarcely achieve a tenuous unity, a precarious balance: the contradictions of its language are too great. Perhaps sensing this potential disintegration, the poet resorts to self-deprecating irony; in his prose continuation of "In Praise of the Masters," he admonishes his imagined audience, think "before you call the ambulance."

Chapter 2

Poet as Ragpicker: Browning
in Pound's Early Poetry

The moralist, the artist, the saint, and the statesman may well be troubled when they see that all foundations are breaking up in mad unconscious ruin and resolving themselves into the overflowing stream of becoming; that all creation is being tirelessly spun into webs of history by the modern man, the great spider in the mesh of the world-net.

—Nietzsche, *The Use and Abuse of History*

Endlessly unraveling webs in the stream of history. The poet as spider in the ruins, as thief, as the jester in motley, the ragpicker, the flâneur, the exile. Each of these figures is remarkable for its equivocation, for its claim to find truth in the detritus of history and its claim that such truth is at best a fragment, at worst a lie. In each the artist is an exile, a reject, even a joker. Pound vividly captures this situation in "Webs," a brief prose fable he sent to Viola Baxter in 1907:

> There was once a man who lived in one room and it was very dusty and full of webs that folk call cobwebs, but for him they were the word webs of the singers of old time, and none but the man looked at the webs. "For," they said, "they will be full of dust and very ugly."
> And there came a wind and blew the roof from that man's house, and heavy dew fell upon the webs. And at sunrise many people marveled. But everybody forgot to look for the man. And there went forth

a rumor that the man died at false dawn of a chill. But I know that he
became a spider and made webs in other men's houses. (Pound, early
typescript)[1]

The outsider, through an ability to escape ruin, becomes the one who
spins "webs in other men's houses." He is by turns the exile and the
insider, the escape artist and the heroic maker of the world net.

Such an artist is the kind Charles Baudelaire would have called a
"painter of modern life" and Walter Benjamin would have called a
"collector"; he is the artist of the metropolitan center, but he is
equipped with an unavoidable sense of its transience and of his own
historicity. He makes his way through the urban crowd of anonymous
people, detritus, and old clothes. Derelict things may retain their
names—like secondhand books recording on their flyleaves their previous owners—but the owners are now missing, perhaps dead.

The ragpicker poet operates not on the heterocosmic analogy—the
poet is to creation as God is to the world—but on the historiographic
principle. Pound owes his place as a singularly important creator of
modernism both to his linguistic virtuosity and to this radically historicized practice of poetic "theft" and construction. His method of
making canons and of making himself a poet was an elaborate form
of thievery. Through translation, imitation, and parody and through
explicit meditation on the processes of poetic inheritance, he collected
a tradition. Like the existential historicist, he found himself constructing historical webs in the endlessly dissolving historical stream. As
his own canonical pronouncements and his own early elaboration of
the web metaphor make clear, this process of becoming a poet involved inherent contradictions—between detachment from and sympathetic participation in history, between the aesthetics of book
production and the economics of authorship, between a pedagogic
relationship to and a contempt for audience. Always for Pound contradictions had to be grasped as technical matters of poetic diction
and form. As his unpublished early poems reveal, he practiced from
the beginning a poetics of contradiction; instead of finding a single
voice he became an ever more capable imitator and thief.

The ambiguous figures of the poet as ragpicker and thief engage

1. "Webs" is contained in the manuscript correspondence of Pound and Viola Baxter
[Jordan], as part of "Poems." In the last sentence, "spun" is written above "made"
and is canceled in pencil. One-page typescript, Beinecke Library, Yale University. In
this passage and in other unpublished works by Pound, I have regularized spelling
and punctuation except where spelling and punctuation are of special interest.

directly the problem of the poet's place in an urban, commodified, and radically historicized world. In these figures we see again the point where Pound links Browning's critique of aestheticism with the art of Pater and his aestheticist successors. As he learned through imitation and translation, Pound not only worked against a doubled nineteenth-century English canon; he also assimilated work of poets in other languages and traditions to the crucial opposition between Browningesque historicism and aestheticist ornamentation. Pound's more mature poetry is a complex version of a poetics grounded in these contradictions about the goals and means of art. In his early poetry, these contradictions are writ large.

The first half of this chapter explores the cultural situation indicated by Pound's figures for the poet, the situation in which, as we have seen, he became an inveterate pedagogue and maker of canons. I begin by attending to the ideological and material conditions in which he began his poetic experiments and by discussing how those conditions were at work earlier in Browning's poetry. In Pound's relationship to audience, as in Browning's, we find the poet conceived as marginal, an exile, a picker of historical rags; like Browning, he challenges his audience by maintaining a posture of simultaneous attachment and detachment which mirrors the historicist's uneasy connection to the past. Following Walter Benjamin and Hannah Arendt, I argue that in ideological and material conditions of alienation from his audience, the poet becomes a collector, a translator who assembles fragments of culture. This ideological condition, I further show, was linked to the material conditions of producing poetry in England at the moment when Pound was first publishing; the artist as collector makes collector's books. The aesthetic reponse to commodification becomes a commodity.

In the second half of this chapter I examine in detail the consequences, for poetic diction and form, of these ideological and material conditions, particularly as they shape Pound's early poetry and unpublished work. As a collector and translator Pound directs his anxieties more toward his audience than toward his predecessors. This being so, I find an approach to imitation based in classical rhetoric more fruitful for understanding his imitations than I do Harold Bloom's model of the family romance.[2] Pound's problematic task is

---

2. Bloom, *Anxiety of Influence*. As I note in detail below, I am particularly indebted to George Bornstein for this anti-Bloomian approach (*Poetic Remaking*), and I also find myself in agreement with Christopher Beach's work on Pound and his predecessors, *ABC of Influence* and "Ezra Pound and Harold Bloom."

not to extend or to wrestle with a tradition so much as to assemble one. Given the ambiguities I have already discussed within his historicism and within such an early poem as "In Praise of the Masters," it should not be surprising to find his imitative art a doubled one. Because Pound like Browning understands himself to be placed in an ambiguous relationship to his culture, he imitates Browning repeatedly in his early poetry when he ponders the proper goals and language of his art. Browning, then, mediates between Pound's own moment and earlier traditions, and Browning's mannerisms are used to resist aestheticism even as his historical concerns enable Pound's encounter with the past. Finally, I argue, Pound moves from what classical rhetoricians would call "exercise" toward the most successful form of imitation—practice. His most complex homage to Browning, "Near Perigord," achieves its own historicist equilibrium, invoking neither Browningesque ironies nor aestheticist detachment. In "Near Perigord," the problem of audience and its attendant difficulties are held in abeyance. Unlike "Near Perigord," however, Pound's earliest poems are more obviously imitation than practice. Though they reveal the beginnings of his more complex historicist practice, their anxieties about audience are evident.

Sordello and the Problem of Audience

From the very beginning of his published work, Pound actively imagined his readers, both present and future. In postulating an audience ambivalent about his art he located himself within the same difficulty he would have found in Browning's poetry; for other than Byron, no nineteenth-century English poet made the relationship of poet and audience so explicit a theme of poetry itself.[3] Right from the outset Pound imagines for his poetry a reception almost as dubious as the actual reception of Browning's *Sordello.* Just as the historicist experiences attachment to and detachment from the past, so the poet both approaches and distances himself from his audience.

3. Byron's importance for Pound has seldom been remarked; yet Pound's early poetry and prose allude to Byron frequently—especially to Byron's criticism of English society. Pound's poem "L'Homme Moyen Sensual" imitates Byron forthrightly (1915; PSP, 256). In America, Whitman also frequently addressed the question of audience, but with less irony and more easy confidence than Browning. And it is crucial to recall in constructing Pound's early situation that he chose not to publish his first books in America but in Europe, thus defining his own project in a cosmopolitan way that owed more immediately to Anglo-European than to American literary traditions. See the discussion in Chapter 3 of Byron and mock epic.

In "Famam Librosque Cano," published in Pound's first volume, *A Lume Spento* (1908), the poet, with some self-ironizing and some seriousness, imagines two fates for his poetry. In the first, the "little mothers" sing his verses to children; at these readers, the world may laugh, not recognizing their seriousness. In the other fate—more directly allied to the anti-epic ironies of the poem's title—the poems become the ragged object of an old and "out at heels" bibliophile (CEP, 22–23). The world also sneers at this reader because "he hath / No coin, no will to snatch the aftermath / Of Mammon." Nonetheless, the old man plucks "a ragged / Backless copy from the stall" as though he has found something strange and rare. The poet comments sardonically on this fate. In "Famam Librosque," Pound imitates Browning's ambiguous imagining of audience in *The Ring and the Book*; for Browning had plucked his old yellow book from among the rags of the Florentine flea market and, suspecting his readers' hostility, insisted on its value.[4] Here at the start of his career Pound projects his own poems' escape from Mammon: the private lullaby (unappreciated by the world) and the ragged, perhaps more ambitious forgotten book plucked by a textual ragpicker from the detritus of a used-book stall. The larger audience, the world, is projected as unsympathetic and driven by commercial motives.

The poet himself in *A Lume Spento* and in other early volumes in certain respects identifies with the special readers he imagines. He seeks a new freshness from old texts, an energy of song from the troubadours, and a delicate intimacy from fin-de-siècle love poetry. Like the old man, he extracts books from a pile of ragged paper and seeks poetry in them. The poems of Pound's early volumes also exploit the ironies of the poet's detachment even from his most sympathetic readers. This ironic, detached voice provides an antidote to aestheticism even as it fosters it. The ironic poet is the cosmopolitan poet in exile. He longs for and rejects in advance the approval of the audience.[5] Like Browning, he is more anxious about his audience than about his poetic predecessors.

4. Both *Sordello* (Browning, *Poems*, 1:148–296) and *The Ring and the Book* locate their initial scenes in urban marketplaces, Venice and Florence, respectively. The young woman who tugs on the poet's sleeve in *Sordello* is poor and disreputable and yet is, if anyone is, his instigation to poetry; in *The Ring and the Book* the old yellow book is plucked from among urban detritus and historical junk. The old man of "Famam Librosque" remarkably resembles Browning's father.

5. Longenbach's *Stone Cottage* treats in detail Pound's and Yeats's attitudes toward audience during their period of closest association. Longenbach demonstrates Pound's growing antipathy to the public or the "mob" and shows how, despite this elitist

We can without exaggeration imagine Pound's early poetry as a repeated working out of positions created and deconstructed in Browning's *Sordello*. With Christine Froula, I would claim *Sordello* as the earliest substantial modernist poem in English. It presents us with the poet as arranger of rags in commercial and historical marketplaces. *Sordello*'s significant confrontation with Palma in Book 3 occurs barely removed from the commercial and political uproar of the Veronese market; the poet's encounter with the nameless poverty-stricken woman who becomes his muse occurs in the Venetian marketplace. The poet presents us with a spectacle of art (or the artist) in the marketplace and with the concomitant question of art's relationship to its audience.

Since the advent of large-scale commercialization in publishing "serious literature," the nature of and relation to audience had been a vexing matter, for poets even more than for writers of prose. As the potential audience for serious poetry grew, so did the poet's uneasiness with its possible demands and limitations.[6] Like Pound's major works "Hugh Selwyn Mauberley," "Homage to Sextus Propertius," and *The Cantos*, *Sordello* deliberately challenges its readers. It requires what Jerome McGann has called "radial reading," a pursuit of significance that necessarily reaches beyond text into context (McGann, "Cantos," 1–4). The contexts of *Sordello* have been as puzzling to Browning's readers as the contexts required by much of *The Cantos* have been to Pound's. *Sordello*, like Pound's poems, deliberately challenges its actual audience and wishfully imagines an ideal one. It exacerbates its concerns about audience by treating this relationship thematically, by doubling its narration in a self-conscious and self-reflexive way, and by relying heavily on obscure allusions.

Sordello's conflicted relationship to audience, to the muse, to politics, and to the poet who creates him prefigures Pound's own challenges in becoming a poet. Though the poem's muse is in the crowd and though the poem is largely situated in scenes of urban strife, *Sordello* presents chivalric love poetry and nature poetry as alterna-

---

stance, he "paradoxically continued to think of himself as an artist who worked for the common good of the people" (95).

6. By "serious poetry" here I mean poetry published in books and magazines, rather than broadsides, music hall songs, and oral poetry. Of course it is precisely this troublesome and loaded distinction between the serious or literary and the popular that vexed the question of a widening audience; as Chapter 6 indicates, the problem of audience reflected gendered divisions as well as complex class distinctions. A full discussion of these complexities is beyond my scope here.

tives to its own central undertaking, alternatives that years later engaged Pound with nearly equal power. Sordello hopes that "nature's strict embrace, / Putting aside the past, shall soon efface / Its print as well" (Book 3, lines 7–9). Browning characterizes such hope as futile. Chivalric love poetry fails equally: Sordello has forgotten his songs—his brain has forgotten its craft, his tongue its tricks (3. 76–77). The poem leads Sordello inevitably toward urban and intensely political conflict; and yet Book 6 suggests that Sordello's last word remains the scrap of song remembered in the natural scene of Goito.[7] The poet himself in Book 3, in propria persona, adjusts the rags of the crowd (739–40) and is called to account by a woman who is its ragged nadir and who yet represents the poet's social and political—if not affective—aspirations.

In its questions about audience and the means of art, *Sordello* engages the issues to which Pound's early poems address themselves. For Pound, the complexities of *Sordello* were mediated through Browning's later poetry and through D. G. Rossetti's and Swinburne's appropriations of Browning's text. In Pound's early poetry, published and unpublished, we see the poet as historical ragpicker and thief. Like Sordello, he must grapple with the social and historical meanings of poetry and with the problem of audience. Like Browning, he takes up the position of the self-consciously modern poet addressing the present while calling up the past. At the outset of *The Cantos*, Pound situates himself in a position precisely analogous to Browning's two generations earlier; he sits on the Dogana's steps worrying about poetry, women, and money.

The Collector, the Translator, and the Contradictions of Aestheticism

The poet in the marketplace—the ragpicker, flâneur, or collector—must capture the evanescent and the almost vanished. It is not simply that beauty is fleeting but rather that all life forms are historical and historicized. No teleology can guarantee their coherence or stability, let alone order them in a hierarchical way. Like Browning, then, Pound is in the situation of the existential historicist. He is, or can be, rapt before the spectacle of the past as he himself has formed it by building a pattern, by tracing threads of his historical web to various

7. The fate of Sordello's poetry is not unlike that of Pound's own, remembered as it often is for the more lyric sequences of *The Pisan Cantos*.

elements of the context. His "webs," as Pound calls them in his early
fable, become a figure for what Hayden White has named "contextualist history" (*Metahistory*, 17). In his creation of a nineteenth-
century canon, Pound associated this historicist project with Browning
and opposed to it the approach he characterized as Tennysonian medievalizing. Yet as we have seen, like Browning, Pound had to reckon
with the aestheticizing tendencies of this historical view.

If the legacy of historicism is antiteleological, if as Leopold von
Ranke said, every age is immediate to God and none therefore merely
preparatory, then historicism invites detachment (Krieger, *Ranke*, 6).
The poet may stand back in awed appreciation of the pattern she has
made, initially rejecting aestheticism, then perhaps coming to practice
it. Before Pound, Browning was especially attentive to this difficulty;
the historical and moral ambiguities of aestheticism dominate portions
of *The Ring and the Book* along with many of his monologues.[8] Detachment before the spectacle of history leads to an aestheticism Browning
as often as not analyzes for its violent potential—the violence inherent
in aestheticizing human relationships.

Opposing Browning's historical view to Victorian medievalizing
provides Pound with a means of resisting aestheticism. Yet he must
contend with the aestheticism even within his own project. For the
contextualist poet, historical coherence can be a momentary, elusive if
not illusory, series of connections (cousins of the "image" or even the
"ideogram"). The historian or poet risks a detachment that, even if he
begins in the critique of aestheticism, easily transforms itself into a
view of history as beautiful patterns, conjunctures, or recurrences. In
resisting progressivist historical narrative, the contextualist historian
may become a collector of the past—a figure Walter Benjamin connects to the idler in the modern city who is detached both from commodified things and from the narrative of progress that would link
them (*Illuminations*, 45).

Pound's contextualist historicism brings together both anti-
aestheticist and aestheticizing tendencies. Such a situation is presented
through the figure of the idler in *Lustra* (1916). In "Further Instructions" he describes his poems themselves as fragments among fragments. He calls them idlers: "You stand about in the streets, / You
loiter at the corners and bus-stops, / You do next to nothing at all"

---

8. See especially "Cleon," "The Bishop Orders His Tomb at St. Praxed's Church," and
Guido's and the prosecutor's monologues in *The Ring and the Book*. See also my
History and the Prism of Art.

(PSP, 95). Pound's urban idler is a living criticism of the "man with a steady job"; at the same time he is the modern embodiment of Pater's sensibility contemplating the past, the past of beautiful fragments. In "Further Instructions," Pound declares—half ironically— that he would clothe his poems with scarlet trousers and dragons, the accoutrements of aesthetic and exotic painting. The poet contemplates his creations, even as he juxtaposes the beautiful with the bus stop; irony resists but can never abandon the aesthetic.

The idler on the streets encounters beauty in fragments and in the faces of unknown women. When Yeats placed Pater's description of the Mona Lisa at the beginning of the *Oxford Book of Modern Poetry*, he confined himself to Pater's description of the woman, omitting his contention that Mona Lisa is "modern" because she sums up the multifariousness of life and of history. Pater cannot resist the fancy that one life can sweep "together ten thousand experiences" (*Renaissance*, 99). It is the unstable crowd of meanings he attributes to the woman which attracts him, not the woman herself or the painted surface. The Mona Lisa is modern; she might as well be the woman Baudelaire glimpses in the crowd, the muse Browning encounters in the marketplace, the shopgirl Pound sees on the streets, or the figure he chooses to personify New York.[9]

In "N.Y." (*Smart Set*, 1913), Pound takes up and resists Pateresque aestheticizing by responding directly to the question of modernity. He plays out the contradictions of the artist's position, evoking a kind of irony more skillfully developed later in the *Homage to Sextus Propertius*. Can the idler still find beauty on Madison Avenue? The poem's argument suggests he cannot; the poem's language suggests he can. New York becomes a type of modern beauty (a white beauty, thin as a reed), and the poet claims he will "breathe" a soul into the woman / city.[10] At the same time, an antithetical voice claims the poet is mad: *"For here are a million people surly with traffic; / This is no maid. / Neither could I play upon any reed if I had one"* (Pound's italics, CEP, 185). The

9. On the idler or poet and the attraction to the woman in the crowd, especially in Baudelaire, see Benjamin, *Illuminations*, 196. Virginia Woolf parodies such scenes in *Mrs. Dalloway.*

10. The "white beauty" of "N.Y." has its own ironies, if we follow Alex Zwerdling's argument that a crucial element in Pound's expatriation was the sense he shared with many of his position and race that the United States was being inundated with nonwhite immigrants, that is, by those who were not from northern Europe (unpublished lecture). The personification of New York may owe something to Pater as well; Longenbach has shown how both Pound and Eliot adopted Yeats's view of Pater's place in the genealogy of modernism (*Stone Cottage*, 170).

poet's stance involves attraction to a single (largely imaginary) beautiful figure, detachment from the crowd, and an ambiguous detachment from his own detachment.

Pound's detachment before the crowd or the flux of history makes irony and even cynicism possible; but rather than attempting an ironic critique of irony as Browning often does in the dramatic monologues, Pound plays out the contradictions in juxtapositions of tone and style. In "N.Y." and other early poems he incorporates in their very language the poems' material and ideological contradictions. His poetry is closer to Browning's *Sordello*—whose tortured syntax serves as "brother's speech"—than to the more stable of Browning's ironic monologues. In a poem as simple as "N.Y."—and a poem as complex as *Sordello*—no final argument can be made about the priority of a single voice.

In his early poems through translation, imitation, and parody—and in the later poems through translation and quotation—Pound multiplies voices. He builds webs in other men's houses. In the process he lends a double force to the past. It is the cobweb spun in the dust of history and a pattern of jewels, the historicist pattern and the aestheticist object. The web is tenuous, subject to immediate destruction; yet in creating a web in the stream of becoming, the poet claims to survive destruction and to weave again.

The spider, the ragpicker, and the collector figure poetry as ineluctably historicized and as marginal to or displaced from the commercial and industrial center of society. Focusing on these metaphors we can see Pound's situation as remarkably like that Walter Benjamin described in his essays of the 1920s and 1930s. Coming to grips with modernity, Benjamin's essays analyze the links among the artist as flâneur and urban observer, the collector, and the translator.

In Benjamin's view, art in the age of mechanical reproduction no longer can claim authenticity, uniqueness, or centrality in communal ritual. Nor, though Benjamin is less concerned with this, is it produced solely for a group of patrons whose taste is known and largely shared by the artist. In short, as Hannah Arendt has pointed out in her introduction to Benjamin's *Illuminations*, tradition can no longer guarantee the significance of art to its audience or the meaning of the past to the present. Hence the collector attempts to substitute the criteria of authenticity and the rarity of the work for the wider guarantees of tradition. Thus he responds to the contradiction between art "embedded in the fabric of tradition" (Benjamin, *Illuminations*, 223) and art as object for exhibition. Benjamin places the collector precisely in the position of the poet who identifies with Odysseus in the final version of Pound's first canto. Benjamin's collector, like Pound's poet, violently yokes the present to the past, raising the shades of the departed: "The genuine picture may be old, but the genuine thought is new. It is of the present. This present may be meager, granted. But no matter what it is like, one must firmly take it by the horns to be able to consult the past. It is the bull whose blood must fill the pit if the shades of the departed are to appear at its edge" (from *Schriften* 2.314; quoted in Arendt, "Introduction," 44). The present confronts the past as the poet wrestles in sacrificial violence.

The collector then, unexpectedly, becomes the presiding presence at a scene of some cultural violence. His situation is not unlike that René Girard has described as the "sacrificial crisis," when cultural or historical distinctions have broken down in such a way that violence can be thought of as a means of restoring distinctions.[11] In Pound's case, as I show in Chapter 5, the poet eventually comes to present himself as both prophet and victim. But in the early poems and cantos, the poet is a collector, rescuing fragments from historical flux and making claims for their importance. His art itself establishes their authenticity and cultural significance.

The search for authenticity, however, is in Benjamin's view contradictory from the start. Authenticity, established by tradition, is orthodox and hierarchical; responding to the predicament of art, as commodity reproducible without reference to its embeddedness in culture, the collector unexpectedly destroys even as he creates. The passion of the collector is to "combine with loyalty to an object, to individual items, to things sheltered in his care, a stubborn subversive protest against the typical, the classifiable."[12] The collector, Arendt asserts, in Benjamin's own time has no longer to break with tradition but only to "bend down, as it were, to select his precious fragments from the pile of debris" ("Introduction," 45).

Pound writes in a similar situation, rescuing fragments from debris: yet his position differs in one significant way. He cannot relinquish his project—discussed in the previous chapter as canon creation—of restoring tradition. From the collector's or the ragpicker's place he enacts a contradictory poetics of nostalgia for authentic hierarchy and "stubborn subversive protest against the typical."

11. See Girard, *Scapegoat*, chaps. 1–4.
12. Benjamin, "Lob der Puppe," *Literarische Welt*, 10 January 1930; quoted in Arendt, Introduction to *Illuminations*, 45.

The contradictions implicit in Pound's poetics can be seen concretely in the production and distribution of his texts. Jerome McGann
has called attention to the Pre-Raphaelite practice of fine bookmaking
as a model for the production of Pound's early poems and the first
thirty cantos. In *The Textual Condition*, McGann notes the break in decorative style of the production of Pound's texts in 1912: the early
books are clearly linked to the "protomodernist innovations" of Pre-
Raphaelitism and of aestheticism, whereas the books after 1912 make
use of vorticist decorative initials and, later, of Chinese characters.
Using Benjamin's analysis, McGann shows how, like some other modernist poets, Pound felt compelled to control all aspects of "textual production" including the physical production of the text itself
(138–39).

In this insistence Pound continued the effort of the Victorian decorated book, particularly as represented by William Morris's medie-
valism and the work of the Kelmscott Press. The Victorian decorative
book as developed by Morris had its own historical and historicist
agenda. It recalled the craft-based production of texts; the Kelmscott
books recalled "that historical moment when a newly discovered tool
of mechanical reproduction—the printing press—had not yet become
an engine of cultural alienation" (McGann, *Textual Condition*, 138–
39).[13]

If this care in controlling the visual aspects of the text and its production shows us Pound's need to reduce the alienation of the means
of production, such a restoration of the artist as maker (for an unambiguous audience) is more problematic when we consider the
means of distribution of the book once it was made. For the decorated
book, by the 1890s, was a collector's item. Ellen Moers has pointed
out that the firm of Elkin Mathews and John Lane (publishers of the
fin-de-siècle aesthetes and of *The Yellow Book*) had by 1892 acquired
the name "Publishers, and Vendors of Choice and Rare Editions in
Belles Lettres." The firm made the most of the collector's mania that
enabled the decorated book to show a profit (*Dandy*, 293–94). And it
cultivated new suburban or bourgeois buyers of books.

By the time Pound reached London in 1908, Lane and Mathews had
separated shops, and as Pound knew, Mathews was Yeats's publisher.
Both Lane and Mathews distributed Pound's pamphlet *A Lume Spento*

---

13. McGann's work on *The Cantos* demonstrates how Pound attempts to set these experiments in a "world-historical scale" by controlling all textual aspects of book
production. Thus *The Cantos* become an epic of language. See *Textual Condition*.

(Wilhelm, *Ezra Pound in London and Paris*, 5). Mathews subsequently published a second printing of his *A Quinzaine for This Yule* and brought out virtually all of his early poetry through 1919–20, the years in which Pound also published private and limited editions of "The Fourth Canto" and "Hugh Selwyn Mauberley" with John Rodker. Rodker's Ovid Press edition of "Hugh Selwyn Mauberley" appealed to collectors willing to invest a substantial amount in a book printed on Japan Vellum, numbered, signed, and ostensibly not for sale.[14] The rest of the small edition was published elegantly, with protective leaves of tissue and a natural silk ribbon marker; twenty of these copies were signed and numbered. When in the same year Elkin Mathews published *Umbra: The Early Poems of Ezra Pound* he issued both ordinary copies at eight shillings and special copies at twenty-five shillings. The audience, fit though few, was in significant part an audience of collectors. Pound's major books of prose, by contrast, appeared under the imprint of larger commercial publishers—Dent, Macmillan, Knopf.[15]

Though Pound made little money by his early poetry, he did cultivate the audience and the book buyers to whom the fin-de-siècle aesthetes and Yeats had already appealed. His books and even his own physical presentation in these early years are congruent with what Moers has called the paradoxical turn-of-the-century openness to the artist as "go-getter" (often a colonial) who attempted to sell his talents by publicity and showmanship and who often published his work in fine limited editions (*Dandy*, 292). At the outset of his career—and indeed for many years—Pound struggled with the contradictory goals of combating commercialism and commodification and at the same time making a living as a writer.[16]

Himself a collector of sorts—a poet who made his work in historical fragments—Pound made books that in turn appealed to collectors. In

14. Donald Gallup quotes Pound's letter to his mother of 20 August 1920 in which he writes, "Signed copies of Mauberley all gone, save 2 or 3 vellum copies, bound in full parchment at £3.3" (*Ezra Pound*, 30). Thus, as Gallup points out, the copies ostensibly not for sale were sold at the higher price.
15. The most significant exception was *Gaudier-Brzeska*, published with plates, by John Lane.
16. See Longenbach, *Stone Cottage*, especially chap. 2, "The Bourgeois State of Mind." We might also measure Pound's opposition to universities as an early grip on a kind of "alienation" of labor in accumulating scholarly apparatus. In "The Logical Conclusion" he gives a sardonic account of the replication of replications of knowledge in modern scholarship (CEP, 274), a replication his later poetry both criticizes and encourages.

the production of his early books as well as in the metaphors he chose for poetry we see his attempt to resolve contradictions. The invention of modernism occurs in the struggle with these contradictions—between collection as destruction and canon making as ordering tradition, between book writing and making as resistance to alienation and the need to grasp the bull of the present by its horns. The task of making *and* selling beautiful "subversive" books makes clear the contradictions that gave rise to aestheticism in the first place. The goals of making art as resistance to alienation and of making a living as a writer were deeply antithetical.

That Pound took so relentlessly to translation should not, in this context, be surprising. The fragmentation of tradition, the contradictions between the conventions of aestheticism and the means of its reproduction, the position of collector as destroyer: these are among the conditions, for Pound, of expatriation. And even self-exile makes the exile, necessarily, a translator.[17]

Translation for Pound was yet another form of ragpicking, of collecting, another response to fragmentation. As we have seen, he assembled his Victorian canon to include numerous translators. Unlike most readers he also insisted on the significance of Browning's translations. For Pound, as for Benjamin, translation was a significant response to modernity. In "The Task of the Translator," Benjamin describes the translator's effort not as capturing the spirit or integrity of a work but as a reconstitution of the already broken: "Fragments of a vessel which are to be glued together must match one another in the smallest details, although they need not be like one another. In the same way a translation, instead of resembling the meaning of the original, must lovingly and in detail incorporate the original's mode of signification, thus making both the original and the translation recognizable as fragments of a greater language, just as fragments are part of a vessel" (*Illuminations*, 78). In this early essay, which according to Arendt displays his theological bent, Benjamin goes on to relate

17. For Pound's concerns with exile, audience, commercial success, and his hopes for an American renaissance despite the decentralized or fragmented nature of American culture, see "Patria Mia." He claims that from his European vantage he hears "the creaking of a scattered discontent. Hardly a week goes by but I meet or hear of someone who goes into voluntary exile—some reporter who throws up a steady job to 'come to Europe and breathe'; some professor from a freshwater college who comes away on scant savings. Our artists are all over Europe. We do not come away strictly for pleasure. And we, we constantly-railed-at 'expatriates' do not hear this with unconcern" (SP, 133).

the "greater language" to logos, as Pound was to weld translation in *The Cantos* to his private pantheon and to his notions of political order.

If the poet is to engage with fragmentation rather than to make the translation closely resemble the original, then translating a language in which one is not altogether at ease makes perfect sense. It is arguable that Pound's greatest translations—*Cathay* and "Propertius"—were undertaken, paradoxically, without great concern for a thorough grasp of the language. Apart from modern Italian, the languages most attractive to Pound as translator of poetry were those that exhibited the most fragmentary character, the dead languages—Anglo-Saxon, Latin, classical Greek, Provençal, classical Chinese. The translator from dead languages is, precisely, the spider who spins webs in others' houses. Benjamin's metaphor of the vessel reconstituted from fragments captures the relentless historicization of translation and hence its significance for the language of modernity.

Such a view of translation also explains why Browning's translations, like his *Sordello*, should have been Pound's especial favorites and a special puzzlement to Browning's Victorian readers. Both *Aristophanes' Apology* and *Balaustion's Adventure* examine the reception of the Greek plays they translate, and both construct situations that foreground the position of art in times of social fragmentation. *Aristophanes* is set during the fall of Athens, and *Balaustion's Adventure* during the fall of Rhodes. Euripides, celebrated in both translations, is recognized primarily by exiles and foreigners:

> Alone, unless some foreigner uncouth
> Breaks in, sits, stares an hour, and so departs,
> Brain-stuffed with something to sustain his life,
> Dry to the marrow 'mid much merchandise.
> (*Balaustion*, 300–303)

The exile engaging in translation or gathering up cultural fragments overcomes the deadening pile of "merchandise" by discovering sustenance.[18] Pound the translator himself resembles Euripides' disciples.

18. George Bornstein discusses in detail the significance of *Balaustion's Adventure* and *Aristophanes' Apology* in Pound's early understanding of the process of poetic creation. Not only does *Aristophanes' Apology* provide Pound with the metaphor of the ragbag in the early versions of the first three cantos; Browning's translations also provide the focus for Pound's speculations on poetic influence in his early "journal" and the related poem "To R. B." *Balaustion's Adventure*, Bornstein argues, "enacts the premises of Balaustion's notion of literary influence, in which a later poet both

To read Pound thus as a thief, idler, ragpicker, collector, or translator is necessarily to write the history of early modernism reading
back through *The Cantos*. The conflict between fragmentation and order which is played out through translation in *The Cantos* is less clearly
drawn in the early poems, where imitation and translation are equally
important. Through imitation the poet engages conflicting understandings of poetry and of history; and he confronts the material and
ideological contradictions of the poet's situation. He works in, rather
than resolving, the contradictions between aesthetic detachment and
subversion, between appeal to an elite audience and larger claims of
cultural centrality.

Following Browning as collector and ragpicker, Pound challenged
simple notions of originality, inspiration, or poetic voice. As often as
not, he wore his pieced-together garments with their seams showing;
he displayed his vessel without concealing its cracks and glue.

Models of Poetic Beginning

It is only logical that a ragpicker should have no definable point of
beginning, no spectacular moment of discovering a singular voice.
Indeed, Pound's early poetry challenges both received notions of originality and Bloomian constructs of inheritance. It engages the task
Browning also attempted of rewriting the romantic notion of the poet.
Pound's early poetry is understandable both in terms of the classical
tradition of imitation as it is brought to bear on romantic aesthetics
and in terms of Lawrence Lipking's model of poetic self-making.

Pound's early practice of imitation and translation should not be
seen as simply a stage in his career, to be passed through and gone
beyond. In his *Life of the Poet*, Lipking has persuasively argued that
living as a poet is a complex process in which poets read themselves
and induce their subsequent audiences to read their early work in the
promise, and eventually in the context, of later work. Thus Dante
reads himself or we read his *Vita Nuova* in the promise or the context
of the *Commedia*. Similarly, Pound fashioned himself as author in the
promise of a poem of epic scope. And in fact his early poems, read
backward from *The Cantos*, do not invite metaphors of development

---

takes power from an earlier one and simultaneously revivifies his work. We have
only to think of Pound's *Cantos* to ponder another long poem which depends on
masks, both draws power from and actually translates a Greek work, and insists
on the social efficacy of literature." See *Ezra Pound among the Poets*, 111–12, 121.

toward a single monologic and mature voice, but metaphors of multifariousness become more so.

Pound was unusually, if not uniquely, a modern poet who made himself a poet through imitation. And here, I believe, is a key to what George Bornstein has rightly observed about Pound's poetry, that his postromanticism is not a Bloomian anxiety of influence (*Postromantic Consciousness*, 16–17). One has only to compare Tennyson's relationship to Keats or even Eliot's to Tennyson to see the differences. Herbert Tucker has demonstrated the repeated ways Tennyson implicitly rewrote Keats. Tucker speaks of Tennyson's determination to have "no other texts before him" and of his declaration that after the college prize poem "Timbuctoo" he never imitated (*Tennyson*, 50–53). T. S. Eliot's early poems are remarkably circumscribed rewritings of Byron, Ben Jonson, and Jules Laforgue, plus occasional album verse in a hortatory Victorian tradition. It seems perfectly apt to speak of apprentice verse, from which Eliot turns away (Litz, *Eliot in His Time*, 474), and to maintain as Walton Litz does that Eliot returned to Tennyson in his later poetry as the result of a "changed sense of poetic self" (480). Tennyson's "Mariana" or Eliot's "Prufrock" can be regarded, if too simply, as marking a move from imitation to what each poet recognized as his own legitimate beginning.

Pound's poetry is not nearly so susceptible to identification of a moment of beginning; for his was a very different approach to imitation. Unlike Tennyson, Pound could hardly have claimed that after, say, *A Lume Spento*, he never imitated; he might better have said that by 1915 he had become a more able imitator, a more voracious assimilator of traditions. To cite Pound's own favorite metaphor, one could say he became a more accomplished thief. His effort was not to have no other texts before him but to have all other texts before him. He wished at least to acknowledge the many texts he found worthy of inclusion in his canon. By various means—imitation, translation, quotation, parody—he lays them before the reader. Pound's early poems, for all their aestheticism and archaisms, are when taken as a group also remarkably disparate and multifarious. Inclusion, by way of imitation, is, from the first, the guiding principle of Pound's poetic self-definition.

Pound's early poems show the complexity of departing from the kind of romantic authorship that Harold Bloom has characterized through his agonist model. The poet harbors an ambition to "out top" previous poets—the ambition to be original, some form of belief in genius—and a conviction that poetry is fundamentally a matter of

extending, multiplying, sharing, imitating. It is not just that, as Wordsworth argued, the poet makes the taste by which he is to be appreciated, but that the poet requires the reader to accept the writers of
his own created canon as his "brother" laborers and to meet them,
insofar as possible, on their own terms. In this connection Pound follows the model of Sordello's "brother's speech." As Pound puts it in
an early poem, "To R. B.," which he never published, he himself and
Browning, Cavalcanti and Sordello stand in analogous relationship:
each makes the poetry by which the other is read, each in Pound's
metaphor, "but a part of some greater thought tree, seen before in
some other part and not known to us to be the same" (introduction
to "To R. B.," typescript, Beinecke Library).

The insistence with which Pound promulgates his canon and that
canon's eccentricities reflect his pursuit of originality; yet he insists,
equally, that from a god's eye view, all technical innovations or new
uses of language that characterize the greatest poets are simply
branches of one great tree.

This notion of poetic invention—though it allows for genius and
originality—cannot be accounted for on the Bloomian genealogical
model, as both Christopher Beach and George Bornstein have shown.
In his interesting discussion of Pound and Bloom, Beach contends
that Bloom's genealogical model is deterministic and exclusionary,
privileges one kind of poetry, and emphasizes poetic "power"
or "strength"; Pound's approach to poetic influence, in contrast, emphasizes choice, inclusiveness, and matters of poetic technique.
Pound's poetic tradition, Beach argues, is both a matter of poets'
choices and a cyclic process of technical innovation ("Ezra Pound and
Harold Bloom"). The donative artist, as Pound asserts in *ABC of Reading*, creates something truly new, a new technique in answer to the
requirements of poetic tradition and of his own time; he is followed
by artists who build on his innovation and then by those who are
mere diluters and starters of crazes. A remarkably similar construction
of cyclic poetic history occurs in Browning's essay on Shelley (which
is itself a product of a dualist romantic aesthetic accounting both for
inspiration and innovation).[19] This historicizing of poetic tradition
leaves a young poet not with a Bloomian family romance but—to keep

19. See my discussion of the "Essay on Shelley" and the aesthetics of antithesis in
History and the Prism of Art. For fuller treatment of how Pound's emphasis on techne
allows for canonical inclusiveness (other poets constructing their own canons on
his model) and for poetic influence of the sort Pound's poetic has in fact had, see
Beach, *ABC of Influence*.

to the family metaphor—in the position of the young person who seeks outside the family for adults who represent for her the world she wishes to grow into. A young poet of Pound's inclinations is in an ambiguous position with respect to his forebears, at once their companion and their successor. The young poet's ambiguous place is not compounded simply of genealogical anxiety but rather is shaped by the encounter with poetry as part of a larger history of languages and technique.

For Pound, the poet's ambiguous place is precisely that of the existential historicist who seeks to represent the past on its own terms but whose own position as historian (or poet) necessarily remakes the past as precursor to the present. Pound's difficult double task is to answer repeatedly the question he asks in "Three Cantos," "What's left for me to do?" and to answer it in a way that gathers up, selects, and even does homage to a poetic tradition as he sees it. Because Browning, too, was faced with this ambiguity, because (like Shelley) he approached his art as a matter of experiment and technical innovation, and because of his historicized sense of the poet's role, Browning was especially well suited to become Pound's most significant poetic predecessor in English. A careful examination of Browning's place in Pound's early and unpublished poetry shows Pound both explicitly raising the issue of poetic tradition and taking his own part in tradition through a deliberate process of imitation.

The process of Pound's coming to terms with Browning is less interesting as a teleology of poetic development than as a key to dynamic tensions that constituted Pound's art long after allusion to Browning's texts was replaced by more eclectic processes of quotation and inclusion. Indeed, there is a danger to the critic in following uncritically Pound's own tale of self-definition or his "réforme" through encountering the diction of Browning or Flaubert. For the very conflicting strands of Victorian tradition as Pound defined them by contrasting Browning's poetry with late Victorian aestheticism can be seen to keep twisting and unraveling themselves in his later work.

The persistence of this complex and conflicted tradition is not surprising given the large role Pound accords imitation and all matters of technique. In many of his published and unpublished early texts he exhibits an attitude toward imitation that is more nearly like a classical stance than a modern romantic one, and this despite the profusion in his early work of what he later called Pre-Raphaelitish "stale cream puffs" (quoted in Martz, "Introduction," CEP, vii). The number and variety of Pound's imitations, moreover, indicate that as in the tradition of Quintilian or Seneca one learns through imitating more than one model. Pound's practice of imitation extended to quotation, translation, and parody—a trio not unlike the imitative practices of memorization, translation, and paraphrase recommended in Quintilian's *Institutione oratoria*.[20] Though for brevity's sake I frame this discussion of classical notions of imitation with Quintilian as an example, it is clear that Pound knew the classical rhetorical tradition of imitation both through original sources and through Renaissance proponents of imitation.

Both in pedagogy and in practice, from the classical era until the demise of memorization and other imitative techniques in the twentieth century, imitation meant not replication of the model but imitation with difference.[21] This difference is emphasized in Quintilian's discussion of translation as enabling the translator to learn to speak more effectively in the mother tongue; a benefit of translation is that it enables one to test the limits of one's own vocabulary and to think of new figures of speech in order to create in one's own language the virtues of another (Donald Clark, "Imitation," 19). This understanding of translation and imitation allows us to see the continuity among Pound's imitations of English poets and his translations of classical and Provençal poets. All were in the classical sense exercises, though as Edward Corbett remarks of imitative exercises generally, it is often difficult to distinguish imitation exercises from "practice" in which the imitator subsumes the model in a project of his or her own.[22]

20. Pound had evidently read his Quintilian; he does not deal with Quintilian's notions of imitation but dismisses him for his damaging influence on style in the "mid-Renaissance." That influence, in Pound's view, encouraged "rhetoric and floridity" and " 'did for' the direct sentence." See "Affirmations," *New Age* 11 February 1915, rpt. in *Gaudier-Brzeska*, quoted here as reprinted in PPC, 2:17.

21. See especially Clark, "Imitation," and Corbett, "Theory and Practice of Imitation." Pound's own education, of course, in addition to numerous translation exercises, would have emphasized the traditional disciplines of memorization and imitation.

22. Corbett, "Theory and Practice of Imitation," 246–50. Pound's critics—following the poet's own lead—have used the metaphor of the mask to account for this process of imitation and its consequences; for such a metaphor allows us to sidestep the question of originality and genius. But the classical notion of imitation is equally useful as it focuses our attention on issues of literary canon and poetic technique rather than on a presumed poet who stands behind the masks and casts them off one by one. Humphrey Carpenter's description of Pound as a congeries of masks, however, is a compelling one. Carpenter quotes Wyndham Lewis's pungent opinion that Pound "is that curious thing, a person without a trace of originality of any sort ... yet when he can get into the skin of somebody else ... he becomes a lion or a lynx on the spot" (*Serious Character*, 53). Here a comparison with Browning is instructive; for of major Victorian poets, Browning was the one accused by readers

In Pound's early poetry, both published and unpublished, the issues of originality and of poetic influence are repeatedly raised, and for the most part Pound is willing to set aside originality as an important and immediate goal. In early unpublished poems including pieces titled "To Shelley," "Disappointment," "Pageantry," and "Rex," he attempts to situate himself in poetic tradition and to see how to claim it. In his introduction to *Ezra Pound among the Poets*, Bornstein quotes Pound's dictum in "A Retrospect": "Be influenced by as many great artists as you can, but have the decency either to acknowledge the debt outright, or to try to conceal it" (LE, 5; quoted, xii). This formula could be taken as a retrospective description of Pound's own practice in his early years, though he more often succeeded in acknowledging the debt outright than in concealing it. In his delight in writing poems about poetry the early Pound seems at pains to find as many ways as possible to acknowledge debts. These poems, like other early ones, also show the double nature of the canon as Pound seeks to make it: Browningesque roughness alternates with Pre-Raphaelite aestheticizing.

The early poem "To Shelly" (*sic*) exists in two versions in the Beinecke Library, the more heavily amended draft dated 25 October [1906]. Two pages of Shelleyean doggerel, it is interesting primarily as an early version of Pound's relationship to a predecessor poet. In one of the two drafts, probably the first, the poet admits he is greeting Shelley, whom "I never read afore." If as Bornstein has argued, Pound first seriously read Browning beginning in 1902, one can conjecture with some certainty that Pound came to Shelley through Browning's comments on Shelley's significance for himself. Pound's imitation of Shelley remains at the level of quotation he derides in "A Retrospect" as mere ornamental borrowing of vocabulary—or here, of Shelleyan symbols. More interesting, however, is the way Pound raises the question of influence. He first cites Shelley's verse as coming to him as "some echo of a older song that quite forestalleth mine." But he is not forestalled for long; for in the next strophe he begs of Shelley that "thy ryming to my ryme / Shall be preceptor." Then the Poundian word "preceptor" is canceled in pencil and the more properly Shelleyan "inspirator" is substituted; in what appears to be the second

---

from Henry James to J. Hillis Miller of having no personality, of being composed wholly of masks themselves. Perhaps a better explanation of Pound's poetics is to see, as Bornstein does, that Pound and Browning both have an unusual freedom from the anxiety of authorship. Such freedom enables Pound's imitations.

Epic Reinvented

typescript version, the whole line is canceled, possibly to make less abrupt the transition from Shelley as "my master" to Shelley as "my brother." Both versions end with the poet claiming brotherhood with Shelley and promising him, "Even so I follow, loving where thou has loved."

Like "To Shelley," another unpublished poem written in a vein of aestheticism about poetic influence is "Pageantry," a product of Pound's days in Crawfordsville, Indiana, and one he signed with his aesthete's nom de plume "Weston Llewmys." "Pageantry," too, invokes past poets, a whole procession of them. Written roughly in three-stress couplets, the poem begins by invoking Spenser and Browning:

> Spenser in broidered vair
> Where is thy spirit? Where
>
> Is the naked truth
> That standeth in Browning's line
>   'Thout ruth?
> Dante, amid the spheres
> Where in the flow of years
>   Thy following?
>   (typescript, Beinecke Library)

Pound goes on to invoke Chaucer, the Provençal troubadours, Saxon poetry, Villon, Shakespeare, Jonson, Marlow, Carew, Lope de Vega, Cervantes, and Calderon and to ask rhapsodically enough, "Who among you is so bold / As dare to follow them / That be gone with the wind?" Spenser's "vair" is a clear indication that, despite Browning's naked truth, Pound is presenting a poetic pageant clothed in Pre-Raphaelite medievalizing. His *vair* comes more immediately from Rossetti than from Spenser. The poet who dares to follow these predecessors obviously is the one who typed "Ezra Pound" and signed "Weston Llewmys" a page and a half later, the poet who sought at the end of the poem for one who would "make a song of his living / Spite the preface of prose." It is likely that Crawfordsville seemed to the young Pound to be a preface of prose and about as distant from pseudo-Spenserian vair as it was possible to be.

Yet the "preface of prose" does have a place in Pound's poetry of this period. As we have seen, his dramatic monologue spoken by Rembrandt grows from a prose piece, as does the piece from the same period that Bornstein has described in detail in *Ezra Pound among the*

Poets, a piece of mixed prose and verse that Bornstein calls a journal (107–9). Pound's poem "To R. B." at least in its second version also involves a brief prose introduction. Prose introductions appear as well in the poems he published in 1908–9, most elaborately in "Na Audiart," "Sestina: Altaforte," and "Piere Vidal Old," where the Browningesque datelines Pound often favored are expanded into notes (CEP, 13, 108, 109).

The mixture of prose and verse is particularly curious in the early journal Bornstein discusses. Here is one of Pound's most explicit discussions of imitation, originality, and tradition as well as an early explicit questioning of audience. Pound acknowledges that previous poets, Browning particularly, have been near to "life and rooted things" and that poets who come after great dead poets must be in some sense secondary. Yet the audience, the public, has missed the truths or beauties the old poets saw, and the younger poet's task is to take up their vision and attempt to make his audience see. Two passages of rough verse in the journal make this relationship clear by taking up the metaphor of the poet in motley and by quoting Robert Browning (who is quoting Elizabeth Barrett, as Bornstein points out):

> As the grass blade in its sheathe
> so are we like in tendency, thou Robert Browning
> and myself. And so take I no shame
> to grow from thee, less near may hap
> to life and rooted things, less "human
> "wish" my "droppings of warm tears,"
> less strong as fits the younger blade
> to be.
>
> The county [country?] of poets, the one royal race
> and shall I swap mine heritage for mess of novelty
> and feed my body's hunger from the land
> my fathers deeded to my very soul.
> Because this trick or that shall sell
> at this or that per word, the jester gets
> some Judas thirty for each noun and verb
> that is a feather tickler to the feet,
> bare feet and canabal [cannibal?] of Baal that laugheth
> to see beauty bare.
>
> (typescript, Beinecke Library)

The mixture of metaphors here is particularly interesting. The great poets are in touch with the essentially human; they are at once kings and jesters, or jesters at least if they sell their souls to the devil of popularity—to the clamor for novelty and originality.

Pound's journal inhabits the same metaphorical territory as his unpublished poem "Rex," which also has a "preface of prose." In "Rex" he imitates Browning more complexly; one can see him actually working his way toward the pentameter couplets Browning used to such good effect in *Sordello* and "My Last Duchess." The beginning of "Rex" situates the speaker, more or less openly Pound, in his own literal and prosaic place: "Some good eighteen by twelve an six, I think my realm is, wall paper poor, the carpet mediocre" (typescript, 5 pages, Beinecke Library). At the top of the first page is scrawled "ars cellerare artem." Whether this phrase refers to Browning's couplets, which conceal their own artifice so successfully, or to concealing influence is unclear. In any case, the title and initial metaphor of "Rex" are borrowed from Ruskin's "Of King's Treasuries," the lecture on reading published in *Sesame and Lilies*.

In his small kingdom, the poet invites us to behold the treasury, a glass-fronted bookshelf, and the verse moves toward the pentameter:

> Behold the vitreous barriers are wide
> "Poetics of the Sage and the sublime
> Longinus," crafty he
> To hold the ear (and more?) of Zenobe
> Both for a silver thumb-nail, lire-split, a dime
> To worthies and their best.
> To catalogue and under-write the rest
> I waste your time and mine
> You take me?
> (typescript, Beinecke Library)

Beginning "Rex" in this prosaic and Browningesque way with a modest move toward self-irony, Pound goes on to a disquisition on painting which revises Browning's "Fra Lippo Lippi" by praising Fra Angelico over Monet; he comes at last to more metrical couplets and to praise of Dante. Here the question of poetic influence, the "debt of words," gives him pause: "But HO!! an I praise Dante, all this scrawl / had better not begun itself at all." The "dime" of the poem's first section reappears as the poet refuses to "twine" his wealth in the golden hair of a poetic idol (a reference to Samuel Daniel and possibly to Browning's "Gold Hair"). Seeking the sublime rather than the "dime," the poet declares his wealth is "men." But having reached this conclusion, which Lippi, Browning, and Ruskin might share, he rejects men's "circumstance and petty things" and chooses to write of "their spirits highest flounderings." Looking for high prophetic and romantic "signs / of wonder," the poet arrives again at Dante. He refuses to be so "beggared" that he cannot praise Dante or, in painting, Michelangelo. But he fears the audience who would object to Dante's putting a pope in hell and Cunizza in heaven. He suggests by having Ibsen make an incongruous appearance that such an audience "chose Dame Grundy for their God."

The tonal incongruities of the sublime/dime rhyme, or the Dante/Ibsen pairing, or spirits' "highest flounderings" are repeated in the twenty-one-line "Envoi" that ends the poem. Here the poet questions himself, "But Ezry, doth this strain run on all night? / Well, I'll conclude it." As if in a first step toward making this poem dramatic, "Ezry" is canceled in pencil. And the poem's tonal instabilities are continued in "Ezry's" determination to avoid "baking gold bricks" in favor of being "mid great men's souls high scavenger." Ezra Pound, Weston Llewmys, and Ezry all have a propensity for high scavenging. The multiple self-namings also represent the young Pound's doubled allegiances to poetic tradition; the scavenger has a taste for Browning's roughness and historicization *and* for an aesthetic sublime.

At the level of explicit statement, "Rex" is much more concerned about an unresponsive audience than about the act of thievery or the incongruities of the language it steals. In "Disappointment," another unpublished poem of this period, the poet speaks cheerfully of "we who pilfer Dante" (typescript, Beinecke Library).

In "Rex" a desire for sublimity is matched by an attempt at dramatic self-irony, though the result is closer to tonal instability than to a thorough remaking of poetic language. The poem, if unrevised, unpublished, and somewhat incoherent, reveals the processes of Pound's making a poetic tradition and in it a place for some of his recurrent themes. He attempts Browning's diction and meter, Dante's symbols, late-romantic sublimity, and a kind of ironic self-mockery. He records these encounters with illustrious forebears in metaphors of economics, of treasury, of coinage. His later poems would return obsessively to the rhyme of sublime and dime, but in the economy of Pound's poetic ancestry, thievery—imitation acknowledged or concealed—is no crime.

Pound's "Piazza San Marco" inhabits similar metaphorical territory and works through a like relationship to literary forebears. Pound never finished the poem, which was written in fair copy and continued in pencil in the San Trovaso notebook in 1908. Like much of his early verse it is a pastiche, with diction borrowed from Browning, Villon, and Burns; its third part is a full-dress imitation of Shakespeare's Sonnet 98, larded with liberal borrowings from Chaucer:

> When proud-pied April leadeth in his train
> And yellow crocus quick'neth to the breath
> Of Zephyr fleeting from the sun-shot rain,
> Then seek I her whom mine heart honoureth.
>   (CEP, 238)

In Quintilian's sense, this is imitation by paraphrase. Yet despite its admiration of Villon's thievery and like "Pageantry," "Piazza San Marco" cannot escape the effect of too many too present forebears at once. The very process of imitation seemed for Pound at first to embody the sublime, and thus the purpose of his earliest imitations was imitation itself.

When Quintilian advocated imitating the best features of each model, he implied the subsumption of these models in a larger rhetorical purpose. Pound's best imitative poetry, as I shall suggest, achieves this relation between model and imitation. Many of the fragmentary efforts he chose not to publish were a poorer kind of motley, a garment loosely patched together from previous texts, its multiple seams and textures showing. For Pound, however, achieving a mature style was not a matter of making a Bloomian swerve away from strong precursors but of turning to account the poet-in-motley, the thief, the Browningesque ragpicker.

The necessity of respecting, even of recapitulating, tradition I believe explains why Browning is crucial to Pound's definition of and response to the Victorian canon. For Browning's historicism provided Pound with a way of constructing his own poetic past. He frequently invokes Browning as kind of mediator between his own needs and poetic tradition. As a poet who himself assumes masks and engages in transcriptions and translation of previous texts, Browning has a key role as preceptor. Like the classical teacher of rhetoric he both is a model and offers other models. Pound, appropriately, coined the word *predefessor* to describe him (letter to Viola Baxter [Jordan], Paige typescripts, Beinecke Library).

Among Pound's early published poetry, four poems from *A Lume Spento* (1908) deal significantly with poetic influence and the possibility of fame: "Fifine Answers," "Mesmerism," "Famam Librosque

Cano," and "Scriptor Ignotus." All four owe their poetic premises to Browning and turn upon metaphors of masks and mesmerism. "Fifine Answers" and "Scriptor Ignotus" borrow their titles and something of their dramatic method from Browning; in "Fifine Answers" the speaker embraces life via exile and disgrace, recognizing as an artist/ actor that he cannot entirely know the "work shop where each mask is wrought." "Call," he concludes, "eh by! the little door at twelve! / I meet you there myself" (CEP, 18). But one might ask who is this "speaking"—a "semi-dramatic" character, one might say, following Pound's characterization of Browning's Sordello ("Three Cantos," PSP, 231).

Both "Mesmerism" from A Lume Spento (1908) and "Histrion" published in A Quinzaine (1908) pose the problems of "Fifine Answers" in terms of the influence of one artist upon another. "Mesmerism" obviously is both Pound's most affectionate tribute to Browning and a deliberate taking on—through parody—of Browning's manner. Browning is acknowledged as a poet of epic proportions, a "long-tonsilled Calliope" (CEP, 17–18). In parodying Browning's diction Pound both enacts and mocks the possibility of poetic influence as mesmerism, while alluding to Browning's poem of the same title. In "Histrion," Pound presents the possibility of mesmerism seriously, and interestingly here Browning's influence is pervasive though his name is omitted. Unlike "Mesmerism," "Histrion" does not imitate Browning's diction but is closer to the characteristic archaisms Pound frequently favored. Its central though muddled metaphor owes much to Browning's golden ring metaphor in The Ring and the Book, even as its list of those whom the poet personates combines Pound's particular heroes, Dante and Villon, with Browning's characters ("Christus, or John, or eke the Florentine") (CEP, 71). The speaker declares that the souls of great men and his own individuality melt into each other (CEP, 71). The poet's "I" is a clear space, taking the forms of others' spirits even as Browning's wax melts away in Book 1 of The Ring and the Book, leaving the design etched on the ring as the molten gold hardens. Although Pound shares Browning's figure of molten gold taking shape into a poem, he takes mesmerism or spirit possession rather than resuscitation as the metaphor to describe how the poet speaks. Thus Villon or Dante, even Christ or John, should possess and speak through the poet. The convergence is a Pateresque moment: "This for an instant and the flame is gone" (CEP, 71).

In these early poems that clearly borrow from Browning, Pound uses the earlier poet as model, as object of parody, and as a mediator of a tradition that is yoked to—but often contrasted with—the tradition of Pateresque aestheticism. As Pound balances or vacillates between ironic historicization and the aestheticization of history, Browning furnishes him both a kind of language and one set of lenses for viewing poetic tradition.

The Doubling of Tradition

The poems I have discussed to this point, both published and unpublished, borrow from and imitate Browning in order to come to terms with the nature of authorship and with the relationship between originality and imitation. The poet who views his craft as ragpicking or as building webs in others' houses, I have indicated, is necessarily committed to a complex relationship to past artists; he must have an affiliative and inventive relation to traditions. Pound's valuing and achievement of inventiveness in his own work rests paradoxically on this affiliative respect for traditions. It also rests, for better or worse, on his profoundly doubled assimilation of poetic traditions, on his ability to entertain contradictory conceptions of the past and contradictory approaches to poetic language.

Although Browning was, I believe, the single most significant predecessor for Pound in his coming to grips with the meanings of authorship, tradition, and relationships to audience, Browning's poetry—as Pound understood it—formed only half of the poetic tradition in English as he created it for himself early on. We have already seen his tendency to assimilate a doubled tradition in his complex relations to Pater and Ford as he created his nineteenth-century canon. In his early poetry, these tensions play out in mixed diction and tonally uneven imitations. Browning mediates between the present and the past as the most important figure in one of the two strains Pound identified in the English poets who were his immediate predecessors.

These two strains we may for convenience call by the names of Keats and Browning. The first strain, the Keatsian, flows for Pound through Keats, Tennyson, Swinburne, and the Pre-Raphaelites to the Georgian aesthetes, including the early Yeats. The second is represented by Browning, by Landor and Beddoes, possibly by Wordsworth, and by the "harder" language of Yeats's middle period. It is also, as we have seen, the prose tradition in verse. Behind the Keatsian line we may of course see Spenser and what I will call Pound's paradisiacal Dante; behind Browning's line he surely places Villon, the "infernal" Dante, and aspects of Chaucer, Shakespeare, and Whitman. The two strains as Pound identified them can be seen fighting it out in his early poetry. Ultimately, neither side wins, but Pound comes to yoke them together, to create the tensions, the lyric toughness that characterizes his later work. In the early prose this doubling is amply evident, particularly in the short piece "Imagism and England," in which he attempts to construct a unified English lineage for imagism. He begins by opposing lyricism to imagism. He goes on to describe as imagist "The Seafarer," the works of Chaucer and Shakespeare, *Sordello,* and the early books of Wordsworth's *Prelude,* and he argues for the inclusion of the best of Keats while remarking that for some (himself in his avant-garde mood?) Keats's language is not always "hard" enough (PPC, 2:19).

Pound's unpublished early poetry suggests that he recognized the potential conflicts in his own way of assimilating tradition. Perhaps it was this doubling that also attracted him to Sordello, who is himself torn in two by contradictory urges. Certainly in several early notes and poems Pound quotes and paraphrases Browning's line from *Sordello,* "You get no whole and perfect Poet" (5.116). In Pound's college notes from 1907 is a typescript sheet that comments significantly on the conflicted nature of his own work. This short prose piece, addressed to "gentlemen of the craftsmen," seems to be an imaginary letter designed to preface enclosed poems. The poet asks, "Here enclosed an oddity? Well no I, I admit the first flee-bitten (*sic*) with Browning and the second, to superficial reading, insanely rhapsodic" (college notes folder, Beinecke Library).

The unpublished poem "Pageantry" places Browning in the pivotal position between Spenser and Dante, and "To R. B." establishes Browning as a key element in the analogy among Sordello, Cavalcanti, R. B., and Pound; but the most astonishing instance of Browning's mediating role in the development of Pound's poetic tradition comes in an unpublished poem beginning "Bah, would I have loved her had she lived?" This poem, like "Pageantry," is found in the Beinecke Library in a folder of Pound's college verse. It is a dramatic monologue in the manner of Browning, spoken by Dante, who is reflecting on his unsatisfactory wife. Here we have a Browningesque voice speaking for one side of the double-voiced Dante. In this brief poem Dante seems closer to the monk of Browning's Spanish cloister than to the poet invoked in "Rex" or translated in "La Nuvoletta" (*Canzoni,* 1911, CEP, 151). Dante crudely declares:

Better this uncomprehending brute that looks at me (as)
half master half some rare wonder to be boasted of to her
gossips.
      Gad yes ! better she. her . it
than Beatrice growing old. as I do
   loving life for its hate
     taking my joy in paining others. with some thought of good
      PERHAPS !?
                 (typescript, Beinecke Library)

After the poet asserts parenthetically that these words have been
"jerked out" with "gloating and bitterness," Dante returns to declare
cynically in the last line: "ghh. Even a poet must have some one to
keep his house and cook." This poem is not merely an irreverent look
at Dante but a process in which the poet exaggeratedly assumes the
stance of Browning in order to present the speech of Dante. The earlier
poet is mediated in the language of the later one. And the whole is a
far cry indeed from the aesthetic verse Pound was still publishing in
Canzoni (1911). The unpublished poem presents the Dante of the in-
ferno as having a touch of the infernal himself. In *Canzoni* the poet
delicately sets a rose in his copy of the *Paradiso*, "between the empaged rime's high holiness / Where Dante sings of that rose's device /
Which yellow is, with souls in blissfulness" ("Rosa Sempiterna," CEP,
152). The Dante of "Bah! would I have loved her" is a Dante even
Browning would have hesitated to imagine; Pound for his part hesitated to revise and publish his imagined speech.[23]

A similar doubling can be seen in two unpublished early poems
about Shakespeare: one is a dramatic monologue by a sometime contemporary playwright who asks colloquially, "Small pay in sonnets,
eh?"; the second is a sonnet "For Mistress Ann Hathaway" that deals
in archaism and ends with an evocation of the "maid of the Avon
with wind in her hair" (college folder, Beinecke Library). The distance
between these two Shakespeares, the distance between the Dante of
"Gad yes! better she. her . it." and the Dante who made "the empaged
rime's high holiness" is a measure of the two strains Pound identified
in nineteenth-century tradition.

23. Browning, at any rate, was unlikely to imagine the misogynist tone of Pound's
poem, but he was perfectly capable of presenting an infernal Dante. Ironically, the
clearest depiction of Dante in this light among Browning's poems comes in "One
Word More," Browning's dedicatory poem to his wife, Elizabeth Barrett. There
Browning describes Dante writing on the brows of the wicked in hot ink, so that
the wretches would go "festering through Florence" (*Poems* 1:738, line 41).

A group of sonnets from the same period illustrates such a dichotomy very clearly. The three Italian sonnets vary markedly in tone—by turns rhapsodic or flea-bitten Browning. The first, titled in a handwritten flourish at the bottom of the page, is called "The Improvisator." It could make any aesthete happy. The sonnet begins:

> From out the temple of one perfect chord
> I sought to draw the image of thy soul
>
> In gray and crimson, as the music stole
> From out the shadows 'bove the ivory board
> (typescript, Beinecke Library)

The decorative periphrasis of this effort makes it a curious companion to the sonnet following, which despite its sacrifice of diction to meter and its lapse into archaism, generally runs in Pound's flea-bitten Browningesque mode:

> You prate of joy, bah! joy, and think you know
> or feel, or think to any reach of love,
> sad fool, oh fool, the outer edge thereof
> thou scarce hath tained unto. Cheap flowers blow
> about that borderland.
> (typescript, Beinecke Library)

These sonnets exhibit radically differing diction with no apparent attempt at connection. They prefigure the more radical and often more accomplished juxtapositions of Pound's later work. Here the two languages are simply juxtaposed without any attempt at a larger structure.

These sonnets, in turn, could easily enough be the poems alluded to in another and more interesting piece of Pound's college verse. "Have I Not, O Walt Whitman" was written several years before the more polished "A Pact," which was addressed to Whitman in *Lustra* (1916). In "A Pact," Pound uses the same metaphor—describing himself and Whitman as limbs of a tree—that he used in "To R. B." to describe his relationship to Browning (PSP, 90). In the unpublished "Have I Not" the link to Browning is more obvious, and the self-critical description of Pound's own poetry is clearer. The poem begins with the poet asking Whitman, "Have I not cursed thee for the hitching / roughness of your abominable versification"; in pencil on the typescript Pound then amends "thee" to "you." He goes on to allude to Browning's "One Word More," saying he has, unlike Whitman, made a "century of sonnets" which attempted to match "with lyre and harp strings the divine / and mellow music of the wind." But imagining Whitman evokes the telling admission:

> And yet confound it
> When I have some real thing to say
>   I blurt it out bald as Browning
> no tom foolery, no tinsel
> no pre-raphaelite zitherns and citoles
> to make ecstatic holes in the pants of my meaning
>   (folder of college verse, Beinecke Library)

It is interesting that Pound did not choose to publish a version of this poem in his early volumes and waited until *Lustra* to write openly about Whitman. Perhaps a Whitman so obviously mediated by Browning could only raise but not resolve the question of Pound's relation to America. That Whitman and Browning could be paired in this early effort may in part be a consequence of Pound's conception of Browning as more exiled than English. The doubling of Pound's tradition, in any case, kept national distinctions subordinate to distinctions of poetic craft.

This doubling is apparent not only in the tonal oscillations of the early poetry but also in the arrangement of *Canzoni*, the volume Pound published in 1911 and the last volume that as a whole still takes seriously his apprenticeship to the style of the 1890s. James Longenbach has shown the value of Pound's own claim that he organized *Canzoni* in a rough chronology. The poems move from matter of Provence, to Tuscany, to the Renaissance, to the eighteenth and then the nineteenth centuries, to what Pound calls "external modernity" and "subjective modernity."[24] This is the volume that made Ford Madox Ford literally roll on the floor in pretended agony. Pound ever after claimed that Ford's disgust at his "stilted language" and jejune provinciality (Ford's description) saved him "at least two years, perhaps more. It sent me back to my own proper effort, namely toward using the living

24. Pound's phrases "external modernity" and "subjective modernity" may originate in Browning's opposition in his "Essay on Shelley" between subjective and objective poets. Longenbach's quotation from Pound's "Status Rerum" (1913) makes a similar distinction: Pound opposes Yeats's subjectivity to Ford Madox Ford's (and Flaubert's) "objectivity" (*Modernist Poetics*, 65–75). *Canzoni* may be found entire in CEP, 127–74.

tongue" (P/F, 172). Perhaps Ford would not have rolled quite so long had Pound not cut out in proof five of the more satiric poems he originally intended to include toward the end of the volume. He later admitted the volume as not as good as his others and explained its failures this way: "I was affected by hyper-aesthesia or over-squeamishness and cut out the rougher poems. I don't know that I regret it in that case for the poems weren't good enough, but even so the book would have been better if they had been left in" (P/J, 285).

Canzoni is in large part a potpourri of imitations—the canzoni imitate various troubadour forms, a sonnet declares debts to Cavalcanti, and the volume contains translations or adaptations of Propertius, Dante, Pico della Mirandola, Joachim du Bellay, Leopardi, and Heine. "Sonnet" is Pound's version of a Shakespearean sonnet. A great deal of the volume is mediated through or comments upon the nineteenth century: the Renaissance section presents Paracelsus, whom Browning had already recreated, and it represents "Speech for Psyche" from Apuleius, whom Pater had already recreated; the Dante of "La Nuvoletta" in its turn owes much to D. G. Rossetti. Shelley appears among poems about the nineteenth century in "A Prologue," which is—of all things—a nativity ode in the manner of *Prometheus Unbound*. The "Victorian Eclogues" are equally odd, the last part being a semi-dramatic poem spoken by Abelard, probably with thanks to Ovid's *Heroides* filtered by way of Landor's *Imaginary Conversations*. "Redondillas," one of the poems Pound withdrew in proof, was originally subtitled "Locksley Hall, Forty Years Further," and the last section of "Und Drang" is a rejoinder to Yeats's "Cap and Bells." "Song in the Manner of Housman" is parody of the broadest stripe. The rejected poem, "To Hulme (T. E.) and Fitzgerald (A certain)" is a self-parody in the manner of Burns:

> Ye see this birkie ca'ed a bard,
> Wi' cryptic eyes and a' that,
> Aesthetic phrases by the yard;
> It's but E. P. for a' that
> (CEP, 214–15)

In the context of these multiple modes of imitation—translation, allusion or quotation, and parody—*Canzoni* is more a testament to Pound's own literary history than to his historical sense. It is no wonder that Pound, parodying Tennyson in the Virgilian hexameters of "Redondillas," announces his antecedents:

> Even this hobbledy-hoy
>   is not my own private invention.
> We are the heirs of the past,
>   it is asinine not to admit it.
> O Virgil, from your green elysium
>   see how that dactyl stubs his weary toes.
>
>   (CEP, 220)

Such self-conscious delight in announcing himself as part of literary history comports oddly with what Pound himself called "hyper-aesthesia"; if we attend to the original plan of *Canzoni* it is clear that the poems were to be organized to move from aestheticism toward something rougher. And this move entailed an increasingly explicit consideration of what poetic tradition means in modern culture.

The four sonnets originally intended to be published near the end of *Canzoni* under the title "Leviora" debate questions of language, form, and audience. The first section, "Against Form," could be called an antisonnet. The second section, "Hic Jacet," debates the relationship of art and life in terms taken from Browning's "Essay on Shelley"; "we" poets can be classified "subjective egoists, objective makers . . . the true and false partakers / Of semi-fame" (CEP, 213). The third sonnet, the only one retained, was titled "L'Art," and, like "Redondillas," it can be characterized as Pound's ironic self-commentary on his own propensities to imitation. Imitation comes off better than aestheticism, and again the unmentioned Browning mediates these issues. It is Browning's poem on Keats and his audience, "Popularity," that furnishes Pound's epithet for Keats. Pound's sestet runs:

> Horace, that thing of thine is overhauled,
> And "Wood notes wild" weaves a concocted sonnet.
> Here aery Shelley on the text hath called,
> And here, Great Scott, the Murex, Keats comes on it.
> And all the lot howl, "Sweet Simplicity!"
> 'Tis Art to hide our theft exquisitely.
>
>   (CEP, 163)

The ironies of "L'Art" are most accessible in the context of Pound's short essay "M. Antonius Flamininus and John Keats: A Kinship in Genius," published in February 1908 in the *Book News Monthly*. Pound likens the Renaissance Latin poet Flamininus to Keats for their "kinship in classic desire," their revivification of the "old Pantheon," and their "loving the wood-wild fairness for itself alone." This, he comments, is "poetic poetry with no strong optimism as Browning's to make it vital, or to cause it to be slandered with the name of prose in verse: a beauty so sweet, so unreal, that we may not have it with us always without cloying" (445–47). The last line of "L'Art," a recapitulation of the "ars cellarare artem" of "Rex," encapsulates the doubleness of Pound's position here, which would defend imitation and decry the weakness of Keatsian verse. The merely exquisite, this sonnet sequence suggests, is useless and dishonest, and rank imitation may become "some second stew / Of many pot-lots with a smack of all" (CEP, 163). Surely, there is some self-reflection here; *Canzoni* is many "pot-lots" indeed. But there is also solidarity with Keats, or more properly with Browning's Keats.

The last poem of *Canzoni*, "Und Drang," curiously combines these two strains in Pound's canon, being at once an exercise in aestheticism, a meditation upon it, and a multiply mediated questioning of it. The numbered parts of the poem take up a series of positions until, in the fourth part, after the "Elegia," the poet exclaims,

> How our modernity
> Nerve-wracked and broken, turns
> Against time's way and all the way of things,
> Crying with weak and egoistic cries!
> (CEP, 169–70)

By the eleventh and twelfth parts of the poem an ironic tone pushes back against this world-weariness, and the meter and lineation become, accordingly, more forceful:

> I suppose, when poetry comes down to facts,
> When our souls are returned to the gods
>   and the spheres they belong in,
> Here in the every-day where our acts
> Rise up and judge us;
> (CEP, 173)

Here ironically all we can know is the verity of the salon—where we'd like our tea. The conclusion of "Und Drang" brings these two tones together in the twelfth part, "Au Jardin." This last section is both a response to Yeats's "Cap and Bells" and a reply to the beginning of *Canzoni*; for the third "Canzon" is subtitled "To be sung beneath a window." "Au Jardin" places the poet as jester in the garden, refusing the role of poet/lover: "Well, there's no use your loving me / That way, Lady; / For I've nothing but songs to give you." And the whole enterprise ends in a questioned quotation: " 'The Jester walked in the garden.' / Did he so?" (CEP, 174). This doubling of tone, the questioning of past images of poetry, and the metaphors of history as webs, threads, and mirrors in "Und Drang" are given direct historical referent five years later in *Lustra*, particularly in "Near Perigord."

In "Near Perigord" (1916) we see history itself as a kind of exile. To encounter history in a poem the poet must act as collector of fragments, as translator of and commentator on the words and images remaining in the historical record, and as the creator of links between present and past. This historicist method may involve deciphering documents, concretely envisioning place, or—most important—imaginatively recreating the fleeting subjectivities of the past. In "Near Perigord" as in the early cantos, imaginative reconstruction is hedged about with questions even as the poem's subject Bertrans is himself surrounded by the castles of superior powers. Because "Near Perigord" makes no claims for its own cultural centrality, but only for the pleasures or insights of the existential historicist moment, Pound can leave the poem's questions unanswered, implying the limits of historical, and of all human, knowledge. The poem invokes both Dante and the troubadours; it is also Pound's most powerful homage to Browning. Despite or because of all these forebears, in its own accomplishment it moves from imitation to practice. Pound works out his own peculiar blending of the narrative techniques of *Sordello*, with the dramatic techniques of Browning's monologues, and with the lyric immediacy of the poems Browning called "romances." Pound's multiplication of genres allows him to achieve at once the detachment associated with contextualist historicism and the lyric intensity of the romance.

"Near Perigord" does in one poem what *Canzoni* took a volume to attempt; it presents history in a new light, takes up poetic tradition, mixes diction, raises questions about the possibilities of historical knowledge. It continues the matter of Italy which Pound had earlier treated through translation, aesthetic invocations, and dramatic monologues in Browning's manner.

Although the third section of "Near Perigord" is a dramatic monologue of a sort, its distinctiveness is clear in contrast with Pound's earlier Browningesque monologues, the most notable of which are "Cino," "Marvoil," and "Piere Vidal Old." Like many of Browning's monologues, "Cino" includes a dateline, "Italian Campagna 1309, the open road." As in much of Pound's poetry, historical and literary context are inseparable. Pound asks us to identify his allusions to Whitman and Browning. The imitation of Browning's manner is immediately striking: " 'Bah! I have sung women in three cities' " (CEP, 10). Cino's own words are interrupted by his recollections of people who have asked after him. They remember Cino in Browning's manner too, catching Browning's rhythm, diction, ellipses, and parentheses:

> "Cino?" "Oh, eh, Cino Polnesi
> 'The singer is't you mean?"
> "Ah yes, passed once our way.
> "A saucy fellow, but . . .
> "(Oh, they are all one these vagabonds),
> 'Peste! 'tis his own songs?
> "Or some other's that he sings?
> (CEP, 11)

One might ask the same of Pound's song, with multiple historical answers.

"Marvoil," another complicated questioning of history and literary history, begins with an echo of Browning's "Fra Lippo Lippi" ("I have small mind to sit / Day long, long day cooped on a stool / A-jumbling o' figures for Maitre Jacques Polin") (CEP, 94). Like "Near Perigord," it is scarcely a straightforward approach to Provence. The troubadour addresses an apostrophe to the "hole in the wall here" where he will put his poetic testament, but the poet pulls the rug out from under him by confessing in fine print that he does not have Marvoil's parchment. Like Marvoil, who evokes Villon and Browning, or Cino who evokes Whitman and Browning, Piere Vidal (*Exultations*, 1909) is left with questions. His lament against his age—and Pound's—prefigures succinctly the tensions of the *Exultations* volume as a whole: "O Age gone lax! O stunted followers, / That mask at passions and desire desires" (CEP, 111). And the poem ends in a Browningesque flurry of ellipses even as "Near Perigord" does.

"Near Perigord" takes up the materials of the Browningesque monologues and yokes to them the lyric strain Pound associates with the Keatsian tradition and with fin-de-siècle aesthetics. Indeed the manuscript of the poem in the Beinecke Library reveals how in the process of revision he tightened the poem considerably. In Part 3, Bertrans's monologue-romance, Pound omitted the aesthetic and Yeatsian moments that were at first interwoven with Bertrans's recollection of speech. The lines that form the second strophe in the final version read as follows in manuscript:

> "Why do you love me?
>
>   Will you always love me?
> "But I am like the grass, I can not love you."
> Had I run mad among the faery roses . . . .
> Or drunk with music found a woman in her.
> Or "love, and I love and love you
> And hate your mind, not *you*, your soul, your hands."
>
> (or moved, or swung a scarf with dancing feet,
> And cut the twilight like a dancing leaf,
> light and as free.)
> [break]
> And then this last estrangement, Tairiran.
>   (typescript, Beinecke Library)[25]

On the typescript the two lines "Had I run mad" and the parenthetic passage are canceled in pencil. The typescript reveals Pound deleting the Yeatsian images in order to emphasize the drama of the incident and to focus on the estrangement between Bertrans and Maent rather than on the poet's response to Maent's beauty.

In "Near Perigord," Pound borrows and discards Yeatsian images. He not only borrows from Browning's monologues but, more immediately, from *Sordello* and from Browning's romances. This strategy allows him to engage topoi of aestheticism without writing in the style of an aesthete. His use of ellipses and parenthetic asides is characteristic of Browning's narrative technique in *Sordello*, and like the narrator of *Sordello*, Pound's narrator intrudes to make direct links between his present and Bertrans's past. More subtle, but equally striking, is the similarity in versification of "Near Perigord" and *Sordello*. Though Pound eschews the couplet, his understated pentameter owes a great deal to Browning. "Near Perigord" breaks the back of the pentameter not through imagist concision or through the satiric excursuses of Pound's vorticist poems but by working off of a pentameter norm. Like the subtle ironies of the poem, the breaks in the pentameter are subtle too. The last strophe is exemplary, containing

---

25. Interestingly, the draft also contains an insert, deleted in the final version, which compares Richard to Achilles.

in its second line complex synaloepha; in line three a headless line; in lines four and five substitutions of strong syllables and a feminine ending; and in line seven an abrupt ellipsis. Only line six establishes an unambiguous pentameter:

> There shut up in his castle, Tairiran's,
> She who had nor ears nor tongue save in her hands,
> Gone—ah, gone—untouched, unreachable!
> She who could never live save through one person,
> She who could never speak save to one person,
> And all the rest of her a shifting change,
> A broken bundle of mirrors. . . !
>
> (PSP, 154)

Like *Sordello*, which remakes the pentameter couplet through a series of subtle effects including substitution, enjambment, and ellipsis, "Near Perigord" recasts unrhymed pentameter.

The language and historical strategies of Browning's *Sordello* and of his monologues are significant antecedents to "Near Perigord," but it is Browning's romances that furnish Pound the stance for yoking historicist questions to personal vision. Though the third section is a monologue spoken by Bertrans de Born, it alludes directly not to Browning's monologues but to his "romance" "The Last Ride Together." "Might she have loved me? just as well / She might have hated," Browning's speaker says of a woman. Browning's poem begins as the speaker and a woman set out on their last ride, leaning together for just a moment at the beginning, as Bertrans and Maent do in "Near Perigord." And Browning's speaker finally is driven to ask, "What hand and brain went ever paired? / What heart alike conceived and dared?" (lines 56–57, *Poems* 1:609). Pound's poem sets the same problem of the relation between thought and action or poetry and love. Bertrans avows he and Maent believed "we should meet with lips and hands." But then comes "the counter-thrust," of " 'Why do you love me' " and " 'Love, and I love and love you, / And hate your mind, not *you*, your soul your hands' " (PSP, 154). No more than Browning does Pound resolve these oppositions; it is their very entanglement that attracts. Ultimately, like the reader of "Near Perigord" or the reader of "Und Drang," Bertrans as Pound imagines him is left with a "broken bundle of mirrors."

The processes of translation, of piecing together historical fragments, of distinguishing apocrypha, of uniting historical knowledge with personal vision are yoked in "Near Perigord" through Pound's allusions and through his combination of genres. Experimental narration and a monologue-romance are juxtaposed in the poem's three sections. The rough Browningesque diction of Pound's early monologues is united with the visionary, if fleeting, evocation of the lady. By leaving his questions open, Pound finds his own balance before the past; it is neither the ironic stance of Browning nor pure Pateresque appreciation, but his own peculiar balance. Because "Near Perigord" deliberately limits its claims and because it ignores, for the moment, the modern poet's relationship to his audience, the poem remains open ended, more invitational than pedagogic.

Because it historicizes both love and war, "Near Perigord" can hold in abeyance the question Pound was asking at about the same time in the drafts for early cantos: "Am I let preach?" "Near Perigord," instead, is one of the most interesting instances of Pound's "brother's speech." It imitates without anxiety and, like the finest imitation or translation, makes something new, its own poetic practice.

The fragmented and "broken bundle of mirrors" reveals not Maent and Bertrans but the poet as collector, translator, and ragpicker. In "Near Perigord" and in Pound's early poetry, imitation—whether it functions as allusion, paraphrase, translation, or quotation, as exercise or practice—is a complex and fragmentary assembling of the past. The poet who makes himself by imitation, in a context of romantic authorship, must become a ragpicker or a jester of great curiosity and skill. He must steal ever more interesting or beautiful rags and stitch his motley with ever greater intricacy. The poet who would write a poem of epic scope, attempting to reconstitute tradition and to establish the authenticity of his fragments in order to claim their cultural centrality, this poet must go beyond the delicate equipoise of the ragpicker. *The Cantos* are a record of struggle between the ragpicker—by definition a creature of the margin—and the inevitable centrality of epic claims. To *The Cantos*, Pound brought both the multifarious languages he learned through imitation and the monologic voice of the visionary; he brought the collector's delight in fragments and the pedagogue's desire for order. Neither Browning's existential historicism nor its cousin, Pater's aestheticism, could provide an all-encompassing model.

Chapter 3

Browning in the Early Cantos:
Irony versus Epic

But now I will begin my poem. 'Tis
    Perhaps a little strange, if not quite new,
That from the first of Cantos up to this
    I've not begun what we have to go through.
. . . .
I thought, at setting off, about two dozen
    Cantos would do; but at Apollo's pleading,
If that my Pegasus should not be foundered,
    I think to canter gently through a hundred.
                —Byron, *Don Juan* (12, stanzas 50–54)

        and Lorenzo Valla,
"Broken in middle life? bent to submission?—
Took a fat living from the Papacy"
(that's in Villari, but Burckhardt's statement is different)—
"More than the Roman city, the Roman speech"
(Holds fast its part among the ever-living).
"Not by the eagles only was Rome measured."
"Wherever Roman speech was, there was Rome,"

Wherever the speech crept, there was mastery
          —Pound, "Three Cantos" (PSP, 242)

If "Near Perigord" establishes equipoise before the past, it provides only such balance as enables a series of questions. How much of the past can we know? What can we guess of Bertrans's motives? Similar questions are carried into the early cantos: *"Se pia? O empia?"* the poet asks about the murder of Alessandro Medici (5.19, 6.21).[1] Even Benedetto Varchi, Pound's historical source who originates this question, can only speculate about the answer. In this instance as in other historical episodes, *The Cantos* begin by questioning the relationship of fact and value, present and past, vision and the often brutal realities of history.

Essential as they are to an existential historicist conceptualization of the past, these questions threaten fundamentally to destabilize the project of what Pound called his long "poem including history." When the poet situates his long poem in the epic tradition these difficulties become acute. As Pound's early evocation of Roman speech in "Three Cantos" makes clear, he felt challenged even at the beginning of his project to write epic as a poetry of cultural "mastery" in a scene of cultural fragmentation. As we shall see, Browning's long poems *Sordello* and *The Ring and the Book* stood as Pound's most important models for a modernist transformation of epic. Yet precisely because of their historicist foundation, Browning's long poems were problematic. *Sordello* was notoriously inaccessible and, worse, it analyzed the poet's failure to unite vision and history. *The Ring and the Book* when most accessible was least usable; for its belief was less persuasive than its skepticism. The drafts and notes for the early cantos and the early published versions of the poem show us how Pound delighted in Browning's ragbag and yet groped for ways to bring new order to its contents.

Although the connections between "Three Cantos" (1917) and the *Draft of XVI Cantos* (1925) have been discussed in detail, the full extent of Pound's encounter with Browning and with existential historicism becomes clear only in an analysis of his unpublished drafts and notes. The various early notes for and versions of *The Cantos* reveal that the process of creating a long poem was, for Pound, both a multiplication of questions and an increasingly urgent attempt to answer, evade, or ignore questions of historical knowledge and poetic authority. The shape of Pound's answers to these questions is the subject of the last half of this book, which argues that a tropological rhetoric best enables

---

1. This and subsequent quotations from *The Cantos* are taken from the 1991 edition; the epigraph to this chapter from "Three Cantos," originally published in 1917 in *Poetry,* and all subsequent quotations from "Three Cantos" are taken from the revised edition of *Personae,* ed. Baechler and Litz.

us to account for the poem's contradictions. Here my purpose is not to focus in detail on the final version of *The Cantos* but to examine how, in his encounter with Browning, Pound came to ask the questions about poetic authority, epic, and history for which *The Cantos* became an answer.

I begin by situating Pound's desire to write a long poem in the context of his larger sense of the problem of epic in an age that seemed antithetical, possibly even hostile to such an undertaking. Pound embarked on his long poem in the context of a dominant aesthetic that consigned epic to earlier cultures, but he imagined a renaissance that might make a modernist epic possible. I sketch in this chapter, then describe more fully in the second half of the book, the way this struggle with poetic form in itself had implications for Pound's politics.

As we have seen, questions of form and language emerged for Pound in the context of an existential historicism that complicated most claims to unmediated vision or cultural centrality; his uneasy experiments with epic, like his other early poetry, developed within a tradition fraught with contradiction. As he proceeded uneasily with the paradoxical project of a historicist epic, he initially shaped and reshaped his poem through a prolonged encounter with Browning. Here I look in detail at the ways he adopted and departed from Browning's practice in long poems, arguing that Browning's poet personae, his diction, and his formal experiments initially offered Pound an attractive model of inclusiveness and experimentation; at the same time, Browning's ironies and his Christian teleology were inadequate to the kinds of coherence Pound increasingly sought. For Pound the crucial question remained: how does the epic poet claim authority? For him, I contend, neither the idiographic juxtaposing of particulars nor irony could establish such authority; Pound could not be completely satisfied with either critical or monumental history (to borrow Nietzsche's terms).[2] I conclude this chapter by suggesting that Pound sought to attain poetic authority while maintaining a radically individualist approach to culture. He sought to establish a coherent vision through invoking Confucian notions of individual and society, through a neopagan exoticism, and through translation and allusion. Each of these strands has its own knots and difficulties. A detailed reading of early drafts and notes for the eventual Canto 5 and an

2. Here I use "idiography" in the sense of Wilhelm Windelband, explained below; this is not to be confused with "ideography," which concerns the logographic dimensions of Chinese writing. See also Nietzsche, *Use and Abuse of History*.

examination of Cantos 20 and 21 exemplify his simultaneous need for authoritative order and for historicist openness to and even aesthetic detachment from the past. Over the many years of its writing, his long poem became at once a remarkably open and a remarkably closed form. Even the earliest notes and drafts for *The Cantos* reveal Pound struggling with the ways a fragmented culture and a historicist poetry could be made adequate to epic ambitions.

"I have many fragments"

Certainly the most urgent problem of the three cantos Pound published in 1917 was how to write a long poem without a coherent "background." Addressing Browning directly he asked in the first canto:

> And you had a background,
> Watched "the soul," Sordello's soul,
> And saw it lap up life, and swell and burst—
> "Into the empyrean?"
> So you worked out new form, the meditative,
> Semi-dramatic, semi-epic story.
> And we will say: What's left for me to do?
>
> (PSP, 231)

Pound answered this question repeatedly through his poetic practice during the years between 1915 and 1925. The question itself was forming as early as 1910 as he began to imagine undertaking a long poem.

From well before he began writing his long poem the problem of the modern epic was clearly in Pound's mind. Though the phrases "long poem" and "poem of some length" served for many years as self-protective euphemisms, he repeatedly focused on the difficulties of modern epic (see his original title for *A Draft of XVI Cantos*). His characterization of *Sordello* as a "semi-dramatic," "semi-epic" story reveals his belief that Browning's poem tackled the problem that had beset aspiring poets since the dominance of romantic aesthetics. Like Browning, Pound had to come to terms with the juxtaposition of naïve and sentimental art or with various transformations of this dichotomy, all of which suggested that epic belonged to earlier, even prelapsarian, ages.[3] For Pound, as for Browning before him, the effort to write a

3. See my discussion in *History and the Prism of Art*, chap. 2, and for a useful summary of antithetical aesthetics, Abrams, *Mirror and the Lamp*, 235–44.

long poem required, then, the simultaneous renovation of the poetic tradition and of the age. Under such circumstances, he repeatedly asked, what kind of poem is possible.

Pound provides an early, perhaps even prematurely disillusioned, answer in a letter to his mother dated 1 January 1910. Isabel Pound evidently had sent him a prospectus for the new "American Academy of Letters and Arts" as he calls it. He derides the academy gently (for her sake?), calling it a good thing for "the artist who is a bit of a hypocrite." In the next paragraph he inquires whether Isabel has read Browning's "Bishop Blougram's Apology," presumably because it is Browning's most successful study of contemporary British hypocrisy. And this, coupled with Isabel's obvious ambition for Pound's poetic career, brings him to his own work:

> Yeats left this morning for Dublin. He is the only living man whose work has anything more than a most temporary interest—possible exceptions on the continent—. I shall survive as a curiosity. The art of letters will come to an end before A.D. 2000 and there will be a sort of artistic dark ages till about A.D. 2700.
>
> The last monument will be a bombastic, rhetorical epic wherethrough will move Marconi, Pierpont Morgan, Blieriot, Levavasour [sic], Latham, Peary [sic], Dr. Cook, etc. clothed in the heroic manner of Greek imitation. Contending with mighty forces, as giants against god, with "cubic resistance" and "bull pressure" and with "geographical societies of Denmark."
>
> I shall write it myself if threatened with actual starvation. A mixture of MacCawley [sic]—at his worst + Cowley, and Dryden should take the public ear, with an occasional Kiplingesque dissonance or a flavour of cockney. (Paige typescripts, Beinecke Library)

The sort of poem Pound actually imagines for himself is clearly not the "bombastic" epic but something more akin to the mock epic; he implicitly stakes out a position against the modern bombastic epic (and against Macaulay's history) in much the same way that Byron had derided the "lakers" almost a century before. Miles Slatin concluded from examining the early drafts, fragments, notes, and letters leading to *The Cantos* that Pound was at first attracted to a Byronic "epic" in the style of *Don Juan*, even as he was also speculating about the possibilities of a long imagist poem or a long poem somehow modeled on the Noh. By December 1915, Slatin concludes, Pound "had exchanged Byron for Browning as a guide" ("History," 185).

Even as he was moving away from the direct imitation of Browning in his shorter poems, he was returning to Browning as a guide to epic.

Thinking through the possibilities of mock epic is clearly for Pound a prolegomenon to thinking about epic. His letter to his mother clarifies his position as expressed in the same year in *The Spirit of Romance* (1910). He believed he had found in Camoëns [Camões] exactly the sort of epic he feared would be loved by a new American academy. Calling Camoëns the "Rubens of verse" he characterizes *The Lusiads* as "resplendent bombast . . . florid rhetoric" (SR, 216). He goes on to argue, "An epic cannot be written against the grain of its time: the prophet or the satirist may hold himself aloof from his time, or run counter to it, but the writer of epos must voice the general heart" (SR, 216). Pound distinguishes the "general heart" from "fashions," implicitly differentiating the matter of epic from the object of satire or mock epic. Eventually he discovered a way to circumvent satire and to write even epic against the grain of his time—by taking the very route of prophecy he at first believed might exclude epic centrality. As he moved from the possibilities of mock epic to epic proper, he came more and more to seek a way to combine prophecy and epic, to imagine a prophecy (or a politics) so powerful that it could make not only the taste but the age by which it was appreciated. The early cantos rest satisfied with the poet as seer of a corrective or at least a countervailing vision, but the difficulties of poetic and political authority were implicit in Pound's epic undertaking from the first.

Even before he began notes for *The Cantos*, Pound's ambition entailed the need to create in poetry a culturally central story. As a cultural commentator, he reveals this concern in the essays of 1912–13 that became "Patria Mia." The political confusions of these essays are clear; he cannot easily combine democratic ideology, his own brand of patriotism, and admiration for strong leaders and patrons on the model of feudal authority. He wants somehow to make his country ready for a "Risorgimento" or a renaissance; he declares America is at once in the "Dark Ages" and on the eve of such a renaissance. The potential for a new awakening is guaranteed by the resemblance of New York to imperial Rome: "I see also a sign in the surging crowd on Seventh Avenue (New York). A crowd pagan as ever imperial Rome was, eager, careless, with an animal vigour unlike that of any European crowd that I have ever looked at" (SP, 104). Awaiting the moment when this vigor can be harnessed, the true artists are "exported" into exile and can only hope that a center of arts will come about as powerful men of "a certain catholicity of intelligence come into power" (SP, 130).[4] As an essayist and editor, and most of all as a poet, Pound hopes for a new relation to power in order to make his own epic possible.

At about the same time as "Patria Mia," Pound writes to Harriet Monroe on similar themes, making clear his own possible role in such an awakening. As in "Patria Mia," he hopes in these letters for an "American Risorgimento" that would "make the Italian Renaissance look like a tempest in a teapot" (18 August 1912, SL, 43). In 1913 he writes to her expressing his ambivalence about his own poem "From Chebar," in which he says he forsook art for "preaching." Yet, he continues, only half chiding himself, "I want in my rather slinking weaker and sentimental moments, I want, or delude myself into thinking I want America to 'uplift' (come on Ezry . . . , etc.) I know this is a baser passion and that it is nothing to the immortal gods. What have they to do with political geography."[5] Though art has to do with the immortal gods, clearly "Ezry" cannot do without political geography. If there is a form to yoke political geography and the immortal gods, it is the (unmentioned) epic.

Writing Monroe from Stone Cottage a year later, in August 1914, Pound makes explicit the terms of his fantasized renaissance, terms that would situate him as an American poet squarely in the center of political and poetic geography. If uplifting America were possible, he implies, then writing a poem of central importance would be possible as well. Again the impetus to a new political and social order is at one with and even preceded by the desire for epic centrality. Pound

4. I take Pound's concern with capitals, centers, art, and power to reflect not only his need for a patron and a way to make a living but also his concern for the possibility of creating a poem of epic scope. For a discussion of the relationship among great men, patrons, the arts, and power—and Dante's place in this configuration—see Dasenbrock, *Imitating the Italians*, esp. chap. 9. Reed Way Dasenbrock has a very interesting discussion of Dante's *De Monarchia* in which he observes the connections with the *Commedia*: "Just as all of the attacks on corrupt popes reinforce Dante's attacks on the Papacy, the figure of the poet Virgil brings with him all of Dante's sense of the importance and providential role of Rome and of Empire. Virgil is also 'lo duca mio,' Dante's guide, and everything in *De Monarchia* about the importance of hierarchy and leadership finds concrete embodiment in the vision of the *Commedia*." Dasenbrock goes on to draw a parallel between Dante's view of authority and Pound's cult of *il duce* and between Dante's attacks on *cupiditas* and Pound's similar views (181). For discussion of Pound's desire for patronage and patronage in the Italian Renaissance, see 148–53. Pound's interest in empire, cultural centers, and such of course predates his admiration for Mussolini; indeed, as I argue below, this desire to write epic from a cultural center may impel both Pound's concern with hierarchy and his later embrace of fascism.

5. August 1913, Poetry Magazine Collection, University of Chicago.

lectures Monroe on the importance of cultural centrality or omnivo-
rousness (imperium?) to art: "You must get it into the reader's mind
that a capital is the centre of the world, or at least *a* centre, not an
isolated segment. All art comes from *the* or *a* capital. A capital is a
vortex, all invention flows into it, and that makes art, it makes the art
of awakening and discovery. Paris is not less french for being omnivorous. There is no nation without a capital. America is a colony until
she can make a capital."[6] America must make a capital, a center of
the world; failing that, evidently, the poet is left in exile to search for
centrality elsewhere. Pound's most immediate effort is to find centrality in art, to create a vortex in London if not of London, and he
persists in this effort for some time despite his Byronic sense that
English culture is more fit for diagnosis than celebration.

It is conventional to imagine that a poet's social and political views
"influence" his art, but in Pound's case, the shape of poetic ambition
and the teleological demands of epic itself are prior. To seek poetic
authority as vigorously as he did, to attempt to write from a capital
or an "omnivorous" center and to represent its awakening and its
discoveries, the poet must identify, and identify with, a center from
which to write. As Pound saw it, the choices eventually narrowed to
two—the centers of commerce and finance he mocks in the early letter
to his mother (Pierpont Morgan, etc.) and Mussolini's Italy. But this
is to get ahead of the story. In reaching toward epic initially, Pound
approached his difficulty as, first, a problem of art and, second, a
problem of vision meeting historiography. He began by asking
Browning, "What's left for me to do?" ("Three Cantos," PSP, 231).

The early drafts of the cantos keep political geography at bay for a
time by focusing on problems of persona, language, and poetic form.
The unpublished typescripts and notes for the early cantos reveal how
significantly Pound's encounter with Browning was implicated in
these issues of language and form. The ambivalences of Pound's earlier appropriations of literary tradition are not left behind in the early
drafts or in final versions of *The Cantos*; if anything, the dichotomies
in his thinking become more acute as he encounters the difficulties of
modern epic. The doubled nature of the canon as he approached it—
the infernal and paradisiacal Dantes for example—is transformed in

---

6. 5 August 1914, Poetry Magazine Collection, University of Chicago. My reading of
this and similar letters suggests revision of the view shared by Michael André Bernstein and Ronald Bush that Pound was suspicious of "imperium" until after the
first world war; see Bernstein, *Tale of the Tribe*, 59 n. e; he quotes Bush, *Genesis*, 247.

The Cantos through the effort to yoke political geography to the immortal gods.

Pound's Early Personae and Browning's "Semi-Dramatic" Poem

Finding a beginning to *The Cantos* is as difficult as finding the moment when Pound ceased to imitate and discovered his own voice. From the earliest moments he is trying on personae, languages, notions of form. The notes and unpublished drafts of the early cantos and the published "Three Cantos" themselves are extraordinarily processual, self-reflexive, even on occasion cripplingly self-conscious. The more authoritative tone of the final first canto is only made possible by translating an episode from an ancient epic into the rhythms and tonal values of an ancient heroic poem and by keeping a poetic heel firmly planted on the serpent of history. All earlier versions of the early cantos involve a much less authoritative tone than the final Canto 1, partly because they present a complex poet persona.

The vicissitudes of Pound's poet persona are evident in the notes and drafts for the early cantos and in the differences between "Three Cantos" and the final version of the first cantos. As Ronald Bush has shown in *The Genesis of Ezra Pound's Cantos* regarding the differences between "Three Cantos" and the *Draft of XVI Cantos* (and the intervening publication of excerpts in *Poems, 1918–1921*), Pound's revisions gradually moved the poem away from the narrator modeled on Browning's diorama presenter in *Sordello*. The beginning of this move can be seen even in the differences between the typescript of "Three Cantos" and the version published in *Poetry*. The unpublished typescript draft of "Three Cantos" begins with an especially vivid evocation of Browning's *Sordello* and with a clear appropriation of Browning's narrative stance. Pound's narrative voice debates the nature of tradition and the source of poetic authority. Both of these questions are brought forward as questions of historical interpretation and of poetic technique. Browning is the object of the poet's ambivalence both as narrator and as historian.

The typescript begins with a much more elaborate address to Browning than even the "Three Cantos" version published in *Poetry*:

> Hang/Damn it all, Robert Browning, there can be but the one
> "Sordello,"
> But say I want to, say I take your whole bag of tricks,

Cast off restrictions, go back on my own full-formed method,
Let in your quirks and tweeks, slap on the back, punch in the belly
Familiarity. Let's say the thing's an art-form, your "Sordello"
Not merely a freak, a by-path.
                            Say that the present world
Needs such a rag-bag to get all its thought in,
Where were the sin, let in thought, argument, morbo-theorbo for rhymes;
Say I draw up my consciousness and dump the lot,
Drag the past with my net and spill the catch out
All shiny and silvery, like sardines at Sirmione
            (a bit fishy?) that simile
            gravely bad
Come pour the gravy in, just that sort of rhyme and frivolity,
This air: I stand before the booth, just to get
                  your attention,
But the truth is inside this discourse,
This booth—, that's the way you go on,
                  is full of the marrow of learning
Rare saws, pithy business,
I'll have up not one man but a crowd of them,
Living and breathing, gouging (??) and swearing
                  real as Sordello,
Say that I follow you, turn on my own tracks,
Give up carving each stone of my edifice
                  as if it were an intaglio.
Appears: Oh let the lot appear.
. . . .

You had up ghosts, or/and my method comes closer?
I know your Sordello wasn't this and that,
      I have saught [sic] the real man.
            And with no better fortune
Had out my Guido and my Daniel
Knew what they spoke, set forth their content
As you set forth Sordello's?
No? You'd stay, or say you'd stay, hidden.
Gave us "Sordello," make a wild romantic.
Of course he didn't die, the "real Sordello",
Went to Provence, had a wife and castle
Where his most fame reverts, won Dante's praise
For vaunting Blancatz' heart. That is the story
            And you and your Sordello
You glorious and more (incidental) intellectual man
Swooning in victory! Do such things happen?
Oh yes they happen. I have seen . . .

> But no matter.
> St. Praxed's for peace. I have loved fact not fancy
> And sought what is, not so much glorious might-be.
> I have had up my past.
>   (typescript, pp. 1–3, Beinecke Library)

As Bush has indicated, "Three Cantos" was more discursive than the later versions of Pound's early matter because it presented the situation of a defined speaker in a process of narration; this earlier version is markedly more discursive than even "Three Cantos." The poet speaker interjects opinions, questions his predecessor, criticizes his methods, and reflects on the process of the poem itself. Pound even addresses Browning as the Virgil to his own Dante. Ironically, he identifies himself with Browning's bishop of St. Praxed's who, dying, reviews his past.

Other typescript notes, probably from 1917, which are extant in the Beinecke Library, retain something of what Pound calls Browning's "punch in the belly / Familiarity," combining it with motifs that are familiar to readers of the early cantos. As in the typescript draft of "Three Cantos," the tone is unstable, though the notes contain fewer interrogatives than the draft. The poet persona continues his folksy intrusion, though he does not wish simply to establish the equipoise of the existential historicist. Like Dante, he wishes to claim a coherent vision. Yet to do so he must omit the details that circumscribe his claims to knowledge. Pound's deletions on the manuscript and the poem's comments on the deletions indicate that the process of learning to speak through juxtaposition is a complex one, made doubly so because the poet cannot make the romantic claim that nature or the muses simply speak through him. Pound's self-conscious comments show him attempting and failing to reach the point that Michael André Bernstein describes as the tale of the tribe narrating itself (171–172).

In these notes to the early cantos, even more than in Pound's reference to Divus in the final Canto 1, the poet's self-conscious references to his own methods undercut his claims to authority. Conceptually this self-consciousness resembles Browning's equipoise—the circumscribed possibilities of the existential historicist rapt before the past but aware that his vision is fleeting and even subjective. The tonal instabilities or oscillations in these notes, however, resemble those of Pound's early poetry. As in the early short poems, in these early notes the Keatsian and the Browningesque alternate.

An extended passage from the notes will characterize their instabilities. The Beinecke notes section "III" begin with a fine question, "What do I mean by all this resonant rumble?" The line is recast along with much of the section in a new section IV, which I quote here in full. I follow Pound's editorial marks and punctuation, except that I retain the passages that are canceled or bracketed, probably for cancellation, in the typescript. I mark canceled and bracketed passages with { }.

'What do I mean by all this clattering rumble?'
Bewildered reader, what is the poet's business?
Populate solitudes, multiply images, to fill up chaos
Or streak the barren way to paradise
       {(Here was the Renaissance)}
To band out fine colours, fill up the void with stars
And make each star a nest of noble voices.

Let undines hear me, and in cool streams
Redeck the muses' gardens, green herbs and cress
And water-drinking flowers. . . .
{[Rumble again? 'What are the muses' gardens?']}
Oh, take a heaven you know, and make the starry wood
Sound like a grove well filled with nightingales,
And call lights 'souls',
And say: The lights ascending . . . like a covey of partridges.
Thus much I saw above me, and beneath, looking into the water.
Beheld the turret as a pillar of fire reflected,
And thence to God,
To the ineffable, *transhumanar no si potria per verba.*

The soul starts with itself, builds out perfection,
Confucius, Dante.
       Or the best man killed in France,
Struck by a Prussian bullet at St. Vaast
With just enough cut stone left here behind him
To show a new way to the kindred arts,
Laying a method, quite outside his art,
Vortex, dispersal, throw it at history.

{Say that the prose is life, scooped out of time,
A bristling node . . . and I am all too plain,}
Too full of footnotes, too careful to tell you
The how and why of my meaning "here was the renaissance.

Venus intaglio'd in the papal gem.

Lewis with simpler means
Catches the age, his Timon,
Throws our few years onto a score of pasteboards,
Says all our conflict, edgey, epigrammatic,
This Timon lived in Greece, and loved the people,
And gave high feasts, and dug his rabbit barrow.

"And Ka-hu churned in the sea,
{Churning the ocean,} using the (sun) moon for a churn-stick.
                    (typescript notes, pp. 29–30, Beinecke Library)

Pound's self-questionings here could serve as a catalog of the left-over heritage of romanticism. Should he populate the world with nightingales, or reach heaven more directly? Or will this effort simply be a multiplication of images? He faults himself for presenting his "bristling nodes" of the past (or of "prose") with too many footnotes, but clearly he wonders how he can claim authentic knowledge without them. Can he be edgy, epigrammatic, and paradisiacal? Will it bewilder the reader? What voice should or can he adopt? Pound has Browning's difficulties without Browning's many compromises with the discursive: say that prose is life, can Gaudier-Brzeska, Dante, or Confucius be models for "building out perfection"?

The discursive and formal possibilities raised by these notes and by the typescript of "Three Cantos" indicate how intimately Pound's questions about his own place in the poem were connected to matters of poetic language. Bush reasons that in working his way toward the final version of the early cantos Pound gave up the formal device of Browning's showman narrator owing to a variety of significant factors—the continuing encounter with James and the prose tradition in verse, Joyce's radical modernist experiments, Eliot's persona in "Gerontion" and his advocacy of impersonality (*Genesis*, 142–50, 186–224). Longenbach moreover has demonstrated how Pound and Eliot debated impersonality through their comments on each other's work— Eliot suggesting that Pound cut personal pronouns from "Three Cantos" and Pound urging Eliot to eliminate more of the personal in *The Waste Land* (*Modernist Poetics*, 144–51). To achieve impersonality Pound departed from the poet persona of *Sordello*, but in his drafts as well as in the published version of "Three Cantos" his departure was tentative. Much of his tentativeness focused on language itself.

Browning's Mixed Diction and Pound's
Representation of History

It is not only Browning's poet persona that worries Pound in embarking on epic but his language. "Say the things's an art-form," Pound grants in the first of "Three Cantos." "But say I want to, say I take your whole bag of tricks" (PSP, 229). The first of the three cantos, both in draft and published versions, is peppered with the word *say*. Browning's bag of tricks, his mixed diction, presents difficulties for poetic coherence; adopting Browning's manner means for Pound not following a path of poetic decorum but indulging in skepticism about language itself.

Browning's mixtures, unlike Dante's for instance, have disturbing epistemological implications. In Dante's epic, mixed diction was allied to the poet's authority in a representational decorum, ultimately guaranteed by divine order. In Browning's poetry, mixed diction, and particularly the self-ironizing of Browning's poet speakers, are often linked to doubts about the powers of language to represent the present and the past. Not only is the mixed diction linked to the fragmentation of language into increasingly specialized discourses, but Browning's mixtures also grow from a historicist desire to capture the multiplicity of reality.[7] Even though he excised Browning's showman persona from the final cantos, Pound could not so easily be rid of Browning's diction. Such inclusive diction, however, might shatter the poem into mere bewilderment. His challenge was to transform it so as to yoke political geography and the immortal gods. Browning's rough language and the prose tradition in verse enabled Pound to examine how history and vision could be made to meet.

Pound's essay "Translators of Greek: Early Translators of Homer," originally published in parts in 1918–19, suggests how he attempted

---

7. On Browning and specialized language see Loy Martin's argument that Browning's monologues include distinct vocabularies "of interest groups, of aristocracies, of scientific and aesthetic elites, of distant cultures, both primitive and exotic, of the educated in rhetoric or in logical processes." Thus, Martin explains, we see a specialization of language akin to the specializations and class interests newly developing in Victorian culture: "In the monologue, therefore, we find the opposition of poetic discourse to other specialized discourses; the opposition of specialized discourse itself to generalized, popular, or even colloquial Victorian speech; and the opposition of generalized discourse to idiosyncratic discourse. This . . . raises, as we have seen, complex and difficult questions about the nature of communication." In Gibson, *Critical Essays*, 97. On mixed diction and historicist multiplicity see Froula, "Browning's *Sordello*," and also Gibson, *History and the Prism of Art*.

these connections. Not only does the essay consider the problematics of translation; it also enables Pound to come to terms both with Henry James and with Browning; for Browning of course figures as one of the translators of Greek. In discussing translations of Greek drama Pound praises Aeschylus's "agglutinative syntax" even while he criticizes Browning's translation of the *Agamemnon*; Browning, he says, falls into the error of imitating in a relatively uninflected language the syntax of a highly inflected language. Pound contends, "One might almost say that Aeschylus's Greek is agglutinative, that his general drive, especially in choruses, is merely to remind the audience of the events of the Trojan war; that syntax is subordinate and duly subordinated, left out, that he is not austere, but often even verbose after a fashion" (LE, 273). Pound uses Aeschylus as a platform to argue both for elliptic juxtapositions and for discursiveness. On the one hand, Aeschylus's inclusiveness—and the better moments of Browning's stilted version of it—enable Pound to imagine epic discursiveness without bombast. On the other hand, Aeschylus's syntax is linked to vision.

Bush asserts that Pound discovered in Aeschylus an extension of the prose tradition that brought together "past and present, history and myth" (*Genesis*, 181). Pound's comments on Aeschylus show how difficult such a combination might be; for like the infernal and paradisiacal Dantes, Aeschylus's nature is double. Aeschylus's agglutinative syntax is for Pound a poetic equivalent of James's endless sentence (C, 7.24) and is therefore also linked to Browning's poetry. At the same time, the choruses of the *Agamemnon* provide the closest analogue to those passages of *The Cantos* where the poet wishes to evoke a vision of the gods (these same choric effects are largely excluded when Pound comes to define either a modern hell or the murky details of Malatesta's past). Is it Aeschylus's choric language rather than the syntax itself that Browning could not get right? A comparison of Pound's excerpts from a Latin translation of Aeschylus with a section of Canto 4 makes the similarities in choric effects clear.

Pound quotes the following Latin lines (line numbers follow his marginal notations):

> 'Apollo, Apollo!   (1095)
> Agyieu Apollo mi!
> Ah! quo me tandem duxisti? ad qualim domum?
> ....
> Heu, heu, ecce, ecce, cohibe a vacca   (1134)

Taurum: vestibus involvens
Nigricornem machina
Percutit; cadit vero in aequali vase.
Insidiosi lebetis casum ut intelligas velim.
. . . .
'Heu, heu, argutae lusciniae fatum *mihi tribuis*:
. . . .
'Heu nuptiae, nupitae Paridis extilales   (1165)
Amicis! ehue Scamandri patria unda!'
                                        (quoted in LE, 271)

Compare the central sections of Canto 4:

The dogs leap on Actæon,
        "Hither, hither, Actæon,"
Spotted stag of the wood;
Gold, gold, a sheaf of hair,
        Thick like a wheat swath,
Blaze, blaze in the sun,
The dogs leap on Actæon.
Stumbling, stumbling along in the wood,
Muttering, muttering Ovid:
        Pergusa . . . pool . . . pool . . . Gargaphia,
Pool . . . pool of Salmacis."
        The empty armour shakes as the cygnet moves.

Thus the light rains, thus pours, *e lo soleills plovil*
The liquid and rushing crystal
        beneath the knees of the gods.
                                        (4.14–15)

The incantatory repetition of this passage, like that of the Aeschylus, is manifest. The multiple repetitions of the same word in Canto 4—much denser repetition than in the condensation of Aeschylus—compensates for the lack in English of the near repetition of sound achieved through the word play of inflected syntax, the acoustic crossing of such combinations in the Latin as "percutit; cadit" or "heu nuptiae, nupitae." But of course Pound's repetition goes beyond the repeat of words—it extends to repetition of whole grammatical units, to paralleling of syntactic elements, and to the complex repetitions of sounds in a phrase like "e lo soleills plovil." Bush points out that in revising "Three Cantos," Pound retained this phrase in Canto 4 even though he removed the context that might have allowed us to understand the allusion (*Genesis*, 199). Surely the allusion was retained as much for its acoustic structure as for its idea.

Aeschylus provides both an agglutinative syntax for inclusive juxtapositions and a repetitive structure for establishing the authority of visionary moments. Browning's translation of Aeschylus's "dust, mud's thirsty brother" which Pound quotes approvingly has closer links to prosaic, even violent inclusiveness, than to vision (LE, 269). But in Pound's essay on Aeschylus, Browning figures in one further link among language, the vicissitudes of history, and the possibility of visionary coherence. Pound's most obvious borrowing from the *Agamemnon* is the description of Helen; he both appropriates it in the original (2.6) and, in "Early Translators," renders it twice: "Helen, destroyer of ships, of men, / Destroyer of cities" (LE, 273). Browning's translation of this phrase is surprisingly apt to Pound's purposes, though it is not cited in *The Cantos* or in the essay on translation. Browning translates the passage, "Helena? Since—mark the suture!— / Ship's-Hell, Man's-Hell, City's-Hell." (Browning, "Agamemnon," 1898, lines 708–9). As Browning's Anglo-Saxon style combinations emphasize, Helen is the chaos at the back of order, the point at which the heroic striving of epic meets the endless errors of romance. Helen is the subject rhyme for Pound's Eleanor and for all the errors of romance included in the stories of Ignez de Castro, or Actaeon, or Seremonda. As an ambivalent muse she represents the intersection of passion with power.[8] Helen is a "Venus intaglio'd in the papal gem" (typescript notes, Beinecke Library).

In taking over the epithets from Aeschylus, Pound evades Browning's mannerism, precisely the mannerism that calls attention to the poet's role in connecting error and epic. "Mark the suture," Browning admonishes the reader in his translation. Pound would ignore the "suture" and call on the reader to image seamless connections between Helen's terrible beauty and the poet's vision of wholeness and coherence. As in Pater's historicism, the details are trusted to convey

8. Elizabeth Bellamy offers an interesting Lacanian reading of epic and romance in which she argues that "the *translatio imperii* is inherently 'neurotic' . . . because its translations of power are dependent on an unrepresented that persists in leaving its repressed traces in epic history. Even as the genre of romance eludes full appropriation within representation by epic ideology, so also does Troy lurk not fully represented within epic narrative" (*Translations of Power*, 35). Epic, for Bellamy, is a translation of power or empire, because epic poets confirm the founding of empire when they assume that historical truth is intrinsically epic (26 n. 51).

their own significance. Such language—like Aeschylus's and Browning's—is not austere; neither, for Pound, can it be understood primarily as epistemological play. The language of vision and "dust, mud's thirsty brother" resist each other, but the poet claims to yoke them into a coherent whole. The reader is left to "mark the suture."

The Challenge of Form

The question ceaselessly threatening to unravel *The Cantos*, the question made explicit in the early drafts and notes, is, aesthetically, a question of form and language and, politically, a question of how beauty and power, passion and order can cohere. If prose (or history) is a "bristling node," the poet's problem is to make patterns of the lines radiating from it. As Pound writes in another set of notes labeled "Fragment / Modern World," the difficulty is to connect diagnosis and pattern, fact and "daemons":

> Predit [predict?] Napoleon from condottieri
> "some obscure place, behind the times"
> after other places, and sovrans are too tired,
> have too much sense,
> all types die, the archetype, then readjustment.
> Catullus, Horace, Musorus,
> circle from self. vortex of Romoe [*sic*], spider web,
> realism in lit. diagnosis, and patter[n]s, reason for realism.
> daemons, Leonardo.
>
> (typescript notes, Beinecke Library)

The question raised in this set of notes is the relationship between what Pound calls a vision that would "pierce the cosmos" and "your microcosmos." Stitching a "suture" between microcosm and macrocosm, diagnosis and pattern, realism and "daemons" is his challenge in attempting the epic. As he puts it in another note, "You have no cosmos until you can order it" (typescript notes, Beinecke Library).

In the drafts for and published version of "Three Cantos," Pound captures his anxieties about form in the metaphor of Browning's ragbag. Browning's form is at once the ragbag of historical scraps, the ragbag of radically mixed poetic diction, and the bag itself—a shapeless shape, a form that fits itself to its contents. One way of understanding the formal problems of the cantos is to come to grips with this foundational metaphor: the ragbag is both container and its motley contents. Both aspects of form or method of course present problems to the poet—who as wearer of motley or as ragpicker must then find a way of achieving epic seriousness. Yet *Sordello*, Browning's ragbag, presents itself to Pound in the typescript as a formal model. In another passage of the typescript which was excised from the published "Three Cantos," he makes it clear that he thinks of Browning as a guide to form:

> Well you'll be my Virgil, for you had the form,
> Ex nihil, nihil fit. Must I make new form,
> Ere I can set my crotchet and my wit
> To take the whole catch of my phantasy?
> Or say I've done it, must I still turn back,
> Send for the baggage that my scouting party
> Couldn't bring up, until they found land open;
> Use your by-phrases?
>
> (typescript, p. 4, Beinecke Library)

As Dante has Virgil, so Pound has, or might have, Browning. It would seem at the outset that the inclusiveness of Browning's form is requisite for the poet if he needs to "send for the baggage" he's left behind. The bypaths of history here turn into the "by-phrases" of language.

In a tortured passage some lines later, Pound again praises Browning's form, again wondering how it may serve his need:

> Or need I texts to hang my music on?
> No. (Can I prach [sic])? Oh that's only half too easy.
> Can I hold off from preaching. . . . I like your form.
> Isn't it loosing all my girthstrings, letting me breathe out,
> You had so much to settle.
>
> (typescript, p. 5, Beinecke Library)

Browning's form is at once attractive and problematic. Pound repeats several times that this "semi-dramatic, semi-epic story" is in fact a form even though it is a "rag-bag" and a "hodge-podge."

In his drafts for the early cantos Pound is clearly as interested in the formal qualities that make *Sordello* a "rag-bag" as in the qualities that lend it coherence—its contrivance of the showman's booth, its basic if confusing narrative line, its brilliantly experimental couplets. After all, Pound characterizes his own situation in "Three Cantos" as modern fragmentation. Although he contrasts his "many fragments" with Browning's "one whole man," he goes on to show how Browning too has fragments, how Sordello, the "real" Sordello, is the product of historical attrition (PSP, 230). The past, taken in its most concrete sense, is fragments. The explicit thematic concern with fragmentation of course continues into the final version of early cantos, in Pound's famous rejoinder to Eliot, "These fragments you have shelved (shored). / 'Slut!' 'Bitch!' Truth and Calliope / Slanging each other sous les lauriers" (8.28). The question of poetic form, ultimately of epic form, becomes dependent in large part on questions of historical fact and interpretation. Truth versus Calliope.

Not only in the notes but even in the typescript and the published versions of "Three Cantos," Pound's ambivalences about historical knowledge and poetic form are acute. Consistently, they are articulated in his encounter with Browning. In the typescript, he both praises Browning for his historical reality and accuses him of indulging in "glorious might be." For himself he declares, "I'll have up not one man but a crowd of them, / Living and breathing." Almost as if to ensure against historical questions and historical failures he proposes to "have up" a whole crowd of prospective epic heroes. Pound criticizes Browning's version of Sordello: "half your dates are out" (typescript notes, pp. 2–3, Beinecke Library). Yet he has to admit he himself cannot accomplish perfect historical representation, and in acknowledging similar limits he puts expressive quotations around the "real" Sordello, whom he claims to have presented more faithfully than Browning. These concerns continue in the version of these questions Pound presents in the published "Three Cantos." As he says referring to his own attempt to write about Guido Cavalcanti:

> Friend, I do not even—when he led that street charge—
> I do not even know which sword he'd with him.
> Sweet lie, "I lived!" Sweet lie, "I lived beside him."
> And now it's all but truth and memory,
> Dimmed only by the attritions of long time.
>
> (PSP, 233)

The typescript draft of "Three Cantos," like this published version but at greater length, suggests the baffling attractiveness of an ideal of historical knowledge and the elusiveness of a form for epic based in existential historicism.

Pound refers to the problem of historical knowledge using the very formula Browning employed repeatedly in *The Ring and the Book* to discuss historical truth: fancy versus fact. But in the early drafts and notes and in "Three Cantos," he expresses his discomfort with the equipoise of existential historicism. He pushes the internal instabilities within this view itself—the requirement that the historian achieve aesthetic detachment from history without aestheticism, that one proclaim how circumscribed one's own perspective necessarily is and yet establish the significance of the historical view that is offered. Browning negotiated these instabilities by holding aestheticism up to ethical critique and, generally speaking, by both deferring and deferring to the need of an explicitly Christian historical telos. Ultimately Browning balanced chaos and telos on the fulcrum of irony. Such a genuinely ironic posture, however, raises serious questions about both poetic authority and epic coherence. Without a significant diminution of the poem's claims, Browning cannot serve as a Virgil to a modernist epic.

"Am I let preach?"

As has often been remarked Pound cannot return to Dante's religious coherence; neither can he rest in Browning's equilibrium of mingled skepticism and belief. He comments in the typescript that he hates "the Hebrew djinn / That you, R. B. had never quite detested" (typescript notes, p. 5, Beinecke Library). Without R. B.'s "Hebrew djinn" or Dante's "Aquinas map," as he calls it, he must make his own principles of coherence and order, from which the epic impulse is inseparable. As *The Cantos* were taking shape he gradually gave up on his hope that American letters (and society) could have an immediate renaissance, but he did not give up his passion for a new cultural order, the passion he described to his father as a "damned mania for reforming things, due to my Presbyterian training."[9] He needed, therefore, both principles of order and a reformable society. He needed, too, a way of establishing his own poetic authority.

A Calvinist mania for reform without Calvin's God and a historicist equipoise without irony leave Pound with the challenge of establishing poetic authority sui generis. Virgil comes to Dante to guarantee his poetic (and political and theological) authority and, as Beatrice's representative, to lead him on the path through hell to paradise. Virgil stands as a guarantor both of language—that is why he is chosen—

---

9. Letter to Homer Pound, 10 January 1919, Paige typescripts, Beinecke Library. No doubt Pound's ambivalence about his Presbyterian legacy as well an intellectual judgment led to his placing Calvin in hell in Canto 14.

and of the fact that the poet has been chosen. He is at once Dante's insurance against hubris and his link to greatness. Given the historicist beginnings of *The Cantos*, Pound can claim neither Homer nor Dante as a guide, despite their importance to his efforts.[10] He attempts to claim Browning, at least initially, largely because he at first sees his problem of authority in terms remarkably similar to Browning's.

We can see Pound's difficulties with poetic authority more clearly in the context of Browning's own struggles with this issue. For Browning as for Pound, poetic authority is linked especially to calling up the dead. Longenbach has pointed to the fundamental importance of the "ghostly visits" Pound creates in the early cantos: the visit figures for the "workings of historicism" (*Modernist Poetics*, 136). In his construction of poet personae, Browning, like Pound, engaged the metaphor of ghostly visits. At the beginning of *Sordello* the poet summons the ghosts of Shelley and Dante (lines 31–373), and in the beginning of *The Ring and the Book* he describes the summoning of ghosts in ambivalent and ambiguous detail (lines 739–56).

In *The Ring and the Book*, Browning's most obvious attempt at epic, the poet speaks at the outset of his historical attempt; he evokes the investigation, translation, and representation of the documents that found his poem. He at once endorses and undercuts the poet historian's position as seer and maker of visions. The central question is the merging of the poet's soul with dead fact, with the inert metal of his ring metaphor, and with his historical document, the old yellow book. Browning's poet persona claims a great deal for himself even as he admits his resuscitating power is only "galvanism" for life:

> For such man's feat is, in the due degree,
> —Mimic creation, galvanism for life,
> But still a glory portioned in the scale.
> Why did the mage say,—feeling as we are wont
> For truth, and stopping midway short of truth,
> And resting on a lie,—'I raise a ghost?"
> 'Because', he taught adepts, 'man makes not man.
> Yet by a special gift, an art of arts
> More insight and more outsight and much more
> Will to use both of these than boast my mates,
> I can detach from me, commission forth

---

10. Rather than taking Homer or Dante as epic guides in the way that Dante takes Virgil, Pound can only appropriate their texts, and that via a complex process of translation that calls attention to the historicity of the texts themselves.

Half my soul; which in its pilgrimage
O'er old unwandered waste ways of the world,
May chance upon some fragment of a whole,
Rag of flesh, scrap of bone in dim disuse,
Smoking flax that fed fire once: prompt therein
I enter, spark-like, put old powers to play,
Push lines out to the limit.

(1.739–56)

Browning's first "mage" is Faust; the poet goes on at the conclusion of this passage to rewrite Faust as Elisha. The ghostly visits of *The Ring and the Book* lead directly to moral questions about resuscitating the past—is the poet historian finally Faust or Elisha? The metaphor of resuscitation also forces the poet to ask how much of the power to make the bones live he can command. Browning justifies his galvanism (an equivocal metaphor at best) by recourse to the historical documents themselves. Tellingly, he could not go on from these documents, empowered as a quasi-Elisha, to write a poem that fit comfortably into the epic tradition.

Nor did Browning succeed in the one relatively long poem in which he claimed unmediated vision. *Christmas-Eve and Easter-Day* is a testament to the modern disjunction of visionary poetry and social satire. The poet attempts to represent in realistic detail a visionary experience in which he is transported through space to Rome and to a Göttingen lecture room. Here his assertion of personal vision and poetic authority is much less ambiguous than in *Sordello* or *The Ring and the Book*, and yet the poet's authority is not convincingly established. Interestingly the early notes for *The Cantos* show Pound exploiting almost exactly the same premises as Browning's in *Christmas-Eve* and with no happier conclusion. Pound fancies his vision in the metaphor of a magic carpet ride (his version of Browning's "Hebrew djinn"?): "All from the genii's bottles, all this talk / Great heads bear up the carpet, heeling along, / we float out of the lecture rooms, over the city, / truth's in the lot?" (typescript notes, Beinecke Library). Pound's carpet ride like Browning's magic flight in *Christmas-Eve* is eventually abandoned; Pound seeks other suitably epic guarantees for vision; Browning maneuvers within the constraints of historicism.

Within those constraints, poetic authority must, it seems, be established by indirection—through historical mediation and irony. Alternatively, the poet can rhetorically obliterate compromising circumstance. Browning claims authority in *The Ring and the Book* while protesting that art must tell a truth "obliquely"; he avers "I disappeared / the book grew all in all" (1.681).[11] In *Sordello* and *The Ring and the Book*, resuscitating ghosts, breathing life into flesh rags, and pouring the whole into a ragbag, a container that takes the shape of the contained, are the tasks of the existential historicist who stands rapt before the spectacle of history. Such a historian or poet cannot forget the standpoint from which this encounter with history occurs. Remembering his standpoint, the poet is ironically placed, and consequently, a positive epic coherence must remain elusive unless, as in Hardy's *The Dynasts*, irony itself is taken as the fundamental principle of order.

Because it invites irony and undercuts the poet's authority, existential historicism is incompatible with traditional forms of epic coherence. As Hayden White shows in the case of Burckhardt, the historical field becomes a "satura," a medley, a stew of fragments the historian puts together through his own wisdom. It can be controlled by no telos, guaranteed by "no epiphanies of law, no ultimate reconciliation, no transcendence" (*Metahistory*, 250–51). Burckhardt and Browning both appear early in *The Cantos*, opening possibilities for the poetry of history; yet Pound never attempts in *The Cantos* the ironic equipoise of either writer. Though visionary claims may be troublesome in a historicist view, Pound is loath to give them up; historicist irony is too protean, too potentially unstable to serve as foundation for his reforming zeal.

The early cantos and, still more, the unpublished versions of them, could be described as uneasy epic. Longenbach has shown that Pound allowed in the early cantos for ambiguity, for the necessary self-consciousness of the existential historicist about the historian's own

---

11. This last declaration only superficially resembles the claims of positivist historiography; for Browning has just provided a lengthy demonstration of the process by which the historian poet situates himself, a demonstration unnecessary for the historian who believes herself to be in ready possession of all discoverable facts and that these facts implicitly carry their own interpretation. On this reading it is little wonder, then, that Pound found *Sordello* more useful than *The Ring and the Book* as a starting point for *The Cantos*; in *Sordello*, whatever the circumscription and self-consciousness of the poet speaker, Browning's principal focus is on the possibilities and difficulties of the artist-as-hero. Browning raises the questions of romantic poetics with which, over and over again, modernist poets had to begin. *Sordello* entertains more clearly than *The Ring and the Book* the possibility of an order of art or aesthetic character being translatable into political order. In *Sordello* of course this attempt ends in failure; *Sordello*'s epic possibilities are reduced to a remaining song (see also Froula, "Browning's *Sordello*," on these general points).

place as a historical being. Pound "toned down" the "visionary historical sense of the early *Cantos*" (*Modernist Poetics*, 138). And he attempted to appear himself as a historian "who leaves blanks and declines to pass judgment" in Canto 5 (141). In these respects, as in particular passages and details, Browning inhabits both the early Cantos and, still more, the notes and drafts. But, Longenbach argues, Pound went on to a more "positivist" historical method "predicated on the questionable belief that anything we could call a 'fact' exists independently from the interpretive strategy that presents it" (143). Though I agree that Pound's "facts" are insistently juxtaposed, I would characterize his method not as "positivism" in the usual sense but in Wilhelm Windelband's term *idiography* (White, *Metahistory*, 381).

"Idiography"—the notion that the precise description of particulars is itself a sufficient history or that such particulars, when combined, create a context or atmosphere of richly varied texture—is characteristic of the romantic historiography of Carlyle and Michelet and is also crucial to what White calls Burckhardt's "contextualist historicism" (*Tropics*, 64–65). The facts of idiographic history, were a purely idiographic history possible, would be like the contents of an infinitely expandable ragbag. Like the multitudinous details of Pater's writing, the facts of idiographic history are potentially atomistic. As we have seen in the case of existential historicism generally, idiography can easily become empiricism or aestheticism, and thus it presents a difficult problem of order to a would-be epic poet.[12]

Browning's circumscribed claims to vision and his ironies—and his willingness to give up epic claims—stand against such potential

---

12. Christine Froula has argued persuasively that Browning's *Sordello* may be viewed as an early modernist poem and that Pound's poem "reenacts Sordello's aspirations, struggles, and paradoxical success-in-failure." The problem Browning explores in *Sordello*, Froula argues, is "the problem of force in poetic and political authority"— a problem also presented to Pound both by his own poetics and in the history of his time. Froula contends that whereas Browning's Sordello "spurns the temptation to political force even as he fails to make persuasive his dream of a common language, Pound, reaching what Hugh Kenner names the 'fault line' of the Italian cantos, falls prey to this temptation when his own 'Maker-see' poetics fails" ("Browning's *Sordello*," 988). I find Froula's the most persuasive discussion—because the most clear in its understanding of Browning's methods—of Pound's appropriation of *Sordello* in *The Cantos*. Froula's argument can be extended, however, into the early cantos themselves. It is not only the "fault line" of the Italian cantos that Pound somehow crosses; the problems of poetry and authority were at issue in *The Cantos* from the first.

chaos. Carlyle's emphasis on heroism becomes his resistance to the dispersions of idiography.[13] For Pound, eventually, the idea of law comes to have such a force. The coherence he seeks in law, however, never entirely overcomes the dispersive propensities of his idiographic examples. Both poetic authority and poetic form remain elusive for a poet who must begin by sorting through a historical ragbag in the world's marketplace.

Although Pound appropriates from the existentialist historicists the technique of juxtaposition and claims an impersonal truth developed through the self-conscious placement of the historian poet, though he borrows the methods of idiography, *The Cantos* do not attempt to recreate the precarious balance of existential historicism or the ironies that seem naturally to accompany such histories. Instead, the contradictions yoked in Browning's historical ironies are played out in *The Cantos* as competing forms of historical and poetic conceptualization. The tensions between dispersion and order, which contribute to the ironies of existential historicism and which are repressed in the general laws of positivist history or in the heroic principle, cause explosions under high pressure in *The Cantos*.

For Pound the desire for moral and political certainty and for poetic authority calls into question from the first the possibility of ironic equipoise. As he wrote and later deleted from "Three Cantos," "'(Can I preach)? Oh that's only half too easy. / Can I hold off from preaching" (typescript, p. 5, Beinecke Library). As *The Cantos* developed he eliminated the circumscribed and Browningesque poet speaker who is condemned to the indirections of irony. Instead of this circumscribed speaker, a moral and presentative voice takes over. The voice that asks, "Can I preach?" becomes necessarily enmeshed in the politics of its time; to one afflicted with Pound's "damned mania for reform," Browning's compromising liberalism could provide no guarantee of poetic authority.

This desire for the voice of certainty need not be seen as arising out of nowhere or merely out of Pound's personal proclivities.[14] The force of epic ambition itself and the necessities of conventional epic forms

---

13. Similarly, Tim Redman (*Ezra Pound and Italian Fascism*, 97) agrees with Fredric Jameson (*Fables of Aggression*, 120) that Pound's view of Mussolini becomes very like hero worship.

14. Another fruitful path for investigation, which is beyond my scope here, is to seek to understand Pound's attempt at epic in the context of contemporaneous developments in American history with the closing of the frontier and the rise of corporate America.

are antithetical to ironic equipoise. Epic makes claims to historical truth and poetic authority and generally claims to represent heroism in a coherent story that has at once historical and political point. The ironies of existential historicists like Browning and Burckhardt are essentially antiheroic even though the historian may admire genius or power. Moreover, the ironizer can seldom completely escape the net of his own irony—a position from which epic coherence and authority become compromised. The contrast between heroic and ironic history was defined by Nietzsche in *The Use and Abuse of History* as the distinction between monumental and critical history, the latter being the vehicle of modern ironists. In Pound's poetry we can see the distinction figured as the fascination for monuments and the (antithetical) need to acknowledge the " 'Beer–bottle on the statue's pediment' " (C, 7.25).

The ambition to view history as epic is essentially anti-ironic even though the poet or historian may employ an ironic critique of the present. One has only to think of Carlyle's assertion that history is "the true Epic Poem" and recall his move away from the equipoise of the early essay "On History" toward later assertions of heroic individualism to see how epic ambition exerts a shaping force on historical understanding (*Works*, 28:176). In *The Use and Abuse of History*, Nietzsche spoke explicitly about the consequences of modern irony for heroism. He delivered a scathing and ironic critique of irony. Modern historiography like modern history, he declared, is a matter of ghosts and bones: it is "the frightful petrifaction of the time, the restless rattle of the ghostly bones, held naively up to us by David Strauss as the most beautiful fact of all" (57). The thinker should direct attention instead not to "masses but at individuals who form a sort of bridge over the wan stream of becoming. . . . One giant calls to the other across the waste space of time, and the high spirit-talk goes on, undisturbed by the wanton, noisy dwarfs who creep among them. The task of history is to be the mediator between these, and even to give the motive and power to produce the great man" (58). One could see Pound's evocation of ghosts in *The Cantos* as partaking both of the historicist delight in the bone shop of history and as an attempt to remedy what he, like Nietzsche, saw as the "petrifaction" of the time—caused in large part by the rattles emanating from the Straussian and ironic bone shop. Insofar as the poem aims at epic authority, it must achieve what Nietzsche called "high spirit-talk"; it must mediate among great individuals or, as Pound called them, "factive" personalities. The ironies of Browning or of Burckhardt render such heroism dubious indeed. The very definition of epic entails a claim to authority and coherence which the ironic poise of historicism cannot offer. A Browningesque Virgil of the ragbag can be no epic guide at all.

The difficulties of Browning's or Burckhardt's works as models for epic may be understood in terms of figuration or dominant tropes, as I indicate in detail in the next chapter. Here I focus on the difficulty of teleological coherence for an epic beginning from historicist premises. The perplexities presented for epic by an ironic history such as Browning's or Burckhardt's are not only those of establishing poetic authority but the political and ideological problems of individualism.

Browning's poetry offers no general prescriptions for a world out of joint, except perhaps the Protestant virtues of individual self-transformation through the moral recognitions afforded by irony or by an intuitive apprehension of human love or Christian truth. Much of his poetry displays an individualism not unlike that of many realist novels, although the monologue form eschews the direct representation of individual development. Browning's poem most important to *The Cantos*, however, is less tied to individualist representation than the dramatic monologue is.[15] *Sordello* is a product not of the 1860s with its dominant discourse of realism and individualism but of the 1830s when both the political situation and the possibilities of representation were in flux. Because Sordello seeks to remake language and politics at once and because the poets—Sordello and Browning—are inextricable from each other or from the effort of the text itself, Browning's poem presented possibilities to epic that lie outside the realm of the novel. (For the same reasons, *Sordello* was unintelligible to many Victorian readers.) *Sordello*, then, provided Pound an ambiguous precedent. It resisted the individualist reading that looked for a representation of the development of character, and yet in other ways it failed to achieve pattern. Browning's poem spoke more to the contradictions between art and politics and within "character" than to a set of patterned relations among politics, nature, and art. Because it examines the problematic of individualism, *Sordello*, not *The Ring and the Book*, provided Pound with a possible model for epic; in grappling

---

15. Loy Martin, however, argues that the versification itself in Browning's monologues forms a kind of antidote to any monologic individualism; it creates a further tension in the representation of languages associated with individuals (who actually are part of various specialized interests), and by making communication problematic it allows the monologue to engage dialectically with the dominant ideology of individualism (in Gibson, *Critical Essays*).

with *Sordello* he was seeking a way to unite "diagnosis" and "pattern."

Although *Sordello* examined the troublesome nature of individualism, it remained within the historicist frame in which the poet must string the threads between present and past and in which he finds it difficult to assimilate the past directly to some larger telos. The persistent disjunction between diagnosis and pattern made room for Browning's liberal and reforming individualism. Pound's other great historicist predecessor, Burckhardt, also developed a historiography that de-emphasized telos in favor of historicist context and individualist explanation. Burckhardt offered a profoundly conservative and pessimistic response to history and contemporary life—a kind of conservative individualism. Both these stances are compatible with irony, and both provide more "diagnosis" than "pattern."

It might seem, consequently, that Pound's effort to escape the limits of historicism would have led him away from individualism altogether; but for him, as I explain more fully in the following chapters, the antidote to irony was not to reject individualism but to embrace a radical individualism reminiscent of Nietzsche and Carlyle. In *The Cantos* we find together the disintegrative force of this extreme individualism and a correspondingly strong desire for coherence and order. Pound's complex project is made yet more difficult because he adopts as his subject not a single story or narrative but the dispersive and antiteleological matter associated with contextualism and cultural history.[16]

16. The beginnings of contextualist historicism can be seen largely to coincide with the birth of cultural history in the late-eighteenth and early-nineteenth centuries. As Maurice Mandelbaum has argued in *The Anatomy of Historical Knowledge*, histories that seek to present the interconnections of cultural forms and forces are more generally synchronic than diachronic in form; they tend to begin with a brief chronological account and then to proceed synchronically. Histories that place greater emphasis on stories of development, on the contrary, tend to begin with a brief establishment of context and go on in a diachronic fashion (40). Burckhardt's *Civilization of the Renaissance* and Browning's *The Ring and the Book* both follow the pattern of cultural history, whereas Browning's *Sordello* engaged in an even more radical sort of synchronicity. *The Cantos* generally attempt a radical synchronicity, though the Chinese and Adams cantos also follow a larger pattern of historical chronology, the second group taking up where the first leaves off. Having no single epic hero and no single teleological action, *The Cantos* set out as a paradoxical, self-contradictory project, an epic of cultural history. Against the disintegrative possiblities of cultural history—a dispersion characteristic of *Sordello* and the anti-climactic last book of *The Ring and the Book*—is Pound's epic search for order. For all his desire to "hold off from preaching," Pound's poem could be called an epic of cultural imperialism, with the poet pedagogue as imperator of one.

Pound's beginnings in existential historicism, his conviction that historical facts and natural details have an idiographic significance, his individualist ideology—all these dimensions of his approach to poetry and history make epic's formal coherence elusive. They militate against the inherent teleological requirements of a long poem. Without a single story, without the comforts of liberal individualism, without a poetic predecessor who could transform a ragbag into an epic structure, Pound was left to invent sources of poetic authority as well as poetic form; his poetic ending and his ethical and political ends were equally obscure.

Epic and Telos

Unlike *The Cantos*, Virgil's epic was national and imperialist; its telos was clear. Dante's and Milton's epics presented a Christian teleology and arguments for Christian political hegemony. Even Wordsworth's *Prelude* had teleological and developmental implications, becoming by default an autobiographical epic with the artist as hero, the epic of self-culture. The political and poetic authority of the epic poet resides in the teleology upon which the epic is founded, particularly in the Christian or openly imperialist epic. An epic founded in, even if departing from, the principles of idiography, cultural history, and existential historicism, however, has no clear teleology or coherent story to guarantee the epic poet's authority. Pound, in short, had to make it up. He became, as it were, the ultimate *inorganic* intellectual.

For Pound, in a work of cultural construction of epic proportions and with ambitions to epic comprehensiveness and coherence, authority could not be found in a recognized religious story or (in 1915–25 at any rate) in the celebration of a successful heroic or imperialist state. The poem itself must construct the basis on which to found authority and to project, if fleetingly, a telos. Telos and poetic authority are grounded for Pound in Confucian notions of the relationship of the individual to the state, in a kind of neopagan exoticism, and in the power of translation and allusion to appropriate traditions. But such authority stands in ambiguous relationship to the givens of Pound's culture, to romantic and Victorian poetics, and to the modern democratic state.

Though he has no tale with an already clear telos, Pound's eventual evocation of Confucian ideals (first clearly evident in Canto 13) is at once individualist and an effort at restoring a cultural center. It is on this point that we can see how his admiration for Confucian ethics and his adoption of Homeric myth coalesce. *The Cantos*, as Jeffrey Perl has shown, are like many modernist texts in being predicated on a *nostos* or myth of return, of which the Homeric nostos of Odysseus is the most striking example (*The Tradition of Return*, 17–33). But even this foundational story is complicated in *The Cantos* if one reads Homer by way of Dante. Ronald Bush has argued that Pound shares Dante's ambivalence about Odysseus—who after all is condemned for the destruction of the Palladium of Athena (*Genesis*, 132). The poet's lot and, most profoundly, the task of the poet of cultural epic is not simply to follow the destiny of Odysseus, the restitution of order (by men and gods) in Ithaca; the poet must restore the Palladium itself.[17]

This act of restoration is in Pound's understanding made possible not only by the poem's claim to vision but also by the posited connections among language, order, and tradition. The Confucian dictum *cheng ming* to which Pound was to return frequently as a normative center for *The Cantos* involves not only right naming, or rectifying terminology, and a guarantee of good government and good art—it carries with it the establishment of proper connections between the present and tradition; collateral terms denote the authorized tradition. Rectifying terminology, then, is connected both to the ghostly visits of modern history's inescapable ironies and to the heroic creation of a new order. It is a form of canon making. As is the case with the modern artist's practice of translation, to attempt to restore a palladium is to name the conditions of its destruction.

The visionary claims of *The Cantos* are as problematic as any claim to the restoration of order, and they are made yet more so by being based in Pound's neopaganism. Though he cultivated epic authority in *The Cantos* to the exclusion of structurally formative ironies, he could not escape irony altogether—the gods of his "azure air" are ineluctably placed by twentieth-century readers of elite poetry in the staler air of Strauss's bone house.[18] The modern poet has at least as much difficulty establishing a rhetoric of vision based on neopaganism as Browning did in creating a visionary Christian poetry. All traditions may be, ultimately, constructed; yet some—the Aquinian universe for Dante for example—may be experienced as given by po-

17. On similar issues with respect to the *Aeneid* see David Quint, "Epic and Empire."
18. The circular irony here—that even the escape from history through vision is ultimately historicized—is indicated in Nietzsche's argument that the modern condition is inescapably ironic.

ets and their contemporary readers. Near the end of his life as a poet, when he was writing the final drafts and fragments of cantos, Pound summed up this situation for Donald Hall:

> An epic is a poem containing history.
> Modern mind containing heteroclite elements.
>
> Past epos has succeeded when all or a
> gt. many answers were assumed.
>
> At least between author and audience,
> or a great mass of audience.
>
> Attempt in an experimental age IS ergo,
> rash.
> (quoted in Hall, *Remembering Poets*, 175)

As the most casual reader of *The Cantos* can attest, neither poet nor reader can assume a pattern to unite "heteroclite" elements. Even the gods of Pound's poetry—in its crucial and authorizing visions—are not given by common tradition but show signs of their own construction. They have the ambiguous status of Pater's "real illusions." Having excised the "Hebrew djinn," Pound still leaves the reader to question the status of his own pantheon. The exoticism of Pound's gods makes them rhetorically striking but also makes it probable for the reader, if not for the poet, that the vision of these gods can guarantee no larger social and political coherence.

From the very inception of *The Cantos*, translation, like neopagan vision, provides Pound with a possible source of epic authority. Like neopaganism, however, translation comes with its seams showing. The price of neopagan exoticism for epic authority is that such claims to visionary truth are purely subjective and idiosyncratic; the price of translation is that it opens epic judgment to radical historicization. Longenbach has astutely observed that we might regard translation in *The Cantos* in two senses: as the remaking of texts from one language into another and in the religious sense of movement from a lower to a higher state (*Modernist Poetics*, 122–23). Translation serves not only the purpose of gathering historical data but also the purpose of creating a cultural palladium. In the early poems, as we have seen, translation allows the poet to come to terms with literary tradition and the wider historical past. In *The Cantos* the mix of translation and quotation in original languages constitutes a linguistic idiography;

through quotation and translation Pound seeks a new empire of languages, a kind of epic esperanto.[19] *The Cantos* intimately connect the epic poet's authority, translation, and state making. Each of these dimensions of Pound's effort is grounded in contradiction.

Although. I focus in detail on the figurative and political contradictions of *The Cantos* in later chapters, an example here from the development of the early cantos can demonstrate in small the difficulties of reconstructing a palladium without letting go the gritty details of a historical and historicized world. One of the most interesting passages of notes or rough draft for *The Cantos* is the five-page typescript titled "Fragment / Modern World" which served as an early nucleus of Canto 5; I have already quoted the portion of these notes that promises to predict Napoleon from the condotierri and that contrasts "diagnosis" and pattern. The remainder is equally revealing of Pound's early ambition; it allows us to see clearly how Browning's version of the monologue, his ironies, and his individualism proved inadequate to epic pattern and yet how at the heart of the early cantos the instabilities of existential historicism remain.

The typescript is dated on the third page in Pound's hand, 9 August 1915. Canto 5 was first published in August 1921 in *The Dial* and in December of the same year in *Poems 1918–21, Including Three Portraits and Four Cantos*. In *Poems 1918–21* the three portraits are (1) "Propertius"; (2) "Langue d'Oc" ("Alba," 1–4) and "Moeurs contemporaines"; and (3) "Hugh Selwyn Mauberley." In the collected volume, then, Cantos 4–7 would have been preceded by historical help in the form of other poems dealing with Rome and the troubadours. Such help would have been useful to readers coping with Pound's ellipses and juxtapositions, which are necessarily part of the early version and which remain at least as obscure in the poem's final form. The early typescript reads, in some measure, like a list of topics later expanded in the final version of the poem; thus the typescript is in part notes and in part a preliminary draft. It is particularly remarkable for passages Pound later chose to omit. It promises directions *The Cantos* does

---

19. See Ezra Pound, *Ezra Pound and Japan*, for various comments on what Pound in the 1930s and 1940s envisioned as a "tri-lingual" system. For example in a piece titled in manuscript "Communicatons, or Cultural Front," published as "Trilingual System Proposed for World Communications" in *Japan Times* (15 May 1939), Pound advocated a system involving ideogram "with the Japanese sound (syllabic) comment," Italian, and English. This combination would enable writers to say virtually all that needed to be said (reprinted in *Pound and Japan*, 150–51).

not follow and inclusiveness on a scale even Pound's eventual om-
nivorousness did not reach.

The typescript begins with a dream vision, a mode of connecting
present and past the poet favored in the early versions of *The Cantos*
but later omitted, preferring fewer mediating devices. The dreaming
narrator, here as in "Three Cantos," disappears in the poem's final
version. In the typescript, however, the narrator begins to take shape
as a Browningesque dramatic speaker. He declares:

> I was the valet to Der [Ser] D'Alviano
> In 1520 in the (Dolomites,) came a bleared evening,
> Snow from the alps, north of Bergamo,
> A wheeze of light, short days, and cringing shadow,
>   al poco giorno ed al gran chercio d'ombra,
> I brought the early candles   set them down
> On the bare table, took an arquebus
> to oil and clean, by the further door,
> piled up the fire (high peak of mantle)
>   arch. term.
>   (typescript, Beinecke Library)

At this point, the draft becomes something more properly described
as notes, and the first-person speaker disappears. As Pound revised
these materials, he omitted the dramatic speaker in favor of the presentative voice that is implied in the notes.

The passage of the final Canto 5 which owes most to these early
notes is a collection of allusions to Renaissance classicism and classi-
cists. These allusions, it is clear from the typescript, were originally
motivated by the creation of something very like Sigismundo's post-
bag: Pound refers in detail to D'Alviano's book bag, his traveling library. In the typescript, the gathering of poets and men of letters is
given a narrative frame both in the description of the library and in
the claim that the dramatized speaker, Bartolomeo D'Alviano's valet,
has seen D'Alviano and Giovanni Cotta (who founded an academy of
the arts) along with Girolamo Frascatoro gathered for a hunting party:

> Cotta had been there
> D'Alviano,
> Frascator, hunting,
> A young chap from Rome with gossip,
> D'Alviano, few books, small for traveling

Marius 2nd. Theocritus idyl
Spain in the time of Martial
Navighero not interested, brings tale of Spain,
Longus, or Gk. novel.
Navghero and Boscan, Granada,
al hambra. what wisdom, honey comb,
plain outside, exquisite interiors, right architecture,
     beautiful squares.
vista on vista, al koran nitche.
Too foreign, italian vs. exotic,
Are Moors to be counted. we accept the greeks,
mix all mythology,
ancient vs. modern., don't start that
Spit on the tomb of Simone de Montfort,
but refrained. what do we know? He's dead.
this re/ Navghero's hate of Martial.
    slave poem
Pico sestina,,, Bembo???? is it Bembo on troubadours,
"Bembo?", Useless says D'Alviano, heard him in Venice,
What *is* the use
     words,
      periodic sentence,
Homer fact. D'Alviano no nonsense.
   Homer of the main line. Plays, Iphegenia, vs. Helen
             (typescript, Beinecke Library)

This catalog of D'Alviano's traveling library and his friends is transformed in the final version of Canto 5 to construct the elliptic ending of the canto. The promise of Iphigenia vs. Helen is also expanded in the final version as Pound compares the troubadour Pieire de Maensac and his lover with Paris and Helen and as he alludes to Aeschylus's *Agamemnon*. Although the complex allusions of the final Canto 5 retain the feel of somewhat arbitrary linkages inherent in the notion of the traveling library, the dramatized Browningesque speaker, D'Alviano's valet, and the narrative device of the traveling library are missing.

Canto 5 as a whole in its final form ponders the links among treachery, romance, and heroism. It takes up some of the matter promised in the next section of the notes—it may not directly predict Napoleon from the condotierri (it leaves that for the Malatesta cantos), but it does forge links between the Renaissance and classical Greece and Rome. Was Lorenzo, the murderer of Alessandro Medici, like Brutus? Was Brutus a traitor? Was Alessandro a Renaissance Agamemnon? In the final version of Canto 5 the murders of Alessandro and of Giovanni Borgia provide the "clock-tick" that "pierces the vision" of the beautiful. History's brutality counters the timeless vision of Helen as source of all romance:

> And Pieire won the singing, Pieire de Maensac,
> Song or land on the throw, and was *dreitz hom*
> And had De Tierci's wife and with the war they made:
>   Troy in Auvergnat
> While Menelaus piled up the church at port
> He kept Tyndarida. Dauphin stood with de Maensac.
>
> John Borgia is bathed at last. (Clock-tick pierces the vision)
> Tiber, dark with the cloak, wet cat gleaming in patches.
>   (5.18)

The place of the poet in recreating this tension between vision and history is ambiguously suggested in the two poets introduced in the final version, Barabello of Gaeta and Giovanni Mozzarello. Barabello, the type of the fatuous poet attempting to be popular, fails to have himself crowned with laurel after attempting to ride the pope's elephant to the Capitol. Mozzarello attempts an epic, but before he can finish he "takes the Calabrian roadway" and is thrown down a well "smothered beneath a mule." "A poet's ending," the voice comments, "Down a stale well-hole, oh a poet's ending" (5.20). Between 1915 and 1921, Pound shifted his emphasis from celebration of D'Alviano and his academy of arts to the ambiguous place of poetry in the modern world, as represented by these poets. These exempla indirectly answer the question Pound asks in the notes, "What *is* the use / words, / periodic sentence." If Homer is "fact," then Bembo's periodic sentences are what Pound derides as bombastic epic. It is not only idiography but the flight from bombast that motivates Pound's ellipses and juxtapositions. The dramatized Browningesque speaker, likewise, had to go in the final version of the canto; Browning's mixed diction and the ragbag (or book bag) as implicit formal model can remain. In the final version of Canto 5 Pound leaves room for the questions of existential historicism: What did, in fact, happen? How do vision and fact connect? But also in that version we see him paring away matter originally in the notes which remained somehow too heterogeneous for inclusion even in so capacious a ragbag. The contents of the book bag or ragbag in his ideal should include materials for drawing a main line.

The notes to Canto 5 reveal the scope of Pound's original epic ambitions. Not only did he intend to include materials concerning the Moors in Spain, the Alhambra's "vista on vista" to match the "ply over ply" he borrowed from Browning; he also intended to invade the territory of the Mahabharata. He evokes "Vyasa's wood," where the epic poet, according to traditional accounts, received the poem. He sketches in the notes a vision of visiting the dead borrowed not from Greek but from Indian mythology:

> Get to your work, say of Vyasa's wood,
> That Ubanuban, or whatever his name was,
> Walked best [?] beneath snakelike trees, a tangle, a jungle,
> That doubled octopus, your indian art, those [?]
>   squirms,
> contortions, what can you hold of it.
> This Ubanasan, plunged down in a cave,
>   full of black dusk,
> Above him clung the spirits, shriveled and querulous
> Dark souls, souls of his fathers,
>   crying for generation,
> Hung by their heels, squeeking with little noises,
> Crying for blood libations
>   (typescript, Beinecke Library)

Here Pound creates another moment of summoning ghosts, a "snake sacrifice" as he calls it on the next page of notes, exhorting himself "oh look up Vyasa." Then he scrawls at the bottom of the page, "an image of the world Come back to it later." As it turns out, he did not come back to it, having little sympathy with the "squirms" of Indian art as he saw it.

Abandoning this possible parallel to Homeric and Dantean visits to the land of the dead, the final draft of *The Cantos* instead keeps to the Greek mythology Pound introduces in the notes. To "pierce the cosmos" as he says in the final page of these notes, he has "a dozen visions." The most appealing one he describes as "spear heads interlaced, a shower of embers, / of fauns and nymphs . . . keeping the one same tread, the one quick measure . . . sweet trees with blossomy branches." The shower of embers is transformed in the final version of Canto 5 as the " 'ciocco,' brand struck in the game" (5.17). The Indian story of libations for spirits, though an obvious parallel to the Greek, presents Pound too directly with the problems of mixing "all mythology." The *Mahabharata* is the greatest epic unassimilated in

The Cantos, and here we see Pound groping for a way to include it. What do "we accept?" the notes ask. What is in Homer's "main line" (typescript notes, Beinecke Library)?

Clearly Pound can draw a line from the Greeks, to Rome, to Renaissance Italy, to the present, a line closely resembling Burckhardt's. To this line he can assimilate Confucius, particularly through neo-Confucian interpretation; for Confucius can mediate questions of order and disorder, microcosm and macrocosm. The multiplicity of Indian stories appeared to Pound, I believe, as a potentially overwhelming disorder—"a tangle, a jungle." It may have threatened too, an image of uncontrolled or multiple sexuality; curiously the only place I can find that he evinces more than a dismissive interest in Freud is in the handwritten memo at the end of this draft, where he wrote "knowledge the inner zodiac= ? / Freud— psyco-analysts—." In the final draft of *The Cantos,* the Mahabharata and Freud were excluded, although as I suggest in Chapter 6, sexuality retained its essential dangers. The heterogeneity, the unassimilable sexuality of Pound's Indian materials, threatened to complicate beyond recognition the "one quick measure" of his Greek dance under the "sweet trees."

If Pound's poem can assimilate epic predecessors, he makes clear, it must establish a "main line." It must provide a "diagnosis" of the modern world and a model for or a vision of order. Neither the Moors nor the Mahabharata could, for Pound, quite be made to fit. For the epic ostensibly to narrate itself, he had to be confident of the main line as he saw it, even if the process of narration obscured the connections. The resolutely historicized monologist, D'Alviano's valet created on something like Browning's principles, had to be excised along with other material that proved somehow too resistant. Yet neither the difficulties within existential historicism nor the threat of chaos is ever excised entirely from *The Cantos.* The heterogeneity of the ragbag cannot be contained by the telos even of Pound's "main line."

Pound's double concern with history and with vision and his continuing struggle for poetic authority and coherent form undergird the project of *The Cantos* as a whole. The elements of judgment and of explanation, I shall argue in the following chapters, bring tensions implicit in the project to problematic though temporary resolution— in the political judgments of *The Fifth Decad,* in the visions at Pisa, or in the long stretches of Chinese and American history whose significances, for Pound, are guaranteed by their exemplary status. By the time he comes to write *The Fifth Decad* the force of a search for order and the nostalgia for a lost order make the equipoise of existential historicism untenable.

The first thirty cantos, however, are more open than the succeeding ones to questions of historical knowledge and more attentive to the possibilities of meaning lost in translation, to vision that is "discontinuous" (C, 21.99). Yet even here the yearning for order, for law, for historical explanation gives rise to the scatology and eschatology of the hell cantos. The early cantos claim both an authority in vision and a vision arising from confusion; they claim historical exemplars in Sigismundo, in Lorenzo Medici, in Jefferson and yet make room for the moral ambiguities of heroism itself. The Este and the Medici and the Malatesta survive by perpetrating violence and embracing culture; even the great Odysseus, from one perspective, could be said to give his men "poison and ear-wax" (C, 20.94).

Cantos 20 and 21 exemplify these complexities. Canto 20 begins with the poet calling explicit and humorous attention to the problem of translation; it modulates into a presentation in which natural beauty is transformed from sound to light, implicitly the light of Italian Renaissance painters, a light revealing female beauty. This vision in turn calls up Niccolo d'Este, who has murdered his wife Parisina and her lover Ugo (his illegitimate son); whatever his violence, he links the founding of the house of Este with the founding of Rome after the Trojan War. In Niccolo's implied monologue, the "jungle," "confusion," and the treachery of beautiful women (Helen, Parisina) may yet be the "basis of renewals" (20.91). His experience recapitulates Greek passion in a Renaissance context, just as in Canto 21, Ficino brings Greek knowledge. Both are in the "main line." Canto 20 ends with a vision of Isotta, beloved of Sigismundo Malatesta. The poet's dream vision and Niccolo's implied monologue coalesce in a vision of a temple emerging from nature above the cliff road. In the "waste hall," a voice—Niccolo's disembodied voice—urges peace (20.95).

Canto 21 continues this concern with the connections between vision and power by focusing more clearly on the poet's place and on the material affairs of governing. The canto implicitly parallels Cosimo de Medici with Thomas Jefferson. Niccolo d'Este's warning to keep the peace returns at the beginning of the canto. It contrasts with the strife in Niccolo's own house and with the internecine strife of Florence. "Another war without glory, and another peace without quiet" (21.98). This line stands by itself in the canto, and thus it can refer equally to the Italian Renaissance and to contemporary Europe. Without overt comment, it forges a connection between the Renaissance and the rest of Pound's main line. The subsequent narration of Lorenzo de Medici's accomplishments in Canto 21, like the narrative of Malatesta's history, is presented paratactically as if to allow Lorenzo's accomplishments to emerge unmodified. But this idiographic strategy is followed immediately by the intrusion of the poet himself (and possibly the reader) in the vision of "we" who sit "by the arena, *les gradins* . . ." (21.98).

The poet by the arena of history, on the Dogana's steps, or near the ruined temple, contrasts the "tesserae of the floor, and the patterns" with "fools making new shambles" (21.98). What holds these details together is the poet's own presence balancing pattern and destruction. His historical place as witness is compounded of historical fact, visionary claim to perceive pattern, and an elegiac impulse that arises when fact and vision undo each other. The poet's vision, extending even to a natural explanation for Homer's "wine dark sea," allows him to see "in the crisp air, / the discontinuous gods" (21.99). In his vision, Athena and Circe figure wisdom and passion; the violence implicit in the process of such visions themselves is figured in Pound's third goddess Persephone. In the midst of the fields of asphodel, "Dis caught her up" (21.100).

Epic coherence, if achievable, must arise here from the patterns within the historical moment and from the way the moment recapitulates earlier patterns. The telos—eventually the utopian force—of the main line remains obscure, although the complexity of Pound's historicist balancing act is evident. The connections between political order and violence, beauty and destruction, became more pressing for him as Europe moved toward another "shambles."

In taking on the job of the epic poet, Pound attempts to reconstruct a palladium, even though he works from the cultural margin. His "damned mania for reform" led him to hope initially for an imminent social and literary American renaissance and for an epic made possible in this new cohesion (letter to Homer Pound, 10 January 1919, Paige typescripts, Beinecke Library). But even as he lost faith in this possibility, *The Cantos* grew increasingly to propose the importance of cultural centrality and coherence. While Pound became more and more inclined to articulate his opposition to the imperial and commercial power of the United States, his poem took on ever more ambitious proportions.

Dante wrote his poem from exile, Milton his in the aftermath of political disaster; both poems can be seen as epics prescriptive for their times. Pound's epic, too, was written from exile, both outside of and within the United States, and certainly *The Cantos* are prescriptive; yet his epic may be the first to require translation—both literally and figuratively—for the best-trained elite readers of its society. It is a curious paradox, and a sign of the multiple contradictions in Pound's effort to write an epic from exile, that even as English, and eventually American English, were becoming internationally dominant, his long poem was becoming both an attempt at an American epic and a polyglot mix of dictions and of international, if predominantly Eurocentric, cultural exempla.[20] The "main line" he identified was, for his readers, both complex and obscure. It was at once a "main line" and what he identified in the same passage as a "circle from self," a "spider web" (typescript notes, Beinecke Library).

The Cantos then remain both epic and ragbag; their roots are in the nineteenth-century traditions of historicism—of idiography, cultural history, individualism, and existential historicism. Yet though Pound retains the juxtapositions of existential historicism, he does so without the structural irony that frequently accompanies such juxtapositions; and although *The Cantos* can be explicated largely in terms of his intellectual and personal biography, Pound generally omits the presentation of the carefully situated and often self-ironized speaker of *Sordello, The Ring and the Book,* and the early versions of the cantos. The contradictions within *The Cantos* can be understood in terms that are formal, political, and figurative. In formal terms, the nineteenth-century traditions of existential historicism combine uneasily with the needs for coherence, heroism, and order which are implied in the traditions of epic. The authority of the epic poet—the ambition for coherence—is difficult to establish in the face of inescapable historicization.

As we have seen, *The Cantos* were a poem long in beginning; perhaps we could say the poem was repeatedly a beginning, so much so

20. By calling Pound's procedure "Eurocentric," I do not wish to minimize his interest in Chinese history and thought, but I do mean that he essentially assimilates Chinese materials to a tradition of high culture that is centrally European; thus his focus is primarily on the most easily (or most frequently) assimilable Chinese materials, those associated with the Western construction of what is commonly called neo-Confucian tradition. Pound displays little and late interest in other Chinese traditions, particularly those associated with Buddhism and Taoism, and no particular interest in ordinary Chinese culture or modern Chinese language. Although in comparison to many poets, he obviously opens the long poem to very diverse cultural materials, the diversity he seeks is assimilable to his own main line.

that *A Draft of XVI Cantos* became at once a draft and the beginning's final form. The actual beginnings of Pound's poem, his early drafts and notes, reveal the complex reasons for this initial tentativeness. His early quest for the persona, the language, the form proper to a "poem of some length," and his repeated encounters with Browning in those early drafts and notes, show him attempting to negotiate potential contradictions. At the heart of his project is a visionary hopefulness, despite Strauss's bone shop, for cultural and political coherence; but in the poem's tropological structures is a contradictory project attentive almost in spite of itself to the discords of its world—discords both tropological and political that are the concern of the rest of this book.

In "sentimental" art, only the poem itself can vindicate the poet's claim to authority; to move from the romantic margin to the tale of the tribe narrating itself required poetic sleight of hand on a grand scale. It implied *a tale* and *a tribe* and, for Pound, a quest for order that might make such unity imaginable. His readers are left with his own early question, Benedetto Varchi's question about the murder of Alessandro Medici: "Se pia ... O empia, ma risoluto e terribile deliberazione"—"whether noble or ignoble, certainly a resolute and terrible decision."[21]

21. I follow the translation quoted in Terrell, *Companion to the Cantos*, 1:21.

Chapter 4

Between Metonymy and Metaphor: Tropological Rhetoric and *The Cantos*

"To hold a . . . belief in a sort of permanent metaphor is, as I understand it, 'symbolism' in its profounder sense. It is not necessarily a belief in a permanent world, but it is a belief in that direction. . . . Imagisme is not symbolism. The symbolists dealt in 'association,' that is, in a sort of allusion, almost of allegory. They degraded the symbol to the status of a word. They made it a form of metonomy" [*sic*].

—Pound, *Gaudier-Brzeska*

For Pound the process of epic ordering was a matter of continuous reinvention. To write a modernist poem of epic scope meant not only to create a form out of the multiplicity of historicist particulars; it meant also to seek a cultural center, and a cultural story, adequate to the poem's epic claims. This search for epic coherence was shaped by paradoxes common in responses to modern industrial capitalism: the fascination with the medieval coupled with an equal fascination for the avant-garde and for technologies of the future; a celebration of the urban center and an embracing of natural fertility and abundance; a disgust at concentrated economic power and a celebration of civic and military power concentrated in the hands of heroes.

Given these paradoxes and the imperatives of epic itself, Pound's needs for judgment, coherence, and a connecting of the past with the present could not be met by the ironies of existential historicism. His epic, as we shall see, could make new form only by yoking the multiplicity of Browning's ragbag to more stringent political and ethical hierarchy. As it developed—and as Europe moved once more to the brink of chaos—Pound's project required not the ironized or compromised individuals of Browning's and Burckhardt's Renaissance but heroic exemplars who could be presented as bringing the force of his visions to political reality. Yet even in *The Fifth Decad of Cantos*, where his search for heroes is crucial, Pound does not simply abandon his idiographic methods in favor of a heroic narrative.[1] Rather, he retains the juxtapositions of the earlier cantos while insisting on the importance of law.

Pound never leaves behind the fundamental tendency to work in contradictory ways which we have seen in his early imitations and in the early cantos. In these last chapters I examine the ways that both formal and cultural contradictions impinge on *The Cantos*. I trace the mutual implications of Pound's doubled tropes, of his combination of epic and elegy, and of his problematic ideological commitments. But first I provide a basis for that analysis by developing what I call a "rhetorical tropology."

Pound's contradictions can best be understood on the basis of a theoretical model that stresses disjunction, tension, and the possibility that a poem or a history can be a site of contention—ideological and tropological—as well as the scene of resolution. Like the analysis of Pound's nineteenth-century canon and his complex relationship to Browning and to epic tradition, a rhetorical tropology provides a basis for recognizing connections between the cultural and the formal contradictions within *The Cantos*. To develop this tropological argument, I depart in the early sections of this chapter from my predominantly historical and historiographic emphasis and engage directly the theoretical presuppositions of Pound's readers. As critics, I believe, we are no more likely to see Pound plain than Browning was to see Shelley so, and we are less likely to see him plain the closer we come to his politics. (Not to mention that reading *The Cantos* at all usually requires the mediation of a sizable scholarly apparatus.) The closer *The Cantos* come to us and to the politics of our own historical mo-

---

1. Most of the cantos following *The Fifth Decad* similarly avoid heroic narrative, though the Chinese and the Adams cantos adopt a significantly different form of narrative coherence by following the order of their sources. "Idiography" here is used in the sense of Windelband and White, as defined in Chapter 3, and should be distinguished from *ideograph*.

ment, the more self-conscious we need to be about the implications of our theoretical paradigms.

Unlike other readers, I believe that *The Cantos* cannot be understood under the model of a single trope; rather, their complexities can more accurately be comprehended through a model that calls attention to their double troping. In arguing for a complex and rhetorical tropology, my analysis departs from the common practice of Pound's critics who have viewed his work under the successive banners of metaphor, synecdoche, and metonymy. I show that each argument for a single tropological model bears with it a set of implicit values. In the context of the critical practices of New Criticism, Hugh Kenner read *The Cantos*, the ideogrammic method particularly, as a species of metaphor; in the context of structuralism, Herbert Schneidau read them as based in synecdoche; and in the wake of poststructuralism, Schneidau and numerous others have promoted a metonymic reading of *The Cantos*.

Each of these tropological readings has had an implicit ethical dimension even though discussions of synecdoche and metonymy are based in a dualist scientific language that, following Roman Jakobson's practice, often ignores the cultural specificity of figuration. Metonymy has been valued as a means of overcoming the possibly theological and certainly metaphysical claims attributed to metaphor. Indeed, arguments that *The Cantos* work metonymically implicitly or explicitly value dispersion, demystification, and multiplications of meaning, and they distrust teleology, synonymy, relations of similarity—all of which are assimilated to "logocentrism." By defining *The Cantos* as predominantly metonymic, critics can describe a postmodern Pound. Moreover, by focusing on dispersion and multiplicity as in themselves valuable, such postmodern readings often allow the critic to veer away from the cultural meanings of Pound's particular figures. A rhetorical tropology, though not without its own limitations, points both to the cultural contradictions and to the formal difficulties of *The Cantos*.

To examine the premises of earlier tropological readings of *The Cantos* is to make clear the limitations of Jakobson's binary tropology, which founds virtually all of these readings. The middle section of this chapter analyzes Jakobson's tropology and suggests how a rhetorical tropology, though it owes something to earlier structuralist and poststructuralist versions, can go beyond these binary schemes. I advocate an approach that brings to bear on Pound's poem notions about language from discussions of natural narrative, ordinary language, and cognitive semantics. Such an approach recognizes the cultural and communal origins of tropes and their political implications. It emphasizes both connections *and* disjunctions among semantic, conventional, and thematic or political dimensions of the poem, rather than seeking to provide a single structural and unifying principle.

Instead of proposing a single trope as unifying *The Cantos*, I argue that Pound's poem works at once metonymically and metaphorically. With a detailed reading of *The Fifth Decad of Cantos*, I show how Pound attempts to order his multitudinous details both through metonymic relationships and through metaphorical exempla. The metonymy of law is crucial in his effort to order the forces of dispersion he describes in *The Fifth Decad*; his metaphorical layering of exempla, particularly of exemplary lawgivers, provides yet a different kind of order. This group of cantos is itself a pivot or hinge between the halves of Pound's poem, and it establishes patterns that are transformed in the Pisan sequence.

The Basis for a Rhetorical Tropology

That thoughtful critics have presented conflicting accounts of tropes in *The Cantos* is owing to the heuristic nature of tropologies, which necessarily reflect the preconceptions of their creators; it also follows from the complexities of the poem and the ambiguous definitions of tropes themselves. To develop a rhetorical tropology I begin here with a brief discussion of definitions and go on to analyze the strikingly different tropological schemes Pound's critics have proposed to describe *The Cantos*.

Hayden White's definitions of tropes in *Metahistory* offer a useful starting place for the reader unfamiliar with structuralist and poststructuralist tropologies. Drawing on Giambattista Vico and Kenneth Burke, he offers one of the most succinct definitions of important tropes and says that four ways of tropological thinking are common in historical and (by extension) literary texts. He selects as basic tropes metaphor, metonymy, synecdoche, and irony. By contrast, Roman Jakobson offers a binary model of significant tropes, dividing figurative language into metaphorical and metonymic poles. My own use of tropes here owes much to White's definition (following Burke's *Grammar of Motives*) and something to Paul Ricoeur's discussion of metaphor, although mine is developed in the context of work in other linguistic areas than they consider (i.e., cognitive semantics and discussions of narrative and ordinary language).

White takes metaphor to establish relationships of similarity among dissimilar wholes, whereas metonymy establishes part-part relationships or suggests cause-and-effect relationships among parts of a thing or system. Synecdoche differs from metonymy; for it typically involves "intrinsic" relations of shared qualities or relationships between a macrocosm and a microcosm. Irony, in this typology, is the odd trope, the trope of negation and reversal.[2]

White's clearest illustration of these definitions is his analysis of the statement "He is all heart," where, he indicates, a synecdoche is superimposed on a metonymy. If we read the phrase metonymically we think of the heart in terms of its crucial functioning in the body—as we would with the similar metonymy "fifty sail" for "fifty ships." If we read it synecdochically we see that being "all heart" refers to a "characteristic of the whole individual considered as a combination of physical and spiritual elements, all of which participate in this quality of the modality of a microcosmic-macrocosmic relationship" (*Metahistory*, 36). If we take the phrase ironically, of course, we assume that the speaker means the opposite of what he or she says, that "he" is in fact heartless. These examples, of course, are at the level of the semantics of the sentence, whereas what really interests White and other critics is the use of tropes to identify larger dimensions or structures of a text. Tropology then is itself a metaphorical use of notions of figuration at the level of the sentence or phrase to define dominant characteristics of whole works.

Because tropology is both metaphorical and heuristic, the various tropologies of *The Cantos* have tended to reflect the critical orthodoxies of their times and, until the 1980s, to obscure the cultural meanings of tropes. Tropological discussion of *The Cantos* began with Hugh Kenner's identification of ideogram with metaphor and continued with Herbert Schneidau's effort to identify *The Cantos* with synecdoche. Both of these critics connect tropes with larger structures. Kenner generally analyzed ideogram as the metaphorical ordering of particulars, adducing similarity in difference, and took ideogram, following Pound's own lead, as central to structure and meanings of *The Cantos*. When pressed to think of ideogram or metaphor as a principle of a whole text, however, Kenner wished to account for Pound's complexity by arguing that "two ideogrammic principles may with advantage be distinguished"—similarity or dissimilarity (*Poetry of Ezra Pound*,

---

2. Standard and substantially similar definitions of these tropes appear in Lanham, *Handlist of Rhetorical Terms*.

91). Here in the first tropological reading of Pound, Kenner is already working toward a double vision of metaphor/ideogram which will allow for discontinuities. Schneidau's work provides an interesting parallel to Kenner's; instead of maintaining that ideogram has a double force, Schneidau claimed, first, that *The Cantos* are ordered through synecdoche and then that they are essentially metonymic. He associates synecdoche with what he describes as Pound's need for religious coherence.[3]

But neither metaphor nor synecdoche is the dominant trope in most recent readings of *The Cantos*. Some years after his synecdochic reading of Pound, Schneidau rewrote synecdoche as a function of Jakobson's metonymic pole of language and argued that *The Cantos* display a kind of "Paleolithic primacy," a renovation through metonymy of the dead metaphors of poetic convention ("Wisdom Past Metaphor," 26). He reads ideograph and ideogram as essentially metonymic, predicative, and verbal; in short, ideogram establishes metonymic relationships of action, of contiguity, perhaps even of cause and effect.[4] Moreover, Schneidau argues following Jakobson that Pound's poetry tends, like the speech of the aphasic with similarity disorder, to be characterized by frequent ellipses and by the display of an abhorrence of "redundancy."[5]

Schneidau's metonymic reading of *The Cantos* remains within the orbit of the poem's own propositions and largely sympathetic to its principles. P. H. Smith and Alan Durant have regarded *The Cantos* in a less sympathetic light than Schneidau and Kenner, reading Canto 47 as an example of Pound's tropological reductiveness. Here the tropological criticism of Pound moves from a structuralist to a poststructuralist tropology. Smith and Durant find Canto 47 "tendentiously reductive." "The primary strategy in this canto is one of metonomy," they argue in "Pound's Metonymy" (329). They acknowledge a ten-

3. In *Ezra Pound: The Image and the Real*, Schneidau bases what he describes as Pound's preference for synecdoche in a religious need for coherence and identifies synecdoche with notions of incarnation. Though his argument for synecdoche and incarnation is clearly wishful, Schneidau describes more persuasively the importance of organicist ideas in *The Cantos*.

4. In *The Rule of Metaphor*, Paul Ricoeur discusses the predicative function of metaphor; his dicussion leads one to conclude that predicative and cause-and-effect relationships can be distinguished (125).

5. When he claims metonymy as the dominant trope of *The Cantos*, Schneidau accounts for Pound's undeniable use of repetitions, redundancies, and metaphors by insisting that they should be seen as "subordinated . . . to a more powerful principle, call it what we will: contexture seems as good a name as any" ("Wisdom," 25).

sion in *The Cantos* by declaring that Pound's metonymic practices are at odds with his metaphysical and teleological ends. They find his chains of meaning, his metonymic sequencing, to be opposed to the "teleological propaganda" by which he presents a synthesis or metaphysical truth. In Canto 47 this teleological propaganda involves Pound's claims of organicist coherence through identifying with Osiris, Adonis, and natural processes. In thus "treating a metonymy as if it were a metaphor," Pound "presumes to transcend the reticular quality of language and takes a god-like overview of the material he is using" (331). His metaphorical equivalences are for Durant and Smith a validation of logocentrism, phallocentrism, and patriarchal culture. Metonymy on this reading is associated with dialectic and with an antimetaphysical stance; metaphor, with an impossible claim to metaphysical truth. Both tropes are characteristic of *The Cantos*, but it would seem that in Smith and Durant's view, metonymy here operates structurally (or syntactically), metaphor thematically and rhetorically (or semantically). Moreover, the judgment implicit in this discussion grants to metonymy the force of truth against the illusions of metaphor.

In an essay building on the work of Smith and Durant, as well as on Max Nänny's essays and Fredric Jameson's treatment of Wyndham Lewis's metonymy, Ian F. A. Bell reads *The Cantos* more single-mindedly than Smith and Durant, though he too values what he calls Pound's metonymic strategies. Focusing on Canto 31 in which Pound combines snatches of the correspondence of Jefferson and John Adams, Bell sees metonymy operating not "merely as a compositional feature, but as part of the poem's very theme" ("Paralyzed History," in Korn, *Ezra Pound and History*, 76). On this reading, the metonymic strategies of combination, citation, and translation are allied to a deconstructive effort of demystification. In Canto 31, Jefferson's letter in cipher, and Pound's free reconstruction of an indecipherable version of the original which he did not have, become for Bell the exemplary language that "deconstructs the confinement of communal discourse" (82).[6] Although Roman Jakobson's structuralist tropology clearly un-

---

6. Here Bell, like other champions of metonymy, engages in a tropological criticism that has its own teleology; metonymy again becomes a pole of value representing the linguistically self-conscious truths that deconstruct "the confinement of communal discourse." "Communal discourse," "organic guarantees," and a "world of metaphors" are figured as confinement or illusion ("Paralyzed History," in Korn, *Ezra Pound and History*, 75–82). Though he is less sympathetic to Pound than Max Nänny, Bell clearly shares Nänny's view that metaphor is suspect; for Nänny has declared

derlies this view of language, the ghost of Paul de Man, generally unacknowledged, haunts this and other celebrations of metonymy.

This critical movement from emphasis on metaphor, to synecdoche, to metonymy reveals the way any critical heuristic bears larger critical and political burdens. The recent claims that Pound's metonymies deconstruct communal discourse at once fit oddly with the poem's own epic claims and allow the critic to avoid the cultural implications of those claims. Such emphasis on metonymy is prepared in the work of Roman Jakobson; any rhetorical recasting of tropological analysis which seeks to account for the ways "communal" discourses work must consequently locate its own departures from Jakobson's binary tropology.

Jakobson's Poetics and the Premises of Tropology

Jakobson's work on aphasia and his extrapolations from it to poetics have had great persuasiveness and beauty as a conceptual scheme. His work appealed to the structuralist desire for a critical science, and more recently it has seemed to dovetail with the poststructuralist criticism of logocentrism. Jakobson's tropology can be appropriated with relative ease by a critical stance that stresses gaps, aporia, miscommunication. If one begins as Jakobson did from pathology and draws inferences from the pathology of aphasia, an emphasis on aporia seems only logical; moreover a Jakobsonian approach tends to lead to the enumeration of stylistic features.[7] If instead one begins from the perspective of ordinary language and emphasizes the conceptual nature of metaphor and metonymy (and the metaphorical nature of many concepts), one comes rather quickly to an examination of the rhetorical force of particular tropes. It is easy to see how a criticism based on Jakobson has a stylistic bent and that based in ordinary language and cognition a rhetorical one; for the examination of aphasics usually emphasizes disorders in the production of speech instances, and the examination of ordinary language and cognition emphasizes the communication of culturally shared concepts or paradigms.

Jakobson has shown that two types of aphasia (or six subtypes) may

---

that Pound's metonymies have the quality of "demystifying the vertical, paradigmatic world of depth, spirituality, and metaphor" ("Context, Contiguity," 396).

7. Schneidau's essay "Wisdom Past Metaphor," for example, both resists and to an extent acquiesces in this tendency, arguing that an exercise like "counting metonymies" is what gives stylistics its bad name.

be classified either as similarity or contiguity disorders based on the bipolar nature of language; he names the poles of language from the traditional lexicon of tropes as metaphorical or metonymic, and he posits that the metaphorical pole of language is typically more significant in poetry, the metonymic pole in prose. Nänny provides a concise summary of Jakobson's argument as it might apply in literary analysis:

> The metaphoric mode of a discourse thus connects one topic or verbal unit with another, though from a different context, on the basis of some internal similarity (likeness, similitude, equivalence, resemblance, analogy). The chief mental operations demanded by the metaphoric mode are selection and substitution of similars.
>
> The metonymic mode of discourse, on the other hand, connects topics and verbal entities by means of external contiguities in space and time. Hence, relationships no longer derive from patterns of similarity but from temporal or spatial associations due to neighborhood, proximity, subordination and coordination. Here the chief mental operations consist in combination and contexture, that is, in a rearrangement or deletion of contiguous entities. ("Context, Contiguity," 386)

Extrapolating from these distinctions, Nänny concludes that though Pound was not aphasic his poetry comes close to the metonymic pole of language and approximates similarity disorder.

Jakobson's examples of aphasic disorders are striking: a woman suffering from similarity disorder, when asked to list names of animals, lists them in the order she had seen them in the zoo—spatial contiguity. A man trying to recall the word *black* says instead "what you do for the dead." A person asked to define *pencil* replies, "to write." A person suffering from contiguity disorder, by contrast, would have no trouble with equational definitions but more trouble with grammar or combination of words. The person with contiguity disorder or "contexture" deficiency will "deal with similarities, and his approximate identifications are of a metaphoric nature, contrary to the metonymic ones familiar to the opposite type of aphasics. *Spyglass* for *microscope* or *fire* for *gaslight* are typical examples of such quasi-metaphoric expressions, as Jackson termed them, since, in contradistinction to rhetoric or poetic metaphors, they present no deliberate transfer of meaning" ("Two Aspects of Language," 107).[8]

8. Paul Ricoeur points out that both Jakobson and Ferdinand de Saussure combine their linguistic notions with an associationist psychology. In Saussure's *Cours de linguis-*

Despite the distinction Jakobson drew between aphasic quasi-metaphor and metaphor in poetics or rhetoric, he bridged the gap between pathology and literature by arguing that, like children who exhibit substitutive or predicative preferences in psychological testing, individuals exhibit their "personal style" in the way they manipulate similarity and contiguity—both in their positional and semantic aspects ("Two Aspects," 110).

Jakobson associated the bipolarity of language not only with writers' individual styles but, as we have seen, with the distinction between prose and poetry and even with particular genres. Thus in "A Linguistic Classification of Aphasic Impairments" he declared that lyric poetry is usually "built primarily on similarity" and epic upon "contiguity." Metaphor, then, "is the inherent trope in lyric poetry . . . and metonymy is the leading trope in epic poetry. In this connection, the lyric poet . . . endeavors to present himself as the speaker, whereas the epic poet takes on the role of a listener who is supposed to recount deeds learned by hearsay" (*Language in Literature*, 297). From his work on aphasia, then, Jakobson charted a series of correspondences: contiguity and similarity allow us to define individual style, particular generic conventions, and the major divisions of prose and poetry. Moreover, such correspondences either assume, or predispose the critic to identify, a coherent paralleling among style, form (genre), and choice of prose or poetry.[9]

---

tique générale chapter on the "mechanism of language" we find, Ricouer says, the "marriage between associationist psychology and structural linguistics. There the syntagmatic and paradigmatic operations are interpreted in terms of combination. Fifty years later, Roman Jakobson sees no difficulty in principle in these interchanges between semantics and psychology, since he grafts his distinction between metaphorical process and metonymic process directly onto the Saussurean distinction, itself interpreted in terms of association by resemblance and by contiguity" (*Rule of Metaphor*, 116).

9. As Ricoeur notes, Jakobson's principle of equivalence defining poetic language is based on a communication model, with poetic language being focused on the message itself (*Rule of Metaphor*, 145). Clearly this is so, but only in a relative sense; for Jakobson's two axes of language which form the structure of the message are based on the model of disrupted communication associated with aphasia.

   In many ways the premise that there is tropological coherence at the levels of style, genre, and choice of prose or poetry has provided critics with an interesting critical tool. Jakobson recognized that all forms of literature—in contradistinction to some forms of aphasic speech—involve both similarity and contiguity, metaphor and metonymy. Hence criticism must take account of the interplay between the two. Critics have taken as particularly suggestive Jakobson's view, based on these correspondences, that literary history can be charted in terms of its dominant tropes. Jakobson

Jakobson's tropological poetic has been quite powerful; critics have particularly taken to heart his admonition that the metonymic dimension of literature has been largely ignored. Yet I think, as Paul Ricoeur does, that Jakobson's theoretical premises provide too limited a basis for a tropological reading of poetry. It is questionable moreover to assume correspondence among style of individual passages, general conceptualization or style of the whole text, and form or genre. The difficulties of assigning a dominant tropological pattern to a poem and in valuing tropes against each other become clear when close analysis replaces generalization. We might take, for example, Pound's short poem "Shop Girl" to explore briefly the problematics of tropological analysis and as a prelude to the more comprehensive rhetorical understanding of tropes which will provide a basis for reading *The Cantos*.

Max Nänny's reading of Pound's poem typifies both the strengths and the weakness of Jakobson's approach to tropes. Nänny's essay "Context, Contiguity, and Contact in Ezra Pound's *Personae*" points to important patterns in Pound's early poetry, particularly in its "reactive" responses to interlocutors, and to the problems of Pound's

---

argued that while the metaphorical quality of romanticism and symbolism had been recognized, the mediating trend of realism "is opposed to both"; for the realist author "metonymically digresses from the plot to the atmosphere and from the characters to the setting in space and time" ("Two Aspects," 111). And Jakobson set up a scheme of "alternative" predominance of metaphorical and metonymic writing.

Jakobson's views have lent special impetus to discussions of modernism, providing the basis for descriptions of Pound's metonymies and for David Lodge's complex history of poetry in English in terms of dominant tropes. Lodge believes that the English romantics saw themselves as replacing an "inauthentic" kind of metaphorical writing with another more authentic form of metaphor and that—despite Jakobson's view of romanticism—characteristically this strategy in Wordsworth could be called metonymic (*Modes of Modern Writing*, 118). In modernism, Lodge maintains, the situation is complex; he discusses for example Eliot's "Prufrock" as pushing to an extreme the metaphorical principle of substitution so that obscurity results (117). Lodge provides an interesting corrective to Jakobson's tropological scheme, by suggesting, first, that a scheme of simple alternation between metaphor and metonymy is inadequate to the complex dimensions of literary history and, second, that a writer's own style may change radically from one pole to the other (as in Joyce's move from metonymy in *Dubliners* to metaphor in *Ulysses*). Lodge modifies Jakobson's arguments by contending that however metonymic, say, a realist novel may be, all literature is at least covertly metaphorical or has a metaphorical dimension (108). Ricoeur would agree with Lodge that metaphor has a crucial role, indeed for Ricoeur a more crucial role than metonymy. Ricoeur argues that "metaphorical equivalence sets predicative operations in motion that metonymy ignores" (*Rule of Metaphor*, 133).

translations (which Nänny sees as "deficient or negligent" code switching on the axis of substitution). But his reading of "Shop Girl" demonstrates in small the difficulty of moving from semantics to stylistics, to the thematics of the whole text and its connection to literary conventions. Pound's poem reads:

Shop Girl

For a moment she rested against me
Like a swallow half blown to the wall.
And they talk of Swinburne's women,
And the shepherdess meeting with Guido.
And the harlots of Baudelaire.

(PSP, 116)

Nänny takes this poem as one of many instances in Pound's early poetry where "one is struck by the frequency and seeming importance of physical, spatio-temporal contacts. This confirms the impression that Pound, almost like an aphasic with a similarity-disorder, was also 'guided by spatial or temporal contiguities rather than similarity' " (Nänny, quoting Jakobson, 395). In "Shop Girl," Nänny argues, "direct physical contact is also favourably contrasted to metaphorical verbalizations and evocations of literary equivalences" (396).

But though the episode this poem presents is certainly one of contact and contiguity, surely its effectiveness turns on metaphor. We could imagine the poem succeeding without, say, one set of the literary women it invokes. We might, with some adjustment for rhythmic closure, eliminate any one of the last three lines (line four more easily than line five). But what would the poem be without the immediacy of its crucial metaphor, "like a swallow half blown to the wall"? The success of the poem hinges on the successful comparison of the woman brushing against the speaker to the swallow brushing or almost touching the wall. The power and vividness of the literary comparisons that follow—and their irony—turn on this metaphor, which itself has an ironic dimension; for the swallow (woman:bird of course has its own literary connotations) and the shop girl are evoked together. Technically a simile, the only obvious metaphor comes in line two and provides the connective between the opening nonfigurative statement and the comments of the last three lines. Those last three lines are themselves connected paratactically with "and," a polysyndeton that can be taken as a species of metonymy. As Jakobson points out, connectives are, with other context-dependent words, the last survivors in cases of aphasics with similarity disorder ("Two Aspects," 247). Yet the polysyndeton, anaphora, and parallelism of these lines are as dependent on similarity as their additive syntax is upon contiguity. When we move from the syntactic and rhythmic to the thematic, again we find it is not contiguity so much as an elaborate series of equivalences that makes the poem: the shop girl, the swallow, Swinburne's women, the shepherdess, the harlots.

It may be that the women evoked in the last three lines of the poem are chosen by their contiguity in some mental construct of Pound's unavailable to us—even as the woman who selects names of animals follows the order in which she found them in the zoo. Swinburne, Guido (Cavalcanti?), and Baudelaire perhaps just happen to be side by side on Pound's mental or physical bookshelf. Indeed the juxtapositions of *The Cantos* often have the effect of details selected beyond our ability to reconstruct their contiguity. One must have seen the zoo, after all, to appreciate the order in the naming of animals. In "Shop Girl," however, we also see the other strategy of *The Cantos*, implied or explicit metaphorical equivalence. Because the equivalences are created by literary (or historical) allusion they require an immediate understanding both of similarity in difference and of context. This is the way, for example, we understand Pound's implied comparison between Helen and Eleanor in *The Cantos*.

This complexity suggests that we cannot move from parataxis or from the possibility of connections by contiguity among the women to the notion that "Shop Girl" is thematically and fundamentally metonymic. Nänny sees as metonymic the poem's implication that immediate physical experience is superior to metaphorical "verbalizations" and "evocations of literary valences" ("Context and Contiguity," 296). Surely the poem does assert the significance of immediate erotic experience, and it refers sarcastically to such experiences as recorded by previous poets. Yet I believe that whatever its metaphors, its contiguities, or its parataxis, the poem as a whole is in a rhetorical sense ironic. And this explains why the "harlots of Baudelaire" must come last. For the poem must be understood in the tradition of urban and sophisticated irony, from Propertius to Laforgue. It simultaneously asserts the superiority of the poet's immediate experience and undercuts its own declaration of superiority by evoking the poetic tradition that makes possible the selection of this experience as a topic for poetry. The class-conscious ambivalences of harlots and shopgirls and the poem's urban flavor control the ordering of comparisons; Baudelaire, as the poet of the urban, provides the obvious place to end. On this reading, "Shop Girl" is anything but a simple defense of contiguity and contact; nor is it metonymic all the way down. Rather, the richest reading of the poem flows from an understanding of its asymmetry; of the tensions within and among syntax, figures of speech, ordering of thematic elements, and rhetorical structure. Its ironies are more likely to establish its connections with Pound's early vignettes than with the larger strategies of his long poem.

This reading of a small poem can begin to suggest how open to question is the presumption of unity of metaphorical or metonymic structures, in Jakobson's sense, at all possible levels. On Jakobson's larger scale—that of literary history or the canon of a single author—there is no greater reason to presuppose such unities. Perhaps only asymmetry can account for change in literary history or in the canon of a single author.[10] Though he claims that every author has a predominantly metaphorical or metonymic style, he himself points out that "a competition between both devices, metonymic and metaphoric, is manifest in any symbolic process" ("Two Aspects," 113). Certainly *The Cantos* are far more tropologically complex than a vignette like "Shop Girl."

Rhetorical Tropology and Cognitive Semantics

Despite his bow toward doubled troping, Jakobson's binary tropology ultimately suggests dichotomies between ordinary and poetic language; it grounds various arguments for a single dominant trope in any given case. A rhetorical tropology based in ordinary language and cognitive semantics, in contrast, can be more attentive than structuralist (and most poststructuralist) tropologies to the place of competing tropes. In *Toward a Speech Act Theory of Literary Discourse*, Mary Louise Pratt has clearly demonstrated the difficulties in the distinction that Jakobson, the Prague school, and structural linguists generally draw between ordinary and literary language. She follows Michael Riffaterre and others in rejecting the notion of the persistence of a dominant verbal structure even when it has "no surface textual realization"; and, following Karl Utti, she argues powerfully that Jakob-

---

10. In his *Pragmatic Theory of Rhetoric*, Walter Beale argues for the principle of asymmetry in understanding the relationships among the elements of his rhetorical typology and that, in effect, asymmetry can be understood to provide a kind of rhetorical energy.

son's definition of poetry in terms of the projection onto the axis of similarity keeps him from doing justice to the connections among ordinary language, literary language, and poetry (36, 75–78). Pratt opposes the intrinsic study of literary language and favors a more obviously context-dependent study.

Recent work in cognitive semantics provides just such a contextualized approach and thus provides a foundation for a rhetorical tropology. From the perspective of cognitive semantics much of the analysis based in Jakobson's theories shows itself to be too rigidly binary. George Lakoff, Mark Johnson, and Mark Turner have recently synthesized work on cognition to suggest that metaphor is as much a part of ordinary language (and cognition) as Pratt and William Labov have shown "natural narrative" to be (see Pratt, *Toward a Speech Act Theory*, chap 1). Their work suggests the crucial role metaphor plays in many concepts, including such basic ones as "time is a valuable commodity" or the spatialization metaphors rooted in cultural or physical experience (e.g., "more is up" or "life is a journey"; *Metaphors We Live By*, chaps. 3 and 4). Similarly, Lakoff and Johnson argue that metonymy also is rooted in ordinary language and culture and has conceptual force. For them, as for Jakobson, metaphor and metonymy are "different kinds of processes" (36). But Lakoff attributes to both metaphor and metonymy what Jakobson seems to arrogate to metaphor only: they both operate through selectivity. In the very process of allowing one thing to stand for another, metonymy involves selection. The choice of a part to stand for a whole, for example, may be culturally determined—in our culture the "face for the person" metonymy is part of a larger conceptual system and mode of perceiving others. Similarly, in the establishment of prototypes or cultural stereotypes one example from a larger category is taken to stand for the whole. In the United States, for example, a biologic mother who does not work outside the home provides the prototype and stereotype of motherhood (Lakoff, *Women, Fire, and Dangerous Things*, 79). Metonymy, in Lakoff and Johnson's view, then, is no more or less than metaphor, a "poetic or rhetorical device" (*Metaphors*, 37); that is, metonymy, like metaphor, is conceptual rather than simply a figure of speech ornamentally or unusually added to an utterance or discourse. Metonymy thus is intrinsically neither more nor less poetic than metaphor.[11] Lakoff and Johnson's work suggests that we profit more from

11. Clearly, Lakoff and Johnson's view does not assign to metaphor the singular role

examining the specific nature of metaphors and metonymies than from labeling texts as one or the other.[12]

In *Women, Fire, and Dangerous Things*, Lakoff posits four types of models of basic human cognition: (1) propositional models, which "specify elements, their properties, and the relationships holding among them"; (2) image-schematic models that specify images, which tend to be spatial; (3) metaphorical models, which "are mappings from a propositional or image-schematic model in one domain to a corresponding structure in another domain" (as in "life is a journey"); and (4) metonymic models, which are "models of one or more of the above types, together with a function from one element of the model to another. Thus, in a model that represents a part-whole structure, there may be a function from a part to the whole that enables the part to stand for a whole" (113–14). In addition to demonstrating how these cognitive models work, Lakoff shows in detail the way culture shapes particular instances. As he examines ideal conceptual models, his examples demonstrate the ethical implications of forms of knowledge we may take for granted—as in the obvious cases of social stereotyping (which works through metonymic models). Lakoff's work provides a basis for reconsidering arguments, such as Ian Bell's, which imply that metonymy stands over against the mystifications of communal discourse; for obviously the metonymic model of cognition underlying the social stereotype is—from the perspective of those stereotyped—a "mystification" perpetrated in communal discourse.

Lakoff and Johnson's work demonstrates the limitations of a simple binary model of tropes in natural language; Lakoff's work on cognitive models in culture can help us see the limitations of the implicit valuation of metaphor and metonomy in both structuralist and poststructuralist binary schemes. Hayden White's tetrad offers a similarly complex, nonbinary tropological model.[13] What is powerful about

---

Ricoeur arrogates to it, in part because they view tropes semantically, culturally, and even somatically.

12. It is easy to infer, too, from Lakoff and Johnson's work that larger developmental schemata that describe literary history as a succession of dominant tropes must be subject to fairly skeptical self-scrutiny; for Lakoff considers both metaphor and metonymy basic categories of human cognition.

13. White's tetrad is obviously not wholly congruent with Lakoff's scheme, though White has left open the question of the "validity of the tropological theory of poetic language itself" (*Tropics*, 74). White cites Jakobson in the notes to this essay as a scientific beginning toward the kind of linguistic work that he believes might come to support his scheme; Jakobson's essays also provide examples in the notes to White's *Metahistory*.

White's approach to history—and to an extent inimitable—is that it operates consciously as a rhetoric and that, except at its farthest reaches, it does not privilege a single tropological mode over the other three. At the farthest reaches of the theory, as Hans Kellner has pointed out in discussing both White and de Man, any such rhetoric of tropes must dissolve in irony (*Language and Historical Representation*). I return to the fundamental question of the instabilities of tropology, but as a path back toward *The Cantos*, the most fruitful basis for tropological analysis is provided—at the level of thematics and structure—by a version of White's tropology combined, at the level of stylistics and particular instances, with Lakoff's emphasis on the cultural meanings of particular metonymies and metaphors.

Competing Tropes in *The Fifth Decad of Cantos*

For an extended instance of reading *The Cantos* in terms of this approach and as a basis for further consideration of ethics and rhetoric in the poem, *The Fifth Decad of Cantos* provides an important point of departure. A tropological reading of *The Fifth Decad* does not imply that the whole of Pound's complex poem takes up a single and unwavering approach to history. Pound's poetics changed over time and, as Rabaté has shown, require a critical treatment alert to these differences (*Languages, Sexuality, and Ideology*, 25–29). Even so, *The Fifth Decad* can be seen to represent the poem's dominant concerns and methods; its examination provides a significant way of describing fundamental contradictions in Pound's poetics and also of understanding the political implications of these tensions. Both the contradictions and the conceptual and formal gaps in *The Fifth Decad* exemplify his antithetical approaches to history.

The Fifth Decad is a particularly significant locus of Pound's characteristic antitheses; for it forms a kind of pivot or hinge of *The Cantos* in a number of ways. As Jean-Michel Rabaté and others have noted, it would have fallen roughly at the center of the poem if Pound's original conception of a poem in a hundred divisions had been completed as originally planned (*Language, Sexuality, and Ideology*, 3–6, 206–7). *The Fifth Decad* also represents a midpoint of the poem's writing and—historically—of Mussolini's power. As critics from Hugh Kenner on have observed, this group of cantos contains both a reprise of earlier themes, an indictment of usury (regarded by many readers, implicitly or explicitly, as a rhetorical apex of the poem), and what, in the Chinese "lyric pastiche" of Canto 49, Kenner describes as the "emotional still point of *The Cantos*" (*Poetry*, 326). The most significant groups of new historical materials introduced in *The Fifth Decad* concern the founding of the Sienese bank, the Monte dei Paschi, the Leopoldine reforms in eighteenth-century Tuscany, and the European career of Napoleon. Pound's historical exempla are designed to give force to the poem's rhetoric and, at least thematically, to harmonize with the lyric moments celebrating natural increase.

In some respects *The Fifth Decad* can be compared with those poems of Browning's middle decades which are only understandable in the context of the political and intellectual controversies of his day. The context in Victorian religious and historical polemics is crucial for such poems as "Bishop Blougram's Apology," "Caliban upon Setebos," and "A Death in the Desert." Similarly *The Fifth Decad* and the Chinese and the Adams cantos, even more directly than the Malatesta cantos, must be read as a mirror of and intervention in history. In *The Fifth Decad* both the Monte and the strong leaders Leopold and Napoleon are given their contemporary coordinates: the Monte is paired with social credit economics and contrasted with Jewish or proto-Jewish financiers, and Leopold and Napoleon are paired with Mussolini. Both the Monte and Napoleon are significantly associated with law.

In its ideological pronouncements and implications, *The Fifth Decad* presents law—in its various senses—in a way fully congruent with what White would call a metonymic conceptualization of history; at the same time, these cantos present their exempla, particularly the related ones of Napoleon, Leopold I, and Mussolini, in a way congruent with a metaphorical conceptualization of history. The dominant theme of these cantos, law, exemplifies Pound's tendency to conceive of historical relations in terms of causal relations between parts and wholes; law acts in these cantos in terms of what Lakoff and Johnson would call "metonymic functions," connecting one element of a conceptual domain to another. Law itself can be understood as the presiding particular metonymy that overarches an implicitly metonymic figuration of the historical field.

Law in *The Fifth Decad* is not, then, law in the sense of Carl Hempel and others who define the possibility of historical knowledge in terms of covering laws (*Aspects of Scientific Explanation*, 231–34); rather it is more akin to what Hayden White describes as the content of the form (*Metahistory*, 7–31). The definitions of the licit and illicit are provided through metonymic relationships. Particular examples of good law are presented to stand for a just ordering of society and of art. Particular examples of evil or corruption are taken to stand for chaos in society

and art—and such exempla are presented in the language of stereotyping, including language referring to perversion and disease.

For all its metonymic emphasis on law, *The Fifth Decad* does not rest
comfortably in a metonymic conceptualization of history. Rather, its
exempla, which figure in a thematics of law, are presented so that
various domains, various historical, natural, or mythical situations, are
metaphorically mapped onto each other. The metaphorical mappings
of *The Fifth Decad* claim to subsume the metonymies of law, even as
the law, for Pound, is subsumed in the authority of the lawgiver. Yet
to read the poem is to test its metaphorical coherence; for these cantos,
like much of Pound's early poetry, can only be read as a record of
contradiction.

The doubling of *The Fifth Decad* cannot be understood as the alternation of lyric metaphorical poetry with prosaic metonymic poetry,
although after the exposition of Cantos 42 and 43 the group roughly
alternates cantos of densely layered quotation with those conforming,
even as pastiche, more closely to the conventions of English lyric poetry or, at least, to the conventions of invective. The matter of law
permeates the entire group of cantos in various guises.

In *The Fifth Decad* the poet presents himself explicitly as the prosecutor in a legal case and his poem as an indictment of usura. It should
be no surprise to find the notion of law and the excoriation of usury
go together; for the prohibition against usury historically posed the
problem of licit and illicit gain whenever there was need of a money
economy or of raising capital.[14] Usura functions variously as the part
and the whole in the metonymic thematics of these cantos. Usury, on
the one hand, is the root of all that is illicit, and on the other hand, it
is the symptom of the disease afflicting the body politic. It is the mon-
ster Geryon absorbing all social ills unto itself, and it is the cause of
all such ills. Rhetorically, usury functions in the various understandings of law that the cantos present, and in this way usury itself becomes a metonymy for all forms of disorder. The extremity of these
cantos is one of fear—and the evil feared is chaos, disorder. It is represented by the swamp. Behind the swamp lies the figure of the
trench, which functions metonymically to represent the destructive
chaos of World War I.

Pound made chaos, the obverse of law, an explicit matter of these
cantos and used this thematics to elaborate self-reflexively on the
poem's methods: chaos in the world must enter and be dealt with in

14. See, e.g., Le Goff, *Your Money or Your Life.*

the poem. The poem itself is transformed into a court of law. The poet prosecutor's voice declares: "This case, and with it / the first part, draws to a conclusion / of the first phase of this opus" (46.233–34) The poem posits the reader as jury, and at the same time it implies that the cases it puts are not so much subject to the jurors' judgment as to an inevitable and mechanistic working out of "scientifically" verifiable principles. Thus what is ostensibly subject to a forensic rhetoric is implicitly a case with a foregone conclusion.

The Monte dei Paschi itself is founded, as Pound presents it, to stand against illicit transactions and hoarding. Here enter both the social credit notions of circulation and the emphasis on the licit versus the illicit:

> OB PECUNIAE SCARCITATEM
>   borrowing, rigging exchanges,
>   licit consumption impeded
>   and it is getting steadily WORSE
>   others with specie abundant do not use it in business
>   (42.213)

Because it is based on natural abundance, the Monte is seen as a source of licit consumption and as a resolution to the problem of the circulation of money. It is congruent with Pound's physiocratic principles of natural abundance and also with what he presents as Leopold I's understanding of good government.

Canto 44, which introduces the Leopoldine reforms in Tuscany, begins the promulgation of law: "And thou shalt not, Firenze 1766, and thou shalt not / sequestrate for debt any farm implement" (223). Immediately a second law, that of Ferdinand II, Leopold's descendant, is also introduced—the law against the exportation of grain. Each of these edicts—the legal founding of the Monte, Leopold's and Ferdinand's laws to protect agricultural production and consumption—each stands metonymically for good law and social order. The Napoleonic Code serves the same function and is explicitly equated with the Leopoldine reforms. Napoleon's code "remains. / monumento di civile sapienza" (44.227). Pound's emphasis on statutory law, and the related figure of poet as prosecutor, results in a kind of functional calculus in which individual measures stand metonymically for social order.

Law in these cantos of course functions more broadly than in its technical and statutory sense. Economic law, natural law, and even astrological law provide instances of the regulative principles of order. Economic and natural law are linked in physiocratic terms, and as Michael André Bernstein has argued, the logic of the poem itself leads to an equation between natural and economic law and therefore probably to a greater emphasis on agrarian economics than is congruent with Pound's broader economic theories (*Tale of the Tribe*, 66). In Canto 46 for instance, the connection between natural and economic law is drawn in the statement attributed to Thomas Jefferson: "No man hath natural right to exercise profession / of lender, save him who hath it to lend" (234). A more subtle pairing of natural and economic law comes in the ways weather and navigation are allowed to stand as metonymies for law or for discriminations of order. Canto 46 begins with a rather puzzling congeries of elements which can be understood on this principle:

> And if you will say that this tale teaches . . .
>   a lesson, or that the Reverend Eliot
>   has found a more natural language . . . you who think
>   you will
>   get through hell in a hurry . . .
>   That day there was cloud over Zoagli
> And for three days snow cloud over the sea
> Banked like a line of mountains.
> Snow fell. Or rain fell stolid, a wall of lines
> So that you could see where the air stopped open
> and where the rain fell beside it
> Or the snow fell beside it. Seventeen
> Years on this case, nineteen years, ninety years
>   on this case
> An' the fuzzy bloke sez (legs no pants ever wd. fit) 'IF
> that is so, any government worth a damn can
> pay dividends?'
>   (46.231)

This passage suggests a sequence in which natural language, the poem's "lesson," the social credit proposal of a national dividend, even the weather stand as exempla of law. The paratactic linking "or" snow or rain, each well discriminated from the open air, shows even nature in discriminable order. This order of nature, where one thing stands beside another in congruence with natural law, is transmuted in Canto 48 into examples of navigation.

Whereas Canto 46 implies that one must be able to discriminate natural states in order to distinguish the licit and illicit in economics, Canto 48 presents examples suggesting that the ablest guardians of culture are those who, literally, are the best navigators: "No trustee of the Salem Museum, who had not doubled / both Good Hope and The Horn. / Sea as if risen over the headland / and there are twin seas in the cloud" (241). Again a law, the regulations of the Salem Museum, stands metonymically for a whole social order. These topoi are contained in the canto with Athelstan's rule that no man shall be "theign" "who has not made three [merchant] voyages" and with the example of the Pacific Islanders' navigations by means of a woven star chart (242). This last metonymy of law may even function as an implicit metaphor for this section of cantos itself. The threads of the poem's "lesson" and the spaces or ellipses between the threads function as navigational tools.

The star chart suggests moreover the links among economic, natural, and astrological law. Clearly, "Falling Mars" in the air (48.243) provides the crucial link between natural and historical law in the cantos. The congeries of particulars associated with Mars and with the vernal equinox—from fishing in Canto 51 (from "12 of March to the 2nd of April," 251) to the Attis / Adonis myth, to the mating habits of insects—represent both war and order. Destruction precedes rebirth, and Mars is the presiding planet. Mars stands metonymically for astrological law and metaphorically is identified with Napoleon and through him with Leopold and Mussolini. In *The Fifth Decad*, then, we find the playing out of the metonymy of law, including natural law, maritime law, and civil law. The whole congeries of laws could be seen to explore the implications of the metaphor that is never mentioned—the metaphor of the ship of state. And we see in the exempla of *The Fifth Decad* Pound's fascination with the "captains" of such ships, including among others, Napoleon.

Despite the ambivalence toward Napoleon expressed in Canto 44, where Pound paraphrases an Italian history of the Monte dei Paschi, in Canto 50, Napoleon serves as an exemplum of order and as a metaphorical equivalent of Mars:

> So that about the time of MARENGO the First Consul
> wrote: I left peace. I find war.
>   I find enemies inside yr frontier
>   Your cannon sold to yr enemies

> 1791, end of representative government
>   18th Brumale, 10th of November
> 14th. June, 1800 MARENGO
> Mars meaning, in that case, order
> That day was Right with the victor
>   mass weight against wrong
>
>   (50.247)

Here in Canto 50 the vexed history of Napoleon's relationship with Italy is simplified: the Tuscan "triumvirs'" failure to restore the Leopoldine reforms is elided, and Napoleon is presented as cleansing France of chaos and Tuscany, at least, of debt. The canto focuses, in the end, on England's and Austria's cynical suppression of the Italian republics. Mars, Napoleon, and Leopold function as makers of law and as exempla of right action. Moreover, like Adonis and like Leopold, who is sacrificed to the Holy Roman Empire in the "hell's bog" of Vienna (247), Napoleon stands as the lawgiver sacrificed to his time. Under Napoleon's sign, under Mars, these cantos are written. In a time of illicit financial dealings, peace is misplaced; so in Canto 51, Geryon or Usury stands in opposition to Mars and sings: "I am the help of the aged; / I pay men to talk peace; / Mistress of many tongues; merchant of chalcedony" (251).

The causal relations in each sphere of law—natural and political—are presented as functional relationships between particulars. Law furnishes the overarching thematic metonymy of these cantos, and its invocation purports to guarantee the poem's coherence even where, as in the case of Napoleon's relationship to Italy, the "case" is not amenable to easy resolution. Mars/Napoleon, too, provides a crucial metaphorical link that seems aimed at countering the dispersive and reductive tendencies of metonymy. Insofar as *The Fifth Decad* coheres, it would provide the means of uniting the varied domains of cause and effect, of part-part or part-whole relationships, on which these cantos turn. Metaphorical equivalence would recuperate metonymy. The overarching metonymy would stand as the linking of the threads of the cantos; metaphorical mappings from one domain of law and from one lawgiver onto another would provide us with the pattern in this web.

Yet a reading like this one cannot recuperate the dispersive difficulties of *The Fifth Decad of Cantos* any more than Pound himself felt order to be wholly recuperated by his own language. For him, the ultimately dispersive force militating against the coherence of the poem is the force that makes it impossible to get "through hell in a hurry" and that literally drives a space between these words themselves (46.231). For many readers—certainly on my reading—the very definition of law which presides over *The Fifth Decad* makes for a poem that tears itself apart at the seams. The licit and the illicit mirror each other and in effect make each other possible, and the description of the forces against law—the description of chaos—brings such an extremity into the poem that in crucial instances (especially concerning Napoleon and the Jews), the poem's thematics provide its own undoing, an unraveling both formal and political.

The forces against order in *The Fifth Decad* are explicitly described in terms of the illicit or the taboo. *The Fifth Decad* suggests that the illicit or chaotic takes the forms of disease, bestiality, sodomy, excrement, prostitution or female sexual power, and the toleration of these forces through hypocrisy or bad law. As the proper working of law in one instance can stand metonymically for proper order in a whole realm of economics or nature, so a particular symptom—an instance of sickness or perversion—can stand metonymically for the diseased state of a whole realm, whether economic, political, or natural.

Usura is of course central to images of disease in these cantos. It and other forms of the illicit are known by symptoms as a murrain (45.229), a canker (45.230), a cause of miscarriages (45.230), "foetid brick work" (46.233), tuberculosis (48.240), pus and sores (meaning probably Talleyrand and Metternich, 50.248), lice (those opposing Napoleon, 50.249), and cancer (51.250). Diseases, especially infectious and spreading diseases, are symptomatic of disorder. The illicit, disorder, chaos are thus to be feared and responded to with revulsion because they are so contagious. In this tropology, disease itself is "contra naturam" and is conceived implicitly as the effect of unnatural relations and of filth. So Napoleon declares himself to be beset by "lice."

With the exception of sacrificial animals, beasts and bestiality are also symptoms of disorder; moreover, they are linked implicitly with female power. Circe becomes the presiding demon of these cantos; for she is seen to provoke, even to celebrate, bestiality. Though the oxen used in sacrificial processions are emblematic of order, the case is different with dogs, camels, and Circean swine. In Canto 46, for example, the American Civil War and World War I are presented as slaughter brought on by bank debt and greed, and Pound reminisces in the same section about seeing Max Beerbohm's drawings:

one of Balfour and a camel, an'
one w'ich fer oBviOus reasons haz
never been published, ole Johnny Bull with a 'ankerchief
It has never been published. .

(46.232)

Through Balfour and the beast (and what, one wonders, would Pound imply Balfour is doing with the camel?), he implies a connection among war, a kind of bestiality or at least unnatural relations, and Balfour's support for a Jewish state in Palestine. The whole modern Middle East, by implication, is presented as a sinkhole, a place of beasts and degenerate religion. The orientalist bent here, the implied thesis that ancient rites have fallen into decay, is presented through Pound's parodic introduction of "Abdul Baha / Third vice-gerent of the First Abdul or whatever Baha . . . in a garden at Uberton, Gubberton," who is unable to drink camel's milk (232). Any religion—Jewish, Muslim, Bahai—that goes beyond the camel driver's inclination to dance is presented as silly, if not suspect.

The English themselves fare no better in Pound's judgment and, through Balfour, are implicated in political bestiality. In the second Beerbohm drawing, John Bull does something unpublishable with his handkerchief, while in the next canto, drugged with uncontrolled desire by Circe's power, the "bull runs blind on the sword" (47.237). The English, and more generally the French and American, lack of good government and economics is connected in the figure of Circe with total disruption of the cosmic order. Circe's power to turn men into beasts is of a piece with usura and with disruption in the heavens. For, we are told, "The stars are not in her counting / To her they are but wandering holes" (47.237).

While beasts stand metonymically here for general disorder, Pound also establishes a complex analogy creating equivalences between Odysseus and himself, Circe/Scilla and the dogs of modern Europe. In Canto 45, usury "gnaweth the thread in the loom" (230); in Canto 47, "Scilla's dogs snarl at the cliff's base, / The white teeth gnaw in under the crag" (236). Against this destruction stand the true law of economics, the true base of credit, and the rites for Adonis (metonymically representing all rites that guarantee proper relations with nature). Scilla's dogs return parodically in Canto 48 when Pound includes a letter from a royal agent probably addressed to the queen (Victoria = Circe = Scilla). The matter under discussion is Dhu Achil,

Black Achilles, and his cairn puppy of somewhat dubious breeding. The male dog, significantly, can boast a legitimate pedigree but the puppy's "dam is unregistered" (241). Thus the puppy is connected by implication both to the prostitute "removed . . . on charge of thievery" from the register of officially sanctioned prostitutes in Siena (Canto 43.220) and to the "whores for Eleusis" in Canto 45 (230). The puppy, though comic, is a diminution of his heroic predecessor, a metonymy for an England fallen into the bestial state of usury and corrupt politics. In the figurative economy of the cantos, the puppy is worthy of his owner, if she is indeed Victoria. By this curious twist, the government of England is connected to illicit female sexuality. As in the case of "bitch" in vulgar English usage, so in Chinese, if Pound is following this train of thought, dogs, and especially black dogs, are connected to illicit sexuality; the words for black dog (*hei-kou*) colloquially stand for female genitals. Whether or not the cairn puppy and his mother— Circe or Victoria—owe something to this linguistic and cultural coincidence, the connections among the illicit, the bestial, and female sexual power are clear. In this context it is no coincidence that Pound's celebration of natural order in Canto 47 ends with both the invocation of Adonis and the "molü" of Hermes that "hath the gift of healing, / that hath the power over wild beasts" (239).[15]

By the time of Canto 50, these strands of invective have come together, and dogs, whores, and filth create the violent name-calling that characterizes Pound's catalog of the illicit. After the fall of Napoleon, Pound writes:

> England and Austria were for despots with commerce
> considered
> > put back the Pope but
> reset no republics: Venice, Genova, Lucca
> and split up Poland in their soul was usura
> and in their hand bloody oppression
> and that son of a dog, Rospigliosi,
> came into Tuscany to make serfs of old Tuscans.
> S . . t on the throne of England, s . . t on the Austrian sofa
> In their soul was usura and in their minds darkness
> and blankness, greased fat were four Georges

15. Terrell, *Companion*, notes this reference as an allusion to the power of Dionysus-Adonis-Tammuz; certainly this gloss is correct. At the same time, moreover, Adonis is identified in the canto with Odysseus; each of them has the gift of healing and power over bestiality, Odysseus by "molü" and Adonis in his power as a dying and rising god.

> Pus was in Spain, Wellington was a jew's pimp
> and lacked mind to know what he effected.
>
> (50.248)

Coming together here in the grossest way are all the elements of the illicit and disorder: dogs, beasts (possibly swine in the grease of the four Georges), infection, prostitution, and excrement. The characterization of Wellington through association with an anti-Semitic slur has been prepared earlier in the canto. Wellington is derided equally for financial naïveté and, implicitly, for his role in bringing down Napoleon. Napoleon in turn is identified with Leopold of Tuscany, who, like Napoleon, was sucked into a very swamp of disorder, in Leopold's case, the Holy Roman Empire:

> and then they sent him off to be Emperor
> in hell's bog, in the slough of Vienna, in
>   the midden of Europe in the black hole of all
> mental vileness, in the privvy that stank Franz Josef,
> in Metternich's merdery in the absolute rottenness,
> among embastardized cross-breeds
>
> (50.247)

The black hole—Circe's hole—breeds illicit mixtures and filth. The bastard, the "son of a dog" (female), like the Jewish financier and Circe herself, are mapped onto one another metaphorically. Each can stand metonymically for disorder, for chaos, and for the forces opposing law.

If we reassess *The Fifth Decad of Cantos* through a tropological rhetoric or through an examination of particular tropes and their cultural work, we can see writ large the polarizations implicit in Pound's early appropriation of Browning's poetry and of nineteenth-century tradition. *The Fifth Decad* clearly shows the strains of achieving epic coherence. I have suggested that any extended and complex instance of language is likely to involve a variety of figurative usages, particularly because figurative language is essential to many basic concepts. At the same time, I have agreed that on the scale of whole texts, a particular tropological strategy or strategies may be fundamental. If we pursue the second notion first, taking the tack of a tropological rhetoric, *The Fifth Decad* presents us with a significant question: Can we identify a dominant trope in *The Fifth Decad of Cantos*?

I believe not. The question, moreover, makes a troubling assumption about texts and, more generally, about a tropological rhetoric. This assumption is explicit in the introduction to White's *Metahistory* (though White's practice when it comes to texts is considerably more complex than this portion of his introduction would necessarily suggest). White significantly complicates Jakobson's binary scheme both by doubling the number of tropes and by arguing for a dialectical tension between what he calls "tropological modes" of historical conceptualization and modes of emplotment, argument, and ideological implication. But White takes the tropology of historical conceptualization as exempt from dialectic, as basic in a fundamental, structural way. According to him, "In every case, dialectical tension evolves within the context of a coherent vision or presiding image of the form of the whole historical field. This gives to the individual thinker's conception of that field the aspect of a self-consistent totality. And this coherence and consistency give to his work its distinctive stylistic attributes. The problem here is to determine the grounds of coherence and consistency" (*Metahistory*, 30).[16] White's assumption of coherence does hold for the majority of nineteenth-century historians he treats; it can ground a persuasive reading of a poet like Browning, for instance. One can see Browning as an ironist, with the tensions within his work ascribable to his nonironic treatment of Christian incarnation.

The Fifth Decad, however, presents a much more fundamental challenge to a positing of coherence; for it pushes the qualities White identifies as "dialectical" beyond recuperation in a single synthesis. It is precisely the presence of alternative modes of historical conceptualization and rhetorical figuration that complicates these cantos. This doubling, or double troping, the combination of metaphorical and metonymic understandings of history, makes it quite difficult for the

16. In *Tropics of Discourse*, however, White insists more strongly on the dialectical nature of historical tropes and argues that histories that are the scenes of harmonious resolution are, after all, doctrinaire histories. He makes this point in speaking of history and the novel, but it applies equally well to *The Cantos*: "The peculiar dialectic of historical discourse—and of other forms of discursive prose as well, perhaps even the novel—comes from the effort of the author to mediate between alternative modes of emplotment and explanation, which means, finally, *mediating between alternative modes of language use* or *tropological* strategies for originally describing a given field of phenomena and constituting it as a possible object of representation. It is this sensitivity to alternative linguistic protocols, cast in the modes of metaphor, metonymy, synecdoche, and irony, that distinguishes the great historians and philosophers of history from their less interesting counterparts among the technicians of these two crafts" (129).

reader to produce a single coherent picture of *The Fifth Decad* and of *The Cantos* generally. Indeed, the Odysseus/poet of *The Fifth Decad* is a man of many turnings, "polytropos" with a vengeance.

This contradiction in Pound's conceptualization of history should not be taken to figure a gap between poetic and prosaic language, or the distance in reading experience between the more lyric and the more heavily documented passages of *The Cantos*. Canto 51, for example, provides an interesting instance of this tension or gap in historical conceptualization even while its coherence seems guaranteed by a familiar lyric voice. On the one hand, in Canto 51 as in *The Fifth Decad* generally, the overarching metonymy of law guarantees a coherent construction of the historical field; the notions of economic and of natural law intersect to create a totalizing conception of the operation of history. The functions from one element of history to another are glossed as part-whole or part-part relationships where the coherent understanding of those relationships is guaranteed by an understanding of causation. Thus, the poet declares, with usura "Azure is caught with cancer," "wool does not come into market / the peasant does not eat his own grain" (51.250). Such multiplying chains of relationships, however, threaten to exceed the readers' powers of association and the poet's powers of creating a totalizing vision, particularly when Pound's vision of order raises the specters of disorder.

On the other hand, history in Canto 51 is conceived equally, and differently, as a series of exempla. If, as Pound puts it elsewhere, history is a school book for princes (or readers), in Canto 51 the school book is given a particularly monitory shape. This school book, as in Chinese histories, works not by adducing some totalizing metonymy of law but by presenting positive and negative exempla.[17] So in Canto 51 a variety of elements, presented for themselves, are either in their importance or in the density of their detail beyond any simple recuperation in a totalizing metonymic scheme. These elements include the paraphrased passages of Neoplatonic poetry, Napoleon's declaration about mud, the description of fly fishing, the quotation from Rudolph Hess, the evocation of the League of Cambrai, and the Chinese characters that conclude the canto (*cheng ming*). They are hard to

17. The Renaissance tradition of teaching through exempla—and the place of exempla in Renaissance rhetoric—also of course is behind this historical strategy. Though his main focus is not on the nature of exemplarity itself, Dasenbrock makes this point about the middle sections of *The Cantos* in his essay on Pound and Machiavelli; see *Imitating the Italians*, chap. 8.

integrate to any particular metonymic set of cause and effect, action and agent, part and whole, except indirectly in the cases of fly fishing and mud, where the two elements are assimilable to cause-and-effect relationships involving natural increase and order. Even here, the loving detail of fly-fishing technique consumes almost a third of the canto, thus overpowering as an exemplum whatever connection it has to the metonymy of law. More obviously, Napoleon and Hess (or Hess's unidentified voice) appear as exempla of order or the attempt at order defeated.

All these details function in a set of metaphorical equivalences which is as basic to Canto 51 as any metonymic relation of law. Moreover, Pound's invocation of Neoplatonic doctrine provides the ideological justification for metaphorical conceptualization. His Neoplatonic doctrine, like his emphasis on leaders as exemplars, is characteristic of what White would call "metaphorical" and "formist" historical conceptualization. Indeed, White's characterization of this understanding of history describes with remarkable precision both Pound's Neoplatonic emphasis on the thing itself and his neo-Confucian invocation of *cheng ming*, calling things by their right names:

> The Formist theory of truth aims at the identification of the unique characteristics of objects inhabiting the historical field. Accordingly, the Formist considers an explanation to be complete when a given set of objects has been properly identified, its class, generic, and specific attributes assigned and labels attesting to its particularity attached to it. The objects alluded to may be either individualities or collectivities, particulars or universals, concrete entities or abstractions. As thus envisaged, the task of historical explanation is to dispel the apprehension of those similarities that appear to be shared by all objects in the field. When the historian has established the uniqueness of the particular objects in the field or the variety of the types of phenomena which the field manifests, he has provided a Formist explanation of the field as such. (*Metahistory*, 13–14)

In the context of White's discussion of metaphorical or formist history, we can see that in Canto 51 neither the specifications of fly-fishing nor the invocation of Albertus Magnus which follows is out of place.

The exempla in Canto 51 are characterized by the idiography of forms, and implicit in them is the notion that the uniqueness of each thing in itself is sufficient explanation of its connections to other things or actions. As Pound puts it in the language of Neoplatonism:

That hath the light of the doer, as it were
a form cleaving to it.
Deo similis quodam modo
hic intellectus adeptus

(51.251)

Each exemplum is godlike in a way, in its particular way.

The move from the godlike exemplum to the authoritative lawgiver is not far to seek. Rectifying the terminology is the obligation of the scholar, the reader, the citizen, but it is the special prerogative and responsibility of princes and poets. Ideologically, *The Fifth Decad of Cantos* asserts that between rectifying terminology or discriminating the forms of things and giving good law, there can be no essential incompatibility. Yet neither formally nor thematically can Pound close the gap between metaphorical and metonymic understandings of history. Nor do his metonymies of law seamlessly cohere. There is not *a* single form clinging to this and other cantos, but forms. Metonymy and metaphor unravel each other.

The tropological polarization of *The Cantos* poses particular problems for a modern and redefined practice of epic, and as I explore in detail in the next chapter, it embodies the polarization of Pound's political vision. Both for the resisting reader (and almost all of Pound's readers have sooner or later resisted) and within the poem's production, the sources of coherence are continually undone by the double troping of history. For a poem to do the work of epic, it must, as it functions intertextually in the epic tradition, present a coherent conceptualization of a historical or legendary moment. And here *The Fifth Decad of Cantos* is symptomatic of the way epic coherence breaks apart, the way the very conceptualization underlying the historical field in its polarity belies the poem's ideological claims to wholeness.

Equally important, for a poem to do the cultural work of an epic it must elicit the reader's assent to many of its important claims. Here, particular metaphors and metonymies of *The Fifth Decad* are responsible for readers' resistances to the poem's historical claims. Whether one is disturbed by the implied comparisons among Leopold, Napoleon, and Mussolini, or by the poem's exploitation of stereotypes of Jews and women to form the congeries of the illicit, the moments that may provoke resistance are multiple. For, as I argue in my concluding chapters, the unreadability of *The Cantos* is by no means simply a matter of formal incoherence or obscurity, nor even of tropological polarization; it is also a matter of the ideological work the poem does.

The Ironies of Tropology

Before we come, as any discussion at least implicitly does, to the political consideration of *The Cantos*, it is useful to return to the question of the politics of a rhetorical tropology. I have defended the usefulness of tropology in critically reading *The Cantos* and at the same time shown that binary tropological schemes tend to be radically limited. As we have seen, work in speech act theory and in cognitive semantics suggests that Jakobson's initial binary opposition between metaphor and metonymy, the poetic and the prosaic is problematic. Moreover, the implicit valuation of metonymy over metaphor has in recent years been directly reflected in the course of criticism of *The Cantos*, with metonymy replacing metaphor as an implicit pole of positive value. In opposition to this view, I have argued for both a rereading of Pound's metonymies in light of their ideological implications and for a nonbinary tropological scheme that would provide a way of naming the complexities and conflicts within Pound's understanding of history. I have contended that Pound rejects the ironies and the historicized narrators of Browning's long poems yet retains the existential historicist's dedication to idiographic detail; he looks both for metaphorical equivalences of exempla and for a totalizing scheme of metonymic relations in order to connect his details. Neither search is more fundamental than the other; neither, more valuable. The metonymy of law, on this reading, is not a guarantee of the poem's value but a key to the area in which the poem is most deeply problematic. A tropological reading of the kind I have suggested indicates the depths of the conflicting conceptualizations of history that *The Cantos* engage.

Although my discussion does offer a new paradigm for understanding the experience of reading *The Cantos*, it is, like all tropologies, subject to two criticisms. First, it is selective; and second, it is subject to its own unraveling into the mode of irony.

The possibility of ironically unraveling any reading of *The Cantos* is especially acute because the doubled conceptualization of the poem can provide a limit text for any tropology. *The Cantos* test the limits of tropological reading because no metahistory, à la Hayden White, can more than provisionally encompass the poem's contradictions or subsume them in some basic notion of coherence, even though both tropology itself and the poem's epic ambitions continually invite arguments for coherence. Even if the reader grants that *The Cantos* or *The Fifth Decad* may be understood in terms of a fundamental conflict between metaphorical and metonymic views of history, the obvious question remains as to what metatropical point of view enables such a reading. The tropologist must always declare herself or deliberately avoid such a declaration. And tropology itself, wherever it starts, tends to devolve toward irony. Hans Kellner has sympathetically but accurately described White's rhetorical tropology as "safe," his readings as "secure in their extraction of meaning"; he characterizes this tropology as a "voluntarist rhetoric restraining a deconstructive antilogic" (*Language and Historical Representation*, 224). Surely my own reading of Pound, even in my revision of White's tropology, is safe and canny, although the seams with which it is stitched together show in obvious ways. In any pronouncement about dominant tropes, or tropological conflict, there lurks not too covertly the ironist's point of view.

No tropology, no trope, is ultimately safe, ultimately canny. Rather, as Kellner has observed, tropes tend to inflation and are caught in the movement of their own logic as any tropological criticism proceeds. As Kellner asserts in a conclusion that is worth quoting at length,

> The tropology, then, *is* a narrative theory; the trope cannot restrain itself from self-explanation. From the small transference of trope itself (a metaphoric process) to the full semantic figurology of discourse that judges and measures each turn of meaning, the tropological movement is the "movement of ironic consciousness." The ironic narrative movement of consciousness is described by Paul de Man: "The inherent tendency to gain momentum and not to stop until it has run its full course; from the small and apparently innocuous exposure of a small self-deception it soon reaches the dimensions of the absolute" ["Rhetoric of Temporality," *Blindness and Insight*, 197]. To allegorize irony like this is to underscore the status of irony as the trope of tropology, but it also points to the allegorical nature of any inflation of the tropes into figures of thought, comprehension, or discourse. Whether it is an allegory of the conventions of language, or of the deep structures of reason, the inflatable trope provides a narrative diagnostic that is distinctly alchemical. (251)

Kellner's summary points to the way in which my argument, like other tropologies, can be shown to have its own tropological agenda; it is conducted from a stable point of view the stability of which is either provisional or illusory.

Though de Man, unlike Kellner, is reasoning from a tropology that is distinctly Jakobsonian, his allegory of reading is the clearest and most compelling demonstration of the antilogic of tropology. Indeed de Man's reading of Proust is the shadowy double of my own reading of Pound; for de Man argues for a conflict between metaphor and metonymy in which metaphorical "seduction" is always betrayed. Thus Proust's metaphor is always becoming allegory (and irony) by way of its metonymic undoing (*Allegories of Reading*, 72).

Even if one posits an understanding of metaphor and metonymy constructed on the basis of communication (cognitive semantics and rhetoric) rather than miscommunication (aphasia and deconstructive aporia), the tendency of tropology is indeed this move toward ironic indeterminancy. It is certainly true that *The Cantos* propose allegories of their own reading, even as de Man maintains that Proust's novel does, and recent discussions of Pound's poem have postulated this moment of allegorical aporia as the moment when metonomy triumphs in its truth.[18] In the different but related formulation of Jean-Michel Rabaté, the "truth of the poem thus appears not just in the adequation with an exterior world, of whose reality no one, not even Berkeley, has ever doubted, but in the process by which someone or something becomes present, for a while, on the background of a structure made up of absence, before the long loop of reference curves back on itself, to complete itself on the blankness of the page" (*Language, Sexuality, and Ideology*, 173). It is possible to read *The Cantos* and, moreover, to read readings of *The Cantos* in this aporia at the end of tropology, as the moment where presence and absence replace each other like the water droplets of the Proustian fountain that Paul de Man invokes (*Allegories of Reading*, 71–72).

Yet there is in the trajectory of tropology, in the speed of its movement which de Man describes, the moment that provokes the equal and opposite reaction. That moment comes when one confronts clearly the issue of power itself. In de Man's reading of Proust we find this moment when de Man takes allegorically the figure of Françoise the cook torturing the suffering serving maid. If this is the figure of the text's status as an allegory of reading, it is equally a figure for the moral ambiguity of de Man's tropology. When the text is understood as self-allegorizing, de Man says, "it will always lead to the confrontation of incompatible meanings between which it is necessary but impossible to decide in terms of truth and error" (*Allegories of Reading*, 76). We can say nothing of the maid's suffering, nothing at

18. See esp. Schneidau, "Wisdom Past Metaphor," and, to some extent, Smith and Durant, "Pound's Metonymy."

any rate that escapes allegory. De Man's reading invokes but does not enact the necessity of ethical decision; tropology remains in ironic aporia.

Why this should be so lies, if we follow Terry Eagleton's analysis, in de Man's revulsion against his own earlier complicity with fascism. Contrasting de Man with Heidegger, Eagleton argues that for de Man, the subject itself is made in a "dubious rhetoric" and that "any hint of metaphorical organicism, in self, history, or sign, is undermined by the blind, aleatory working of a mechanistic metonymy" (*Ideology of the Aesthetic*, 311). Eagleton's argument, whatever its merits with respect to de Man's personal history, usefully brings the discussion of tropes and history back to the point where, implicitly, it began.

If one reads Pound tropologically, one must come sooner or later to identify the reading's own trajectory with the tendency of any tropology toward irony; but to understand this movement in terms of a politics of tropology should, with any luck, present the occasion for a dialectical resistance, a moment of deflating the inflatable trope. In reading *The Cantos* this moment arrives at two points: first when one attends to the ideological work of particular metaphors and metonymies and, second, when one acknowledges the necessity of making a meaningful history so as to imagine an arguably better or at least meaningful future. The necessity of envisioning a future—fraught with danger as it is—returns us directly to the question of power and politics in *The Cantos*.

Chapter 5

The Modernist Sage: Poetry, Politics, and Prophecy

What a Dark-Lantern is history, or worse, even, a Lantern of dark-ness; absolutely tenebrific, instead of illuminative!
—Thomas Carlyle to John Ruskin, 30 July 1874

Any study of Pound has, it seems, an inevitable trajectory. The reader is led sooner or later to a direct confrontation with politics. This is a burden of *The Cantos* which it is impossible, even were it desirable, to escape. Yet what is to be gained after all? Can such a confrontation go beyond a ritual condemnation or defense? Only, I think, when we take seriously the ways politics are implicated both in the very forms of poetry and in the languages of criticism. If *The Cantos* proceed at once metaphorically and metonymically, if this tension is predicated on a more than usual sense of chaos united to a more than usual compulsion for order, and if the poem in clinging to its epic claims entails an explicit politics even when it is most personal, any tropology that accounts for its contradictions must have its own implicit politics. Tropological readings of Pound have often valued metonymy over metaphor and have read all tropes through irony. Yet as Paul de Man's reading of Proust—ironically—suggests, the trajectory of even an ironic tropology leads to questions of power.

In the Proustian episode de Man cites in his allegory of tropes, Françoise the cook tortures a suffering serving maid. I suggest that we take up the position of the serving maid not against Proust but against de Man's deconstruction of truth and error, virtue and vice. When we do so, we are forced back from text to history in the same way that *The Cantos* deliberately force us back from their own furious intertextuality to what we know of the world. As Jerome McGann says of *The Cantos*, they are themselves a "continuous descent into hell, an unending consultation with sources of truth" (*Towards a Literature of Knowledge*, 110). The poem "forces us to the brink of an ultimate spiritual catastrophe that corresponds exactly to what we associate with Pound" (112). If we follow this way of reading, taking the position of Proust's serving maid as the victim of suffering, it becomes clear that virtue and truth, error and vice are not—despite de Man's claim—fully equatable in any meaningful human sense. Though the undecidability of truth and error is endemic in human textuality and epistemology, the undecidability of virtue and vice is a luxury available only to gods. *The Pisan Cantos* raise this problem distinctly—precisely in terms of discourse or naming, error and action.

The Cantos—even *The Pisan Cantos*—because their nature as a political/social document is so insistent, enact a tropological doubling in ways that make the allegory of reading an insufficient response. They build a utopian vision that implicitly claims to be beyond language and yet is so grounded in a dualistic invocation of nature and the female that it demands its own antithetical reading. This reading is the project of the next chapter; here I examine how the metaphors and metonymies I have analyzed in *The Fifth Decad of Cantos* are transformed in *The Pisan Cantos*. The emphasis on law, lawgivers, and cleanser/avengers is to a significant extent replaced by an emphasis on love, healing, and prophets as victims. These transformations, nevertheless, are subject to the poem's larger ambivalences and contradictions. Despite their elegiac tone, *The Pisan Cantos* never give up their epic ambitions or their utopian vision.

Critical Method and the Politics of Tropes

At first glance it would appear that the most explicitly poststructuralist readings of Pound would provide a way of reading his utopian visions against the grain, an approach that escapes the closed circuit of Pound's own visionary language. As I have already indicated, however, the insistently metonymic reading of *The Cantos* has its own limitations. A much more useful approach is Jean-Michel Rabaté's excellent and complex reading of Pound. Rabaté compellingly traces the links among money, text, and sexuality in *The Cantos*; he demonstrates how the Lacanian understanding of the subject and desire (not to mention the Freudian analysis of anality) can reveal the poem's intricate connections. Rabaté has characterized *The Cantos* as a great poem of division, even as he recognizes and rejects the poem's political claims. In *The Cantos*, he argues, division is constitutive of both Pound's "language and his politics, and it appears idle now to minimise the potential rifts and inconsistencies in both; in this creative fissiparity, his writings tend to disrupt the monologist features of our dominant metaphysical discourse while attempting to regain the lost paradise of an utterance that would be able to tell the full truth." Here, moreover, Pound mirrors "our division, a duplication of our duplication, a division of our division, symptomatically living through the tragedy of writing as duplication and division and founding his poetics on it." Out of this division comes the attempt at a private paratactic language and the speech of "a whole people" which will "celebrate" its "vanishing gods" (*Language, Sexuality, and Ideology*, 280). I share Rabaté's conviction that the divisions in Pound's text mirror the divisions of his readers and their society. Yet, again ironically, the very strength of Rabaté's reading of the poem's divisions is its weakness as a political reading; for it suggests too readily that "fissiparity," "division" is the truth of the human condition and that any evocation of "fissiparity" is ultimately a story of truth.

Rabaté's Lacanian analytic framework makes clear the circulation of desire in *The Cantos* and the connection between it and the circulation of money, the glorification of phallic sexuality, and the reliance on writing to create order: a "signature which has to be erected again and again, but in a sacred space: as a temple" (234). Yet that framework, like Lacan's work on feminine sexuality, leaves little outside, little space for an exterior critique. To be caught in this circulation of desire, of money, to attempt to fill the "gaps" with phallic sexuality, a temple, a temple's altar, or with the sign itself appears to Rabaté as "tragic." He thus reads *The Pisan Cantos* as tragic elegy and the larger movement of the poem under the genre of tragedy.

From the point of view provided either by Jerome McGann's ethical reading or by the various feminist responses to Lacan, the tragic reading of the poem's politics appears not to go far enough in its critique. The Lacanian construction of *The Cantos*, like the de Manian irony of all tropology, leaves no space for the suffering servant to speak. It allows us to be taken at once into sympathy for the beauty of Pound's utopian "temple," for the positive female/nature principle, and for the gods *The Cantos* propose. It urges our taking up the position of the prophet. We are then surrounded by the terms of the Lacanian reading itself: in Pound's mythology, as in Lacan's analytic system, the Other is written onto the female by necessity and in a system that rejects history even as it espouses the thoroughly, linguistically or symbolically, constructed order of law and culture. The analyst can no more escape this necessity than the poet. Curiously like Pound in this respect, Lacan espouses "love" and presents himself as the prophet/philosopher excommunicated from the fold. But "love" and "prophecy" are precisely the terms within Pound's own system which must be analyzed for us to locate both the power and the dangers of his way of making poems.[1]

To critique rather than to acquiesce in Pound's prophetic language requires a reading that analyzes both the poem's conflicting tropes and their historical meanings. We must locate the historical meanings of Pound's definitions of love and utopia and historicize the connections among "the altar," prophecy, and poetry. This is to take tropes— in the context of the previous chapter—as involving both cultural constructs and ordinary language, as embedded like all figuration in history.

McGann's explicitly moral language allows us to question love and tragedy. It calls attention to the inadequacy of tragic elegy as either an ethical or a generic paradigm for reading *The Cantos*, and it emphasizes that we must read the poem against as well as with what Pound loved. As McGann tellingly asks, "Is it a comfort or a catastrophe that what this poem loves, what Pound loves, shall 'not be reft' away—in a word, that its fascism will stay with it for ever, as an essential part of its 'true heritage'? Surely we must see how this is a

---

1. Catherine Clément describes this construction of himself as prophet on the part of Lacan; his prophetic role has an interesting resemblance both to Victorian secular prophets like Ruskin and to Pound's own career. See *Lives and Legends of Jacques Lacan*, esp. pp. 94–111. For the critique, both sympathetic and unsympathetic, of the place of women in Lacan's analytic system see especially Rose, Introduction, and Irigaray, "Cosi Fan Tutti," in *This Sex Which Is Not One*. Jacqueline Rose offers an interesting discussion of Lacan and love. Unlike Pound, Lacan contends that "there is no sexual relation," but he puts "love" in a position analoguous to the one it holds in Pound's system. This double role of the prophet and lover makes still more important the question of where or whether the "other" speaks or has desire. Because Lacan's system has precisely the same problem as Pound's it does not provide a completely adequate standpoint for an ethical criticism of Pound that can go beyond a ritual repudiation coupled with the elevation of the poet to the position of tragic hero/prophet; nor does it provide a basis for questioning the historical or cultural meanings of "love" in Pound's work.

catastrophe, and we do Pound's work a profound disservice if we do not also call it that holocaust in which, like Paolo and Francesca, his work will turn for ever" (*Toward a Literature of Knowledge*, 116).

Following McGann, I wish to suggest the contours of reading *The Cantos*, particularly *The Pisan Cantos*, under the sign of catastrophe. I provide an explicitly political reading of tropes in *The Cantos* by focusing on the transmutation of those in the earlier cantos in the Pisan sequence. This examination suggests that *The Cantos* form a limit text for tropology both formally and ethically and that *The Pisan Cantos* should be read neither as an exception in the poem nor as tragic anagnorisis. Formally, we can regard *The Pisan Cantos* as caught between epic and elegy, the outcome of Pound's radical individualism and radical desire for order when it meets with the chaos of modern history. *The Cantos*, particularly the visionary sections that seem most to escape Pound's politics, are deeply implicated in those same politics.

Pound rejects the ironic equipoise of existential historicism which made epic impossible, if still attractive, for Robert Browning, his predecessor in experimentation with historical inclusiveness and with "unpoetic" language. Instead, like Browning's predecessor Thomas Carlyle, he abandons his early existential historicism (which was always compromised even in his early practice by utopian and pedagogic ambitions) for the celebration of possible utopia which was always underwritten by radical individualism and authoritarianism. Like Carlyle, Pound in *The Pisan Cantos* finds himself a prophet plagued by personal failure who sees himself, even more cruelly, failed by history. If, as Carlyle claimed, history is the "true Epic Poem," *The Cantos* is surely the poem that puts such a contention to the test (Carlyle, "On History Again," *Works*, 28:176). In *The Pisan Cantos* the poem's project is at great risk and can only be reclaimed in the face of history's failures by autobiography and by elegy.

The Transformation of Tropes in *The Pisan Cantos*

The Pisan Cantos reiterate and extend the tropological configuration established earlier in the poem in ways that point to the naïveté of reading this section as political or poetic recantation of the poem's central concerns. Indeed *The Pisan Cantos* offer striking parallels to and extensions of the tropological patterns I identified in *The Fifth Decad of Cantos*. The metonymy of law and the metaphorical mappings from one domain onto another continue as in *The Fifth Decad*. In *The Pisan Cantos*, however, law and the lawgiver are transmuted from the cleanser/avenger to the prophet/victim and from the sign of Mars to the sign of Venus.

This shift in the poem's tropological choices is neither a shift in poetic method nor a recantation. Canto 74 puts it bluntly: "I surrender neither the empire nor the temples / plural / nor the constitution nor yet the city of Dioce" (74.448). Or, " 'Se casco' said Bianca Capello / 'non casco in ginnocchion" (If I fall, I will not fall on my knees, 74.441). Driven by history itself to a possible crisis in his own historical convictions, Pound surrenders nothing except that which must be given up—hope in the fascist order as the great modern exemplum of law.

Thus Pound is driven back on the law he had metaphorically associated with fascist order, the natural law; at the same time, he is driven to identify, oddly and obliquely with victims (women and slaves) and overtly and in self-justification with prophets (who are also victims). The social order that was metonymically connected through the cause-and-effect relationships of economic or political law in *The Fifth Decad of Cantos* is so fragmented as to be connected only through natural law or through the poet's memory. Thus the poet must ask what can be salvaged "from the wreckage of Europe" (76.472); memory, the elegiac movement, is left to reknit the fragments. In *The Fifth Decad* only the forces for evil and disorder had seemed radically fragmented and divided—a chaos. Now even the good is fragmented; the process of knowing or recalling the good is fragmented: "Le Paradis n'est pas artificiel / but spezzato apparently / it exists only in fragments" (74.452).[2]

With the collapse of the guarantee of the good, with the failure of fascist law and order even before, in Pound's view, it achieved the greatest possible economic success, the poet recurs to images of fragmentation and to possibilities of reknitting the world and art that characterized the early poetry and the early cantos. He recalls his own past and recapitulates, selectively, the history of the English lyric.

The poet claims "Arachne mi porta fortuna" (74.460; 76.475). The reappearance of the web and even of the ragpicker is reminiscent of Pound's early poetry, and indeed some of the most moving moments of *The Pisan Cantos* are those that recall his years in London and Paris. The description of Yeats, for example, is a powerful evocation of what is left of meaning for the poet and is wonderfully amusing and con-

---

2. Of course Pound claims in Canto 117 that the vision of paradise coheres even if his "notes do not cohere." As I argue in my concluding chapter, he would envision a cosmos coming out of chaos, even if it is fit "to see," not to "walk on." He does claim wholeness for vision; for walking on, ultimately, he can posit only fragments.

trolled. The chain of memory leads the poet further to the junk shop of Théophile Gautier's daughter, to the webs spun from such rags and junk, to the birds on the wires whose alighting and flitting make a visual equivalent of music. This texture of memory, and particularly the tropes that underwrite it—the birds on the wire, the ragpicker, the junkshop, the web—would seem to be a reinvention of the equipoise of existential historicism.

Yet the poet cannot be the ragpicker or the flâneur; there is little delight in disorder and much disaster. The fragments of English verse are indeed now shelved against ruin. In the triumph of bad government, "fog rose from the marshland"; those who attempt better order find "their works like cobwebs when the spider is gone" (80.515). Outside the stockade "there is chaos and nothingness." Pound quotes Dante in Canto 80 to imply that he too has descended through the malignant air.

The poem claims the task not of reweaving culture but of sorting the world out against the threat of yet further ruin. The poet's goals are, most importantly,

> to take the sheep out to pasture to bring
> your g.r. to the nutriment
> gentle reader   to the gist of the discourse
>   to sort out the animals
>
> (80.513–14)

Disorder constantly threatens to overwhelm, and indeed historically has overwhelmed, the order of memory and of nature.

The Pisan Cantos then, even with their return to Pound's personal literary past, undertake the process of sorting out the animals—human and natural. Like *The Fifth Decad of Cantos*, the Pisan group present humans, gods, and animals in a tropological mapping that represents order and disorder.

In *The Fifth Decad*, order is represented by the metonymy of law. Lawgivers, including most notably Napoleon and Mussolini, are identified metaphorically with each other and create order under the influence of Mars, in a kind of holy or at least justifiable war. Against order is opposed the disintegrative force of usury, of disease, of dogs, of Circe's swine. In *The Pisan Cantos* these patterns recur, but in the face of the failure of the Axis in the war and through the force of the poem's internal trajectory, the negative tropologies of *The Fifth Decad* come to be matched by their positive poles in *The Pisan Cantos*. The patterns of disease, bestiality, and war are countered, though not erased, by patterns involving healing, "natural coitus," and sympathy with victims. The metonymy of law is replaced, now that the lawgiver is gone, by the metonymy of memory; and yet the metaphorical mapping from one domain onto another, from one figure onto another that would counter the dispersion of metonymy, is still designed to maintain distinctions, to maintain what Pound surely saw as an ethical hierarchy.

The most important transmutation in the dominant tropes between *The Fifth Decad* and *The Pisan Cantos* is that of its astrological influence from the power of Mars to the power of Venus and the moon. The movement from the just war to the conclusion that "in 'The Spring and Autumn' " there are no "righteous / wars" (78.497) matches this astrological movement. So from the tent in the Disciplinary Training Center (DTC), Pound sees the moon, Venus, and Sirius (80.513–14); an ideal of war as vengeance and cleansing is replaced with a new rejection of war for a new time—the season for war has passed.

Venus and the moon (Diana) become part of a metonymy of increase (seen as the Monte dei Paschi in *The Fifth Decad*) built on images of natural fertility. Fertility is promised through invocations of Dionysos and Bacchus, Zeus and Ceres, Kore and Persephone, Gaea and Mary (figured as Pound's Beatrice, as his daughter, and perhaps as the virgin). The metonymy of increase and fertility is constructed of this metaphorical overlaying of gods, goddesses, and female figures, including even Helen, whose breasts are identified with the hills visible from Pound's tent and whose milk provides offerings for the new altars of Pound's visionary temple.

Of all these figures, Helen is still the most ambiguous; she has provided the most famous "casus bellorum" invoked by *The Cantos*—and she may be obliquely identified with "la Clara," Mussolini's mistress, who was so roundly despised by many Italians and who was executed along with him. The invocation of natural increase, nonetheless, is crucial to the metonymic linkages that guarantee order in *The Pisan Cantos*. Under the sign of Venus, the martial appeal for cleansing and vengeance, though still present in these cantos, is largely transmuted.

Not surprisingly, other elements in the metonymy of law are likewise modified. The overriding concern with ill mixtures, with bestiality, with miscegenation, though still present, is in part countered by an "ordering of the animals." The swine, clearly associated with Jews in *The Fifth Decad*, still appear, particularly in Pound's praise for Mussolini's cleansing Italy. In Canto 78, for example, we find an allusion to the spirits of the fallen Fascists; a recapitulation of Mussolini's call for responsible government by people who do have " 'a front name, a hind name, and an address' " (78.493); and a statement that this call to order stands "uncancelled." As for Mussolini, Pound suggests, he created

> merrda for the monopolists
> the bastardly lot of 'em
> Put down the slave trade, made the desert to yield
> and menaced the loan swine
>
> (78.493)

As in *The Fifth Decad*, disorder here is associated with bastards, excrement, swine, and the lack of right naming. Mussolini has, sadly, died like a swine, compelled to this fate by those to whom he might have been a good example.

In *The Pisan Cantos* this congeries of disorder is held up against natural increase (from the union of gods with goddesses or earth), and we are presented with some promise of healing after the war. Homer, we are told, "was a medic" (80.517). Finally, at the end of *The Pisan Cantos*, the young woman who herds swine is allowed the last word on war. Are the American soldiers worse than the Germans? she is asked. She replies that they are the same. The promises of healing and of ordering the animals, then, reply to but do not escape the metonymy of law as it was developed in *The Fifth Decad* and elsewhere. Swine are still swine, bastards are bastards. Redemption is not impossible, but the redeemers, including Mussolini and the poet himself, have become victims.

This complex pattern is also visible in the continued dualism figured by dogs and cats which appears in earlier cantos and more elaborately in *The Pisan Cantos*. Here is a sorting out of animals in their domestic significance and in their metonymic extensions as well. The dogs, which in *The Fifth Decad* represent bestiality and dreadful intermingling of kinds, in *The Pisan Cantos* are partially redeemed in the light of Venus; the dog star is aloft with Venus and the moon (80.513–14). Dogs come to stand metonymically for victims.

Pound admits a certain identity with some of the black prisoners in the DTC, whom he partially accepts if with a still racist patronage; these men are identified with dogs. The poet muses in Canto 79:

> Indubitably, indubitably re / Scott
>   I like a certain number of shades in my landscape
> as per / "doan' tell no one I made you that table"
> or Whiteside:
>   "ah certainly dew lak dawgs,
>   ah goin' tuh wash you"
> (no, not to the author, to the canine unwilling in question)
>   (79.498–99)

Here Whiteside, the black man, and the white author are identified with the dog. Similarly, Miss Matilda Talbot, punningly invoked in Canto 80, is identified with a dog, with the defense of English liberties because she has preserved a copy of the Magna Carta, and with resistance to the decay of venerable English institutions (80.529).

Finally in Canto 81 the poet excoriates vanity and invokes the "beaten dog." McGann has asserted that in the famous declaration "Pull down thy vanity," Pound addresses as a "beaten dog" not himself but the U.S. Army (*Toward a Literature of Knowledge*, 114). Certainly it would make sense that Pound might characterize the army by the very sort of bestiality and illegitimate mixtures he mocked in *The Fifth Decad of Cantos*. The army is after all the American partially integrated army:

>   Pull down thy vanity
> Thou art a beaten dog beneath the hail,
> A swollen magpie in a fitful sun,
> Half black half white
> Nor knowst'ou wing from tail
>   (81.535)

Other commentators have seen this as Pound's address to himself, and the identification with dogs as victims gives a certain probability to this reading. Ultimately, I think Pound leaves any such identification between the poet and the beaten dog, the poet and the black-and-white army, at best ambivalent; the poem is left to the reader's charity.

In Canto 81, the poet claims to have acted *without* vanity in the service of his art: "to have done instead of not doing / this is not vanity" (535). An uncharitable reader—or one who identifies more solidly with the dogs than Pound does and who doubts Pound's self-identification with the soldiers—would not be comforted by the poet's claim to sins of omission: "Here error is all in the not done, / all in the diffidence that faltered" (81.536). If Pound is to be seen as the "beaten dog," it is in admitting errors of omission and in claiming to be himself a victim.

The status of victims becomes less ambiguous as the metonymy of law is transformed in *The Pisan Cantos* into a transhistorical force of fate. In this tropological structure, the place of the lawmaker is taken by the fated prophet who is also a victim. Pound evokes both the prophecies of the Homeric stories and of the Bible.

In Canto 82 the dog as victim is metonymically associated with prophecy, with fate, and with the English poetic tradition; this should be no surprise inasmuch as the poet describes himself in Canto 81 as a custodian and renewer of English poetry. Pound regrets missing a meeting with Swinburne, and he recalls his London publisher, Elkin Mathews's, having once carried Swinburne's suitcase. He recounts the comic story of Swinburne reciting Aeschylus to the French fishermen who rescue him, and he imagines Swinburne quoting them the Greek:

> "On the Atreides' roof"
> "like a dog ... and a good job
> ΕΜΟΣ ΠΟΣΙΣ ... ΧΕΡΟΣ
> hac dextera mortus
> dead by this hand
> (82.537)

Here we have Clytemnestra's words; Agamemnon, returned victorious from the war, is dead by her hand, and "a good job" too. The prophecy has found its victim. Both desiring and having reason to fear a possible return to the United States after the war, Pound too is in the victim's place; he too might now have reason to fear a dog's death.

The addition of a metonymic structure associated with prophecy and fate to the metonymy of law allows Pound to emphasize the prophet's vision at least as strongly as the lawgiver's agency. The dog as social victim or as sign of social corruption becomes less important than a variety of magical cats, bearing their visions from some other dimension of the world. At the very beginning of *The Pisan Cantos*, Pound presents us with Cassandra, whose "eyes are like tigers" (78.491).[3] In the allusion, of course, Cassandra prophesies the fall of

---

3. The New Directions edition should probably read "tigers'" here in conformity to the usage in Canto 78.482.

Troy and becomes a slave and victim afterward. Through the figure of Cassandra he identifies slaves with unheeded prophets.

Cats, vision, prophecy, and persecution, then, form a crucial metonymic chain in *The Pisan Cantos*. Cassandra is connected metaphorically to the goddesses and gods Pound transforms into each other—such "magical" transformations as we have seen as early as Canto 2. Kore, Aphrodite, Dionysos, Hermes, Helios—all are accompanied by cats representing visionary power. The leopard, the lynx, the puma guard the grapevine, the pomegranate field, the possibility of redemptive suffering, and the utopia of fertility. The visionary claim of Canto 81, when the poet is surrounded by eyes in his tent, is a moment of encounter with such eyes as the cat's or the prophet's: "green of the mountain pool / shone from the unmasked eyes in half-mask's space" (81.534).

The poet recalls subsequently what he has loved, and in the next canto he celebrates a union with earth which is also an encounter with the terror of death. He becomes merged with Kore/Demeter, identified with their feline guardian spirit, fed also by "ichor for lynxes." In the next canto, water from the clouds, the gift of Neptune, can be identified with tears from the caged panther's eyes. The poet, then, is associated in a metonymic chain with Cassandra, cats, vision, and victimization. To read the poem we are compelled to feel the pathos of the poet's situation: "No man who has passed a month in the death cells / believes in cages for beasts" (83.544).

The Prophet's Body and Body Politic in *The Pisan Cantos*

In the metonymy of prophecy, prophetic vision is invoked to stand for a natural order and a fate that will eventually right itself despite the prophets who are made victims along the way; this metonymic structure of association is elaborated in the metaphorical layering of the various magical cats and their divine companions in *The Pisan Cantos*. But the motif of prophecy is developed in another, more uncomfortable context and through a metaphorical overlaying of figures whose presence creates disturbing dissonances. As we saw in *The Fifth Decad of Cantos*, the poem's tropology can make contradictory and—at times—untenable claims. The metaphorical identifications that would balance the dispersive character of the metonymy of law (and here the metonymy of memory and fate) make ethical and political as well as emotional claims.

Pound never deserts, even in the face of the chaos of history, an implicit, and sometimes explicit, claim to establish an ethical hierarchy. The poem propels itself uncomfortably into the history of its own moment in the identification of the poet-prophet-victim with the Hebrew prophets and with Jesus (whom we can regard in this context as a Hebrew prophet). At the same time, *The Pisan Cantos* disavow nothing of the anti-Semitism that has come before. Canto 74 strikes this chord at the outset. The poet claims himself to have seen the corpses of souls in Circe's "swine sty" and to have seen gleams of vision. The iniquity that has brought both the poet and Europe to this pass is usury, which itself is associated with Jewish conspiracy. So Roosevelt changes the value of gold, in response to the conspiracy of Jewish financiers (Henry Morgenthau and the Rothschilds):

> doubtless conditioned by what his father heard in
> > Byzantium
> doubtless conditioned by the spawn of the gt. Meyer Anselm
> That old H. had heard from the ass eared militarist in Byzantium:
> > "Why stop?" "To begin again when we are stronger."
> and young H/ the tip from the augean stables in Paris
> . . . .
> the yidd is a stimulant, and the goyim are cattle
> > in gt/ proportion and go to saleable slaughter
> > with the maximum of docility.
>
> > > > > > (74.453)

The "goyim" are made beasts by a conspiracy of Jewish financiers, just as Odysseus' men are transformed into swine by Circe.

These anti-Semitic moments stand curiously beside the allusions to prophecy in *The Pisan Cantos*. The poet sees a continuity of analysis, identifying himself and the other prisoners with victims, with Circe's swine under an evil enchantment, and with prophets who become victims and slaves. But what looks at first to be Pound's metaphorical identification with victims and with suffering, appears on closer inspection to be more complex. Whereas the Jew is by nature swine, the persecuted prophet is treated as, or transformed through enchantment into, swine.

Despite Pound's identification with Hebrew prophets, there can be no identification with the Jew as victim. In the poet's identification with Jesus, moreover, we find a similar complexity. The poem swings between humility and hubris. Although the identification of the poet with Jesus occurs at several important junctures (e.g., 74.427, 76.459), perhaps the most interesting example is in Canto 74:

> I don't know how humanity stands it
>> with a painted paradise at the end of it
>> without a painted paradise at the end of it
> the dwarf morning-glory twines round the grass blade
> magna NOX animae   with Barabbas and 2 thieves beside me,
>> the wards like a slave ship,
>>> Mr Edwards, Hudson, Henry   *comes miseriae*
> ....
>
>> ac ego in harum
> so lay men in Circe's swine-sty;
>> ivi in harum *ego* ac vidi cadaveres animae
>> "c'mon small fry" sd/the little coon to the big black
> of the slaver as seen between decks
>
>>>> (74.450)

What unites these elements of Canto 74 is the presentation of imprisonment and then death and the poet's identification with suffering victims. Here as elsewhere in *The Pisan Cantos*, the poet identifies the DTC with slave ships and expresses his compassion for and appreciation of his fellow prisoners.

But the ideological paradoxes of these identifications are obvious. Jews are metonymically associated in *The Cantos* with chaos, filth, and swine, and yet Pound appropriates the language of Hebrew prophecy and the place of the prophet/victim Jesus. In the DTC the poet is between the decks of the slaver, in the swine sty; and Circe's poison has immobilized him just as usury has poisoned the body politic. The passage continues:

> Robbing the public for private individual's gain ΘΕΛΓΕΙΝ
> every bank of discount is downright iniquity
>> robbing the public for private individual's gain
> nec benecomata Kirkê, mah! Kakà Φάργακ' ἔδωκεν
> neither with lions nor leopards attended
>> but poison, veneno
> in all the veins of the commonweal
> if on high, will flow downward all thru them
>> if on the forge at Predappio? sd/old Upward:
>>> "not the priest but the victim"
>
>>>> (74.451)

Pound identifies his own body both with those of other victims and with the body politic. And this cuts two ways. On the one hand, there is identification with victims, including both Jesus and slaves; on the other hand, there is identification with the state—a state poisoned by the external intervention of the Jew, who is connected metonymically with filth, excrement, and witches.

Pound's evocation of the Hebrew prophets—Elijah, Jeremiah, Micah, and Isaiah—has a similar structure. The prophets are commensurate with the legendary Chinese kings as lawgivers and makers of culture. And they are aligned as well with Odysseus and Aeneas, particularly with the Odysseus who returns from exile to restore order in Ithaca and the Aeneas who goes into exile to found a new temple.[4] The prophet, like the poet and the political hero, is charged with refounding, restoring a temple for what the prophet Micah calls the "remnant" of his people; this is a central, if not hopeful, project of *The Pisan Cantos*. Aligning himself with the prophets, Pound can in retrospect recreate the earlier cantos as an unheeded warning to Europe and, especially, to the United States.

The attraction of invoking prophets, then, is not just as a means of accounting for his own position as victim—as the prophet without honor in his own country. The identification with the prophet also enables the poet to find a position from which to speak within a disastrous situation. This position is particularly important in Pound's identification with Isaiah, who urges the Israelites to return to the law and whose mission is "to redeem Zion with justice" (74.443). Identifying with Isaiah, Pound unites the metonymy of law with the metonymy of prophecy. Justice, or good law, prevents usury: "not out on interest said David rex." In a "regime based on grand larceny," the grand larceny of usury, avoiding the regulations by making the poet a table is an act of charity. Isaiah's justice shall redeem the man "who putteth not out his money on interest" (74.448).

Finally, the position of the prophet converges with the dispersal and chaos endemic to the negative underside of law in *The Fifth Decad*. Evoking the prophets allows the poet to castigate the Jews even as the Hebrew prophets did. There is, however, a crucial difference; for Pound's voice of judgment is not only the voice of an insider in a

---

4. See esp. Canto 74.440: "Rouse found they spoke of Elias / in telling the tales of Odysseus." See also Canto 74.56 where the true king would "have put the old man, *son père* on his shoulders / and gone off to some barren seacoast."

community he criticizes—however soon he may be rejected in turn by that community. It is also the voice of the insider turning against the outsider, the foreigner. The Hebrew prophets whom Pound cites do castigate their fellow Jews for what they see as corrupting traffic with foreigners. For Pound the Jews themselves have become the foreigners. *The Pisan Cantos* maintain a division between the European and the Jew, the body politic and its poison.[5]

It is in this context, then, that we should understand *The Pisan Cantos* as recasting the tropological structures of earlier cantos, as emphasizing healing and empathic identification with victims, under the sign of Venus. The vision that guarantees the poem's ethical hierarchy can be traced from *The Pisan Cantos* all the way back to the Ovidian transformations of Canto 2. And yet the particular metaphorical layerings and metonymic relationships of *The Pisan Cantos* reveal their ethical contradictions even as they connect these cantos to the rest of the poem. To read the poem, we must trace the unstable and problematic pattern that asks us metaphorically to identify the poet, the slave, Mussolini, Cassandra, Jesus, and the Hebrew prophets. The poet as prophet attempts to establish a hierarchy of metonymically ordered relationships based in an invocation of Venus and of healing and a corresponding judgment of the Jew and Circe as the poison in the body politic.

The double tropological structure of *The Pisan Cantos* in itself comes with no positive or negative ethical guarantees, though systematic incoherences or contradictions should surely call for a hermeneutic of suspicion. Rather the particular metaphors and metonymies of *The Pisan Cantos*, the very messy webs they make, demand ethical response. The seduction of *The Pisan Cantos*—for those readers who do not resist or reject them outright—is neither the seduction of metaphor (pace de Man) nor the de Manian ironic aporia at the end of tropology. Instead the pull of *The Pisan Cantos* lies both in its versification and alignment with elegy and in the ultimately androcentric and racist, but nevertheless real, appeal of its utopian vision.

5. It is interesting, too, as Rabaté (*Language, Sexuality, and Ideology*, 158) and Robert Casillo (*Genealogy of Demons*, 35) note, that Pound may also identify with the prophet Ezra, and it may not be too farfetched to suggest that prophet Ezra's rejection of foreigners as corrupting may, curiously, become part of Pound's pattern of castigating modern Jews. See for example the passage in 74.453 in which we are told that the Rothschilds and the Morganthaus get from an "ass eared militarist in Byzantium" their ability to unite usury and war and to create big money as cultural romance.

Epic, Elegy, and Utopian Vision

It is tempting to look for a generic stability in *The Pisan Cantos* and in Pound's long poem as a whole, just as it is tempting to specify a single unifying structural principle. And yet the doubling in the poem's tropological structures, the gaps in emphasis and poetic strategy among various sections of the poem, and most of all the poem's self-conscious creation as a record of struggle and ongoing response to history—these dimensions should warn us away from single explanatory tropological or generic classifications.

Rather than reading *The Pisan Cantos*, or the whole poem, under the classification of elegy or tragic elegy as Rabaté does, I prefer to focus on these cantos as a section of the poem in which epic and elegy are brought most clearly into tension. Here the epic—with a commitment to making culture ordered as it makes poetry new—clearly threatens to devolve into elegy—with a glorification of the grieving or victimized self as the true paradigm of the culture's failures. If we can see Pound early in the Malatesta cantos approaching his task from the Burckhardtian premise that the state is a work of art, and if we agree with Tim Redman (in *Ezra Pound and Italian Fascism*, following Walter Benjamin and Theodor Adorno) that fascism can be regarded as an aestheticization of politics and was so for Pound, then as the Fascist state crumbles it should be no surprise to find as we do in *The Pisan Cantos* that the poet identifies his body with the body politic. *The Pisan Cantos* hold in tension moments of vision, even a kind of disembodiment, with the moment of the body's possible destruction by Circe's poison. The poet's body, the state as the work of art, and the Fascist revolution as the work of the artist become identified. The poem that was supposed to become, possibly, a fascist epic becomes equally a fascist elegy.[6]

This elegiac situation is materially the result of the defeat of Italian fascism; ideologically, the elegiac situation was already prepared in the problematic combination of radical individualism and of radical desire for order which Pound inherited from the nineteenth century. It would not be accurate to maintain that Thomas Carlyle, for exam-

---

6. The pull toward elegy and the elegiac, of course, is a crucial connection between Pound's modernism and the legacy of romanticism. On the cantos as fascist epic see Lauber, "Pound's *Cantos*"; see also Redman, *Ezra Pound and Italian Fascism*, esp. pp. 118–21, and McGann, "*Cantos* of Ezra Pound, the Truth in Contradiction," in *Towards a Literature of Knowledge*.

ple, let alone his descendants Ruskin and Morris, aestheticized politics in the mode of fascist ideology, and yet Carlyle's repeated laments about his own unpoetic age are intimately tied to a sense that poetry must celebrate heroic historical achievement and cultural order. History is "the true Epic Poem," Carlyle declared; or as Pound would put it, an epic is a poem including history. Implicitly, poetry's task is to represent such history. The shape of history itself, then, is integral to the shape of the poem. For Carlyle as for Pound, history can fail epic. For Carlyle such failure is represented by the French Revolution; for Pound the Fascist revolution holds an analogous place. In Carlyle's own time the political failure of the French Revolution and the moral and social failures of the industrial revolution created a situation in which Carlyle saw men fail in the hero's task of ordering society; they were overwhelmed, Carlyle felt, by a disorder that was itself inimical to poetry or to epic. Pound found himself still more thoroughly overwhelmed. Both the French Revolution and the Fascist one, different as they were, attempted to make the world new enough to impose a fresh dating system on history itself. Both at least made claims for utopian hopes which quickly dissolved into the realpolitik of war.[7] True history is no guarantee of epic coherence. For Pound to undertake or to continue writing an epic was to imagine—in the face of world war—a restoration of the culture's palladium.

If history itself must provide the structure of epic, then Pound could not, unlike Milton, turn to a suprahistorical explanation of history for a guarantee of epic coherence. Pound could provide only what Pater called "real illusions," an individual vision that however compelling cannot construct a providential historical end. Unlike Wordsworth in the face of the failure of revolution, Pound could not defend a continuity of memory and tradition—an awkward position at any rate for most American poets. He could not fully transform epic into elegiac recollection. Rather, *The Pisan Cantos* oscillate between epic and elegy, making claims for the poem's utopian vision and for the poignance of recollection and leaving openings to the poem's future task of rebuilding empire, law, historical coherence.

In examining *The Pisan Cantos* we can see how they transform the tropes of *The Fifth Decad of Cantos* without escaping the poem's fundamental dualisms. The assertion of individual vision—by the artist or the prophet—is confronted by radical disorder and dislocation. The

---

7. Pound's practice of dating his letters according to the years of the Fascist era is well known. See *Selected Letters* and, for further examples, P/F.

sign of Mars may be transformed to the sign of Venus, but natural increase or fertility is, in its turn, dual. One must still sort out the animals. The poet identifies with the prophet and victim rather than the cleanser and avenger, and yet despite the rhetoric of healing he cannot relinquish the pursuit of enemies, though they be victims themselves. The poet's body and the body politic are suffering, and the poem hovers between elegiac lament for lost possibility and the desire for an unambiguous totalizing vision of some future order. Within the very principles of order at the heart of the poem's utopian promise lie the intractable contradictions of its undoing.

Chapter 6

Doubled Feminine: A Painted Paradise at the End of It

ROMA
O   M
M   O
AMOR

—Pound, "A Visiting Card" (SP, 327)

Paganism included a certain attitude toward; a certain understanding of, coitus, which is the mysterium.

The other rites are the festivals of fecundity of the grain and the sun festivals, without revival of which religion can not return to the hearts of the people.

—Pound, "Religio" (SP, 70)

In *The Pisan Cantos*, Pound's hopes survive under the sign of Venus. Yet the invocation of Venus and her equivalents—Demeter, Mary, Gaea, Persephone, Helen—has its own ambiguities. To idealize the feminine and to promote a visionary connection to natural abundance is to evoke this vision's duplicity. As we have seen, Helen is the image of beauty and the cause of war; worse, beautiful Circe sends Odysseus on his way but permanently turns his men into swine. Beauty and natural abundance are intimately linked with violence and destruction. Pound's utopian vision of light as knowledge and of natural union with numinous power, is, like the tropes of *The Cantos*, profoundly problematic. Just as we can see the complexity of tropes in

The Pisan Cantos by attending to their social and historical meanings, so too we can understand the politics of Pound's utopian vision by attending to that vision's historicity.

Even if we call it "mythical method" or "mythopoeisis," we must recognize that Pound's vision has historical meaning and—more significantly—makes historical claims. It is the nature even of otherworldly paradises to make important claims on the living; life on earth can be shaped by a particular hope of heaven. Still more obviously, Pound's utopian vision makes claims on this world; it is a measure of his resistance to a "painted paradise at the end of it." It claims to provide "real illusions" powerful enough to shape social practice. Ironically, though, both this vision and the affective center of *The Cantos* are based in an idealization of the "feminine" that in its own way is a "painted paradise"—both literally and figuratively. The vision that does seem at first sui generis, a personal mythology compounded of diverse elements by a multicultural *bricoleur*, is at heart an insistently gendered vision of society and art which was significantly shaped by late-nineteenth-century culture.

Pound's utopian vision connects an economics critical of underconsumption; celebrations of earth, natural fertility, and the rural (which nevertheless Pound claims is not "pastoral regression"[1]); an idealization of the female and concomitant glorification of male sexual potency; a belief in natural hierarchy; and a conviction that the artist because of his own potency forms the energy of nature into art. These connected themes run with variations all through *The Cantos*, and numerous critics have discussed their ramifications.[2]

Like the metonymy of law, Pound's utopian vision evokes both hierarchy and chaos. It rests on a profoundly dualist apprehension of the world and of the feminine. I trace here the immediate sources of

1. See Pound's observation in "The City" that "Ruskin was well-meaning but a goose. The remedy for machines is not pastoral regression" (SP, 224).
2. Robert Casillo, particularly, has discussed the connections among Pound's ambivalence toward women, his visionary moments, and his anti-Semitism. Casillo says that the meaning of women, like the meaning of usury in the Cantos, is strikingly overdetermined and that women are radically ambiguous. They represent at once the sacred and the profane, the pure and the swamp, the bounty of agriculture and the "polluting, parthenogenetic earth" (*Genealogy of Demons*, 228–29). In their positive aspect, we can see women, particularly Pound's luminous goddesses, as muses, bringers of light, and inspiration for art. In their negative aspect, they are Circe at her worst. This doubling of course is as deep as Western culture. Casillo cites for example Remy de Gourmont's appropriation of Aristotle's view of women as undifferentiated and formless (219).

his vision of the "feminine" in the work of Ruskin and the Pre-Raphaelites and in fin-de-siècle culture. We can see the contours of this cultural construct in the making of modernism, particularly in "Hugh Selwyn Mauberley," in his correspondence with Eliot about *The Waste Land*, in the manifestos of the vorticist period, and in his postscript to Remy de Gourmont's *Natural Philosophy of Love*. As Pound sought a cosmos to enable epic coherence in *The Cantos*, neither his modernist technique nor his epic intentions developed apart from this gendered cultural construct. The idealization of the feminine enabled him to imagine the congruity of beauty and power; at the same time, the feminine was a significant source of disorder. Attention to this structure allows us to see how his utopian vision and his ideology of the feminine were compatible with the domestic policies of Italian Fascism. Such congruity underlies the idealization of the feminine and the praise of fascism in the two Italian cantos, Cantos 72 and 73, and in the Italian notes that served as a prelude to *The Pisan Cantos*. In all these texts, I trace a common thread linking violence and the dualistic ideology of the feminine. It is only when we recognize the violence at the heart of Pound's vision that we can see the catastrophe in his claim that he has found the "Gods moving in crystal / ichor, amor" (91.625).

Utopia and the Idealization of the Feminine: Victorian and Modernist Vision

Pound's utopia with its idealization of the feminine has its roots in nineteenth-century structures of feeling, especially in the representations of women by Ruskin and the Pre-Raphaelites. In Pound's modernist project, this vision of the feminine is not abandoned; if anything it is intensified.

As I have already noted, Pound's early poems make reference to Ruskin's *Sesame and Lilies*, the volume containing "Of Kings' Treasuries" and "Of Queens' Gardens" among other essays. These paired essays discuss, on the one hand, a masculine world of books and ideas and, on the other, a feminine world of nurturing, fertility, and feeling. Ruskin's preface to the 1871 edition, moreover, indulges in the familiar Victorian doubling of good and evil women—or angels and demons. Robert Casillo argues that Pound's idealization/horror of the feminine associates the feminine in its negative dimension with "oriental" horrors and ultimately with anti-Semitism (*Genealogy of Demons*, 211). The beginning of such a train of associations is visible in Ruskin's preface, where he asserts that "the best women are indeed necessarily the most difficult to know" and the worst are "in states of degradation and vindictiveness which opened to me the gloomiest secrets of Greek and Syrian tragedy" (*Works*, 18:47). The worst women, Ruskin says, are compounded of lust and betrayal, like modern Medeas and Salomes.

"Of Kings' Treasuries" and especially "Of Queens' Gardens" are directed as much toward the ideal as toward the negative. And here Ruskin cites literary evidence for the moral superiority of women, including Shakespeare's plays and D. G. Rossetti's translations from the troubadours (*Works*, 18:112–113). The female in this tradition is to know only through feeling; the male, to know systematically and in depth through doing and creating. Ruskin's ideal domestic order, like his ideal social order, is to be founded in the hierarchical articulation of this division, which becomes the paradigm for other social divisions. Moving to Old English etymology, Ruskin claims for the lady the role of loaf-giver and for the lord the role of "law-giver." He would like to imagine England itself becoming the garden that, without destructive passion, avarice, finance capitalism, and munitions building, would be the home of peaceful hierarchical relations among classes and sexes. Women, in this view, are guarantors of moral order and, by a process difficult to imagine in reality, are to become guarantors of the transformation of the social order. For Ruskin, as for Pound many years later, utopia is predicated on an idealization of the female, and such idealization always brings its other side—Circe, Medea, Clytemnestra.

This idealization and its antithesis are played out from the modernist beginnings of "Hugh Selwyn Mauberley" (1920) and *The Waste Land* (1922) to *The Pisan Cantos*. World War I, the war Ruskin might gloomily have predicted, is described in "Hugh Selwyn Mauberley" as a contest waged "For an old bitch gone in the teeth / For a botched civilization" (PSP, 188). In "Yeux Glauques," the section of "Hugh Selwyn Mauberley" following this famous denunciation, we find that Ruskin's "Of Kings' Treasuries" and Pre-Raphaelite art generally are preserved also in their degraded underside; "fœtid Buchanan" set the stage in his infamous essay "The Fleshly School of Poetry." Burne-Jones's model is "bewildered that a world / Shows no surprise / At her last maquero's / Adulteries" (PSP, 189).

Pound celebrates an ideal of physical passion in a way Ruskin never could, and in "Hugh Selwyn Mauberley" as elsewhere he derides Victorian prudery. And yet, in this poem as in *The Pisan Cantos* years later, the Pre-Raphaelite idealization of women still retains its appeal: "The thin, clear gaze, the same / Still darts out faun-like from the half-ruin'd face" ("Yeux Glauques," PSP, 188).

This instability of the feminine is as evident in "Hugh Selwyn Mauberley" as it is in Ruskin's *Sesame and Lilies*. And the double quality of the feminine is particularly apparent in the "Yeux Glauques" section, the text most obviously articulated against its Victorian predecessors. It is no wonder that critics disagree markedly about the tone of this section of Pound's poem; his ironies, here as elsewhere in the poem, are shifting, doubling, and redoubling. But it is not merely the shifty character of irony—which *The Cantos* come to avoid as a structuring principle—it is that the Pre-Raphaelite woman of "Yeux Glauques" is at once the victim of the painter's brush, of Pound's irony, and of his sympathy with the painter's or gazer's point of view. Thus Peter Faulkner can argue against Hugh Kenner that the girl in "Yeux Glauques" is not so suggestive of the "eternal Aphrodite" as Kenner believes. Instead these eyes, in Faulkner's reading, reveal "the impoverishment of an artistic tradition that, in turning away from the world and encouraging aesthetic rhapsody, had left a legacy of bewilderment—an inability to impinge significantly on that 'old bitch gone in the teeth.'"[3] Certainly Pound is critical in "Hugh Selwyn Mauberley" of poetic "rhapsodizing" and of his own earlier Pre-Raphaelite mannerisms, and yet the poem's images never escape the self-circling quality of Pre-Raphaelite idealization of women. Cophe-

3. Faulkner, "Pound and the Pre-Raphaelities," 241; Faulkner also claims that Pound takes issue with Ruskin "in so far as the Ruskinian tradition led towards some form of Socialism" and that the Pre-Raphaelites disappear from the Pound canon between "Hugh Selwyn Mauberley" and *The Pisan Cantos*. As is obvious, I think this view needs revision and that both the Pre-Raphaelite double vision of the feminine and Ruskin's basic principles regarding art and money or economics are fundamental to Pound's work. Of course Faulkner is correct to judge that Pound's obvious imitation of and allusions to the Pre-Raphaelites diminish between World War I and *The Pisan Cantos*. For further explorations of Ruskin and Pound's economic thought see Michael Coyle, " 'A Profounder Didacticism.' " Coyle also calls attention to parallels in Pound's attraction to Ruskin and to Remy de Gourmont: Ruskin attributed "to culture a unified organic life analogous to that which Romantic aestheticians discerned in individual works of art. This way of thinking about culture characterized Pound's work as well. His enthusiasm for Remy de Gourmont, which . . . is no random example, partly derived from his perception that Gourmont shared this way of thinking" (24). See also Witemeyer, " 'Of Kings' Treasuries' "; Surette, "Ezra Pound and British Radicalism"; and Casillo, "Meaning of Venetian History." I agree with Witemeyer and Surette that the Ruskinian tradition was formative for Pound and, like them, take issue with Faulkner's conclusions, which minimize Ruskin's importance.

tua, or Burne-Jones's view of his Victorian model, is faunlike, bewildered, "questing and passive." She is part animal and part woman, part ideal and part victim.[4]

Pound does present the faunlike woman as injured by late Victorian England; Kenner links her to the eyes of Canto 80, saying that "from what painters report of such eyes we can read a time" (*Pound Era*, 363). But this reading of "Hugh Selwyn Mauberley," like the similar reading of eyes in *The Cantos*, is a better measure of the poet's or painter's vision than it is of the time itself. It, too, participates in the idealization of the feminine which, despite all the attempts of modernism to escape its immediate past, recapitulates a nineteenth-century structure of feeling. As Pound's own response to his time became more desperate in *The Pisan Cantos* than it was in "Hugh Selwyn Mauberley," so his idealization of the feminine becomes more marked. As Christina Rossetti observed of her brother's similar tendency in painting, the model appears "not as she is but was when hope shone bright / Not as she is but as she fills his dream."[5]

The feminine in "Hugh Selwyn Mauberley" appears both idealized and doubled, the "old bitch" and the bewildered faun, the dog and the deer. This pairing closely parallels the Actaeon story that appears in Canto 4, by association subsequently, and then in Canto 80. The feminine can be violent or it can serve as the ground of enlightenment. The poet—like Actaeon and the troubadour Vidal—is in danger of being transformed by his desire and torn by his own hounds. The doubling of the feminine, the guarantee of fertility and numinous power in Pound's utopian vision, marks its danger.[6]

I have traced here the doubling of the feminine in Ruskin's text and in the related section of Pound's poem not because Ruskin was uniquely influential on Pound but because a text like *Sesame and Lilies* displays discursively the double construct we see in many instances of the idealization of the feminine between 1850 and the 1920s. This doubling appears more ambiguously in Pre-Raphaelite poetry and art

4. This painting apparently reflected Burne-Jones's response to Morris's increasing concern with socialism as an answer to England's social problems; it is obviously a late version of the response to the "two nations" of the rich and the poor. See *Burne-Jones: The Paintings, Graphic and Decorative Work of Sir Edward Burne-Jones, 1833–1898* (London: Arts Council of Great Britain, 1975), 56.
5. Rossetti, "In an Artist's Studio," in *Complete Poems* 3:264.
6. Diana in Canto 80 appears again with Actaeon, here not as the chaste goddess but as the Diana of Ephesus, the "goddess of the double gates of birth and death" (Terrell, *Companion*, 12, and see also 435).

than in Ruskin's texts; for there sexuality itself has an immediate and dual presence.

Diana the goddess of birth and death, Aphrodite the goddess of love and destructive passion, Persephone bringer of the spring and mate of Hades—these are Pound's double goddesses. Also doubled, though more or less negative in different contexts, are Medusa, Helen, and Circe. In the works of Burne-Jones and Rossetti, the most literary Pre-Raphaelites and the ones most important for Pound, these figures include Helen, Pandora, Aphrodite, Medusa, Vivien, Astarte, Circe, and Lillith.

Indeed, reading through the catalogue raisonné of Rossetti's paintings and drawings is like reading through a list of the mythological or literary female figures Pound invokes in *The Cantos*. Even Rossetti's early paintings of Beatrice, particularly the painting of her denying her salutation to Dante, have something of this quality of simultaneous desire and repulsion. David Riede has discussed this aspect of Rossetti's paintings at some length, pointing to Rossetti's affinity for the "fatal women" of nineteenth-century romanticism and linking his women to the dark women of Baudelaire and to the androgynes of Gautier.[7]

It is useful to recall that this dual representation of the feminine is present also in the work of Pater and the Georgian poets and that an obvious misogyny was often a crucial part of the image of the "poet maudit." Elaine Showalter has traced the ways in which male challenges to Victorian sexual ideology were compatible with misogyny and sexual fear. Avant-garde and male homosexual challenges to convention, she demonstrates, exploited the negative half of the Victorian double vision of the female (*Sexual Anarchy*). At the same time that homosexuality was being created as a category, Showalter explains, a fear of female sexual and social power also helped destroy the illusory coherence of the "masculine"; eventually such apprehensions took the forms of fear of syphilis, of association of sexuality with disease, and often of association of racism with both. In my view this combination of attitudes plays out in the unease already obvious in Ruskin's evocation of Syriac women and perhaps in Rossetti's paintings of "Astarte Syriaca" and "The Beloved" as well. Pound's idealization of the feminine—the representation of the beautiful but fatally powerful

7. See Riede, "Painting, 1859–1882," 233–63. See also Sonstroem, *Rossetti and the Fair Lady*; and Surtees, *Paintings and Drawings of Dante Gabriel Rossetti*.

woman—owes its particular character to these related aspects of nine-teenth-century culture and to their early modernist transformations. Indeed this linkage of desire and repulsion is intrinsic to the texts that most fully defined modernism in the immediate postwar period.

Violence and the Feminine in Pound's Construction of Modernism

Just as the doubling of the feminine is clear in the modernist ironies of Pound's " Hugh Selwyn Mauberley," so, too, is it apparent in the collaboration between Eliot and Pound on *The Waste Land* and in the related imagery associated with vorticism and with Pound's praise of Remy de Gourmont. The feminine stands for fecundity and the swamp, purity and disease, the ground of utopia and the fallen matter of history.

In a fascinating study of *The Waste Land*, hysteria, and sexual identity, Wayne Koestenbaum has shown how Pound's "editing" of Eliot not only engendered but gendered Eliot's poem. *The Waste Land*, under Pound's editing, did truly, as Joyce claimed, "end poetry for ladies" and construct a male reader (Koestenbaum, *"The Waste Land,"* 113–15). Pound systematically suggested alterations to reduce the possibility that Eliot might be identified with lesbian and homosexual writers.

In Pound's "obstetric verses" enclosed in a letter to Eliot about the poem, he claims both to have midwifed and to have sired *The Waste Land*. The two sections following Pound's declaration that he has "performed the caesarean Operation" birthing the poem, chart precisely the territory Showalter has described and yoke racism, disease, and bestiality, which may be countered by assertive masculinity. These lines also demonstrate a certain self-consciousness on Pound's part about his own idealization of the feminine, even while such self-consciousness can only be articulated in a joke about class-based eroticism (reminiscent of Pound's earlier poem "Shop Girl" among others). The lines reveal the fear not only that the birth of modernism may be homosexual, diseased, or deformed but also that it will be Victorian. Whereas Pound rescues Eliot from "inversion," *The Waste Land* is to rescue poetry from the literary past.[8] And yet Pound de-

8. An interesting parallel can be drawn between "Hugh Selwyn Mauberley" as a post-war poem, invoking hysteria and the feminization of men, and Marinetti's postwar

clares he will not give up his Pre-Raphaelite ivory (his own sperm has turned his senses "pachyderm") or his pearl.[9]

Like Browning, who claimed to offend delicate Victorian noses at the end of *Sordello*, Pound claims in the second section of his "obstetric verses" on *The Waste Land* that "he" (whether Pound or Eliot is open to interpretation) is affected by "Bleichstein's dank rotting clothes" and writes of:

> Breeding of animals,
> Humans and cannibals,
> But above all else of smells
> Without attraction[10]

Unlike Browning's relatively undifferentiated smells of nature and of human mortality, Pound's attraction and repulsion is to smells associated with Jews, bestiality, cannibalism, and sexuality—with the crossing of boundaries of all sorts. From evoking such smells to evoking a negative view of female sexuality is only a short step.

In the third section of the "obstetric verses," taking on these ambivalent smells—which are obviously *not* "without attraction"—Pound writes that his own poetry omits harsh "realities." Yet the very writing belies this claim.[11] At issue is something like the Pre-Raphaelite "retouching" of lower-class women, a touch that seems to carry the blinding threat of syphilitic infection:

---

manifesto on "Tactilism." The agressive antifeminism and assertive "virility" of the first futurist manifesto of 1909 is now part of a new program, rejecting "artificial paradises," "sexual perversion (or inversions)," and proposing an antidote to the postwar "malady" of "listlessness, a neurasthenia which is much too feminine, a hopeless pessimism, a febrile indecision of lost instincts and an absolute lack of will." Quoted and translated in Taylor, *Futurism*, 89–90.

9. Koestenbaum discusses "inversion" and the way the homosexual implications of the poem were revised away; see "*The Waste Land*," 124, 127–28.

10. From the manuscript in the Beinecke Library, quoted in Koestenbaum, 122.

11. Koestenbaum quotes the openly misogynist correspondence between Pound and John Quinn on the issue of female smells—which there are linked with death, Jews, and old clothes ("*The Waste Land*," 120–21). Pound's images compulsively identify—and reject the identification between—the ragpicker, the old clothes dealer, the Jew, and the woman. This image of strong smells and of old clothes resembles Browning's images for his poems in *Sordello* and *The Ring and the Book*, where he evokes "cast clothes sweetening in the sun"; but Pound's images, unlike Browning's, are full of fear and disgust.

Angelic hands with mother of pearl
Retouch the strapping servant girl,

The barman is to blinded him
Silenus bubling [*sic*] at the brim, (or burbling)
The glasses turn to chalices
In his fumbling analysis
And holy hosts of hellenists
Have numbed and honied his cervic cysts,
Despite his hebrew eulogists.

Balls and balls and balls again
Can not touch his fellow men.
His foaming and abundant cream
Has coated his world. the coat of a dream;
Or way that the upjut of his sperm
Has rendered his senses pachyderm.
Grudge not the oyster his stiff saliva
Envy not the diligent diver. et in aeternitate][12]

Here Pound plays his own phallic poetry off against Keats's poetic wine, Tennyson's "chalices" or Holy Grails, and Arnold's Hebrews and Hellenes.[13] The birthing of modernism may escape the invocations of the Middle Ages and of the classical past which characterized Victorian poetry. It omits Tennyson's King Arthur and Arnold's Socrates. But the engendering of modernism does not escape the dubious genderings of its predecessors.

In "Hugh Selwyn Mauberley," Pound calls up the double vision of the "old bitch" and the "faun" and reiterates the Pre-Raphaelite fascination with the lower-class woman or prostitute; here he parodies the same set of associations in compliment to Eliot. And yet these associations reveal the terrain of Pound's mental map—the same terrain we again see in his defense of vorticism and in his translation of

12. From the manuscript in the Beinecke Library, quoted in Koestenbaum, "*The Waste Land*," 122–23.
13. Not surprisingly, as Tennyson is Eliot's most important Victorian forebear, Pound is especially eager to eliminate Tennyson from his midwifery, particularly because Tennyson's *In Memoriam*, like *The Waste Land*, celebrates homosocial relationships. Koestenbaum argues that Pound objected to Eliot's epigraph from Conrad because "it records a man's fear of the dark continent" and would seem to be an "emasculated" cry. This is very likely true; at the same time, Pound's echo in his letter of the language of horror alludes to the horror of Tennysonian sonority: "(It also, to your horror probably, reads aloud very well. Mouthing out his OOOOOOze.)" Quoted in Koestenbaum, "*The Waste Land*," 125–26.

and comments on Remy de Gourmont. We must not, then, let our attention to Pound's modernist program distract us from the profound continuity among the sexual ideology of his predecessors, his own idealization/horror of what he took to be the feminine, and his notions of genius.

Even the program of vorticism as Pound discussed it before the war involved these elements, though with a simplistic rejection of the past that does not reflect his predominant practice. In a striking passage in Vladimir Mayakovski's magazine *Strelets* in 1915, Pound distinguished vorticism from futurism, saying, "Everything that has been created by nature and culture is for us a general chaos which we pierce with our vortex. We do not deny the past—we don't remember it. . . . The past and the future are two brothels created by nature. Art is periods of flight from these brothels, periods of sanctity. We are not futurists: the past and the future merge for us in their sentimental remoteness, in their projections onto an obscured and impotent perception. Art lives only by means of the present—but only that present which is not subject to nature, which does not suck up life."[14] The vorticist, or the modern artist, then, "pierces" the chaos of nature, the brothel of past and future, with his "vortex." Pound assumes that the sanctity of art does not imply sentimental remoteness. The very idea of art put forward here rests on a paradox fundamental to all dynamisms, vorticist, futurist, and fascist alike. Art may be sanctity—associated with the divine woman/goddess—but no sooner is it created than it must surely return, a ruined woman, to the brothel of history.

Pound puts forward a similar definition of art in the epilogue to Remy de Gourmont's *The Natural Philosophy of Love*, which he published in June 1921. Not wishing to write, he says, "an anti-feminist tract," Pound defends and expands on de Gourmont's curious elaboration of Aristotle's association of men with form, women with formlessness. This notion becomes a physiological absurdity in Pound's hypothesis that the male brain is something like a coagulation of sperm. Sperm are characterized by the elements of the modernist artistic program: hardness, form, experiment, inventiveness. Genius and invention work on a phallic model, with "man really the phallus or spermatozoide charging, head-on, the female chaos." In a famous sim-

---

14. Pound, interview with Zinaida Vengerova, "Angliiskie futuristy," *Strelets* 1 (1915): 93–94, unpublished translation by John Barnstead, quoted in Isaak, "Revolution of a Poetics," 163–64.

ile, Pound speculates that "even oneself has felt it, driving any new idea into the great passive vulva of London, a sensation analogous to the male feeling in copulation."[15]

The bathing of men's "cerebral tissues" in the "life sap" offers the possibility of making form from chaos; it is not clear whether Pound believes the same benefits accrue to women. If we can judge from his disappointment with London, we would have to say, probably not. In a rather tortured passage, he tries to be evenhanded and not give "disproportionate privilege" to the "spermatozoide"; he says he cannot "introspect" on the possible "cognitive role" of the "ovule." Indeed it is unclear whether he believes that women create their own "ovular" baths of cerebral matter or that, as in his London example, women receive an "ovular bath" from men. In any case he concludes with imagery that in his poetry always has a negative force: "where one woman appears to benefit by an alluvial clarifying, ten dozen appear to be swamped" ("Postscript," PD, 205).

Through a peculiar logic and following de Gourmont's interest in insect copulation, Pound concludes that women are linked with insects and utility, and men with experiment. This in turn leads to social criticism and to another of those moments when the modern and the antimodern in Pound's thought curiously coalesce. In a paragraph directly following a criticism of "money fetish" and "finance," he concludes: "In his growing subservience to, and adoration of, and entanglement in machines, in utility, man rounds the circle almost into insect life, the absence of flesh; and may have need even of horned gods to save him, or at least of a form of thought which permits them" ("Postscript," PD, 206). Here, curiously, women become associated sequentially with swamps, chaos, machines, and even the "absence of [male] flesh"—male artists in the modern age, clearly, risk castration and infertility.[16]

---

15. Pound, "Postscript to *The Natural Philosophy of Love* by Remy de Gourmont," PD, 204.

16. Lawrence Rainey's discussion of Pan is also apposite here; for it shows us the political and cultural context of Pound's embrace of the "pagan" and the roots of his poem's concern with fauns, with Pan, and with various mythological figures for the renewal of society and art. As Rainey shows, the figure of Pan in both Edwardian England and Europe could serve as a "cipher" for reuniting fragmented life, for aggressive sexuality, for claims to ancient wisdom, for primitivism of all sorts. Rainey comments on the connections among Pan myths, primitivism, and fascism. See *Ezra Pound and the Monument of Culture*, 50–56. I might add that Pan often served as a significant myth for homosocial society and homosexual eroticism and—sometimes at the same time—as a mythical expression of misogyny.

From this plight, Pound writes, asceticism, the desire to "super-think," is no escape; more hopeful, more sane, was the custom of seeking a gleam "in the tavern, Helen of Tyre, priestesses in the temple of Venus, in Indian temples, stray priestesses in the streets." Thus women represent desire and threat, the "gleam" and the possibility of castration, the natural seed bed of spermatic genius and the machine, the holy prostitute and the brothel of the past or future. The sane balance, Pound finds in a territory that would have pleased D. G. Rossetti: in Dante's metaphysics, in the "XIIth century love cult," and in Propertius's line, "Ingenium nobis ipsa puella fecit" ("Postscript," PD, 214). The fascination of courtly love for Pound, as for Rossetti, was its apparent resistance to the doubled and frightening prospect of female sexuality. By 1921, Rossetti's blessed damozel was certainly a stale cream puff, but she still lived in Pound's imagination along with her prostitute sister Jenny.

Fascism, the Feminine, and Utopia

This vision of the feminine and this gendered definition of art creating order from chaos are closely compatible with and provide passionate impetus for Pound's sympathy with Mussolini's fascism. The idealization of the feminine, like the glorification of masculine genius, provides the ground upon which Pound's utopian hopes are built. For him, as for many Europeans, World War I only intensified a need for creating utopian hopes and asserting order. For Pound personally, the war was a challenge to the very possibility of an epic poem as a creation of or response to order. The formative quality of "masculine" genius met with the futility of masculine and militarist heroism on a grand scale.[17] The contradiction, though insoluble, worked itself out through ever greater idealization and anathematization of nature and the feminine. Pound's embracing of Italian fascism and of anti-Semitism was obviously overdetermined—by his perception that it was congruent with his earlier economic ideas, by his desire to write an epic poem, by the attachment to Italy in a literary imagination formed by reading Browning, Rossetti, and the Roman, Provençal, and Italian poets. A key element in this emotional/intellectual complex is the engendering of poetic genius and its imposition of order on the troubling nature of the feminine. As Italian fascism promised an im-

---

17. The glorification of masculinity could only have been plunged still further into crisis by the postwar victory of women's suffrage in England and the United States.

position of economic and imperial order, so too it must have attracted
the poet because its domestic program seemed in many ways to match
his ideals. Mussolini's social program and fascist ideology were in
significant ways compatible with and extensions of the nineteenth-
century dualistic ideology of the feminine.

Antifeminism and the idealization of the feminine were deliberate
and significant policies in the Fascist political program. Although
Pound was not explicitly interested in the Fascist policy toward
women, he often praised Mussolini for his drive to increase grain production and for draining the Pontine marshes. These elements of the
Fascist program connect significantly with Pound's utopian faith in
natural fertility and with his belief in the power of male genius to
bring forth order and positive cultural fruit.

Under Mussolini's government, the battle for grain and the initia-
tion of public works were linked with ruralization; the attempt to
eliminate women from the paid labor force; and, through the encouragement of large families, the endeavor to increase population so as
to counter the larger populations of northern Europe.[18] As Lucia Birnbaum has pointed out, moreover, the Fascist policy of large families
dovetailed nicely with the conservative Catholic opposition to birth
control and emphasis on marriage for procreation. The eventual emphasis on natural rural productivity and on women as the moral guarantors and physical providers of heroes resonates with Pound's own
imagined utopia.[19] Pound was—and remained—critical of bourgeois
definitions of marriage and thus was uninterested in the conservative/
Fascist celebration of domesticity. He was not concerned, as the Fascist
government was, that women excel as homemakers. But in a more
fundamental sense, his way of idealizing the feminine was thoroughly
compatible with the Fascist program, particularly as it came to identify fecundity and heroism as the preeminent feminine and masculine
virtues. Male action and female fecundity were the antithetical notions
Pound derived from his predecessors. The Fascist slogan "War is to
man what motherhood is to woman" (Birnbaum, *Liberazione della*

18. See esp. Gregor, *Italian Fascism and Developmental Dictatorship*; De Grazia, *Culture of
Consent*; and Birnbaum, *Liberazione della Donna*.
19. For discussion of these issues see especially Birnbaum and De Grazia. Birnbaum
points out, following the work of Denis Mack Smith and others, that the Fascist
population policy failed. She estimates, following Smith, that abortions in Italy were
running as high as 30 percent of conceptions in 1929 (38). For obvious social and
economic reasons, the birth rate continued to fall during the Fascist era. One wonders how much the reality of this aspect of Italian life could have impinged on the
repeated imagery of abortion and miscegenation in the cantos of this period.

Donna, 34) only restates more crudely the Victorian division of masculine and feminine spheres.

The violence of this Fascist slogan and the obvious physical violence that accompanied fascism are what Pound strove to overlook or to recuperate in many of his pronouncements and especially in his poetry. The difficulties that fascist violence presented to his construction of a utopian ideal are evident in the convoluted arguments of his *Jefferson and/or Mussolini* and in the curious place of Fascist heroes and of figures like Ezzelino da Romano in *The Cantos.*

Without acknowledging the contradiction in his politics, Pound perhaps unintentionally foregrounds the issue in *Jefferson and/or Mussolini* by repeatedly defending contradiction itself; he refuses to be confined to "monolinear" logic, and he disparages syllogistic reasoning. As Gail McDonald has shown, such a defense of contradiction characterizes even Pound's earliest work and persists over the years (*Learning to Be Modern*). In *Jefferson and/or Mussolini* the principled defense of contradiction blends imperceptibly into a defense of Fascist violence. It is precisely in dealing with violence that the breakdown in Pound's logic is most apparent. In his one allusion to Mussolini's Blackshirts, Pound engages not in systematic defense of them but in anecdote. When he encountered them for the first time in Italy in the early 1920s, he says, he did not stand up, as those in the café with him did, for the "cavalieri della morte." And Pound adds, "Nobody hit me with a club and I didn't see any oil bottles" (51). Here, in an obvious effort to ignore contrary evidence, he argues from one limited case, on the basis of which he presents fascism as the will of the people, not the will of some, violently imposed on others.

The most obvious contradictions in Pound's discussion of fascism arise, not surprisingly, in Chapter 26 of *Jefferson and/or Mussolini,* which is simply called "Power." There Pound alludes negatively to Nietzsche and the "will to power," calling him "an ill-balanced hysterical teuto-pollak." The will to power and to enslave others may well be, Pound says, just "simple bossiness, bos, bovis, the bull." Unlike the overman (who is really, Pound implies, a dallying feminized hysterical intellectual) or the bully, the fascist hero recognizes that power is necessary, but the fascist is filled not with the will to power but "the will toward *order*" (99). In opposition to the fascist leader, the inferior professor "toddles in with twaddle about insanity and genius" (99). It is revealing that Pound himself engages here in the very "hysterical" tactics he attributes to Nietzsche. In *The Cantos,* moreover, Pound celebrates Mussolini in the terms he rejects here—

Mussolini is the bull, "bos" or "boss," and the epithet is obviously intended favorably (41.202–3; 74.425).

In *The Cantos*, still more than in *Jefferson and/or Mussolini*, power and violence cannot be openly acknowledged; yet they form the unspoken bases for order. In turn, order is the guarantor of utopia. Pound ends *Jefferson and/or Mussolini* by pairing "ORDER" with the Greek word for beauty, "ta kalon," on which his utopia is built. His aestheticization of politics and his utopian vision take beauty as their justification. In the profoundly disordered world in which *The Pisan Cantos* were written, beauty has become for Pound an elegiac leitmotif. The visions of order, utopia, and beauty are equated in *The Pisan Cantos*, while power and violence are largely ascribed to the U.S. Army. In the last half of Canto 74, introducing the Pisan sequence, the achievement of beauty furnishes a refrain: " 'beauty is difficult,' sd/ Mr Beardsley" (74.458). Beauty is threatened by disorder and by the poet's need to represent a disordered world.

The Pisan Cantos, in common with the poem as a whole, are built on a utopian vision based at once in an idealization of nature and the feminine, in an idealization of order and beauty, and in a willed (or wishful) transformation of violence into order. The agency of this transformation is at once the poet's vision and his "masculine" quality of bringing ideas into action. To bring together the pieces of a broken culture, to act as a ragpicker, a collector, a translator, the poet must directly engage in a violent world; as Pound pieces together that world, he performs his own violent collocation of particulars, all the while claiming that, fundamentally, order is beauty. Epic coherence and Pound's own historical needs require that the tentative and historicized patterns of the existential historicist be transformed in the light of a utopian vision.

To focus on order, forgetting the violence ultimately guaranteeing it, is the great temptation of Pound's utopian vision itself. It is easier to submit to Pound's utopian vision in *The Cantos* than to his explicitly political analysis. Even though few Anglophone readers defend Social Credit, much less fascism, many find an appealing cultural comfort in Pound's invocation of goddesses and in his metaphorical layerings of goddesses and mortal women. Under the influence of Pound's visionary rhetoric, the oscillation between utopian vision and disillusion, between order and lawlessness, love and violence can seem, for a few moments, to be halted.

Despite Pound's visionary rhetoric, we must read against the grain even as we encounter moments in *The Cantos* of undeniable beauty.

What would it mean, indeed, to "build the city of Dioce whose terraces are the colour of stars" (74.439)? Perhaps the most direct, certainly the most frightening, answer to this question can be found in the poems and notes immediately preceding *The Pisan Cantos*, particularly in the Italian cantos, which for many years were absent from the collected cantos and which have only recently been translated. Cantos 72 and 73 and the notes for subsequent Italian cantos are, as Massimo Bacigalupo has contended in "Ezra Pound's Cantos 72 and 73," the prelude to the Pisan sequence; in part because of their political occasion—written for publication in Italian during the period of the Salò Republic—these cantos present most clearly the contradictions implicit in the tropes of the Pisan sequence.

Canto 72 is simply titled "Presence." The title alludes to the presence of dead Fascist heroes, to spirits who appear to the poet, and to the Fascist practice of answering "present" for the spirits of dead soldiers. It is a reprise in a fascist context of *The Cantos'* own beginning. The spirits Pound calls include Sigismundo Malatesta, Tommaso Marinetti, and Ezzelino da Romano. Malatesta is only invoked, but both Marinetti and Ezzelino promise to avenge the losses suffered by the Fascists; Marinetti seeks a body in which to return to battle, and Romano promises future conquest. Perhaps the most disturbing figure here is Romano—who also stands for Mussolini—and whom Browning had used in *Sordello* as the ultimate exemplar of cruelty and tyranny. Here Pound glosses over Ezzelino's dreadful past: " 'Io son quel' 'Ezzelino che no crede' / Che il mondo fu creato da un ebreo. / Se d'altro scatto io fossi reo / poco t'importa ora" (72.429). As Pound translated the lines in the undated version recently printed in the *Paris Review*, "I am that Ezzolino who didn't believe / The world was made by a Jew, / and other outbreaks, that don't matter now" ("Canto 72," 314). Bacigalupo renders the lines less colloquially: "If I am guilty of other sudden gestures / this does not concern you now" ("Annotated Translation," 14). Ezzelino is transformed, finally, into a "paternal" figure who would lead the younger—or more historically belated—poet into the hope that "the regiments and the banners will return" (Pound, "Canto 72," 315). In this canto directly lamenting Fascist defeats in Italy, Ezzelino's tyranny apparently needs no further justification. His spirit is summoned because of its strength.

Canto 73 is narrated by the hero as poet. Guido Cavalcanti returns from the heaven of Venus to tell the story of a young fascist heroine. The canto is structured as a dream vision, again harking back to the earliest versions of the first cantos. The ruthlessness of the Blackshirts is celebrated and has its own continuity with that of such predecessors as Ezzelino da Romano. Whereas Browning's Sordello perished in his inability to make Machiavellian compromises with such tactics as Ezzelino's, Pound's Cavalcanti has no such problems. In Browning's poem, Sordello's love of Palma (Pound's Cunizza) is compromised by her connection to various forms of opportunism and oppression (and Sordello finds that Palma's political opponents have serious shortcomings too); in Pound's Italian cantos, political violence is not an issue but, under the circumstances, a necessity.[20]

Cavalcanti defines love as inseparable from the terror of war. He comes from the heaven of Venus and from Pound's memory, and he calls himself the poet "whom you loved / for my proud spirit / And the clarity of my intellect" (Bacigalupo, "Annotated Translation," 16). The fascist heroine whom he celebrates is likewise characterized as a "proud spirit," and her heroism lies in her suicidal mission. She figures as the modern version of Guido's "pasturella," and she sings, Guido says, of "love / without needing to go to heaven." In the canto, Canadian soldiers have come into Rimini. They ask directions of the girl, who has just been raped by others "of their rabble," and she leads them into the field where her brother has dug holes for mines. The soldiers and the girl die violently near the "Temple of the lovely Ixotta," near the half-ruined Tempio so dear to Pound's heart.

Although Tim Redman argues forcefully that this canto contributes nothing particularly new to Pound's poem and is not, in the context of his work, unusually shocking, I believe it does offer the baldest, the most direct expression of the ambivalences and contradictions underlying Pound's utopian vision. The girl stands as a metaphor for the destruction and rebirth of Italy. As Lawrence Rainey puts it, "The Canadian troops are portrayed as agents of cultural rape—their 'literal' or physical rape of the young girl merely externalizes the motif of cultural violence—whose aim is 'to demolish what little remains of Rimini,' to violate 'the mysterious bed of Ixotta.' " The girl's action "turns her into a second Isotta, a figure who promises another Renaissance of the fatherland and the fascist dream. . . . Yet if the inspiring figure of Isotta is the epitome of 'love' and 'purity,' and if she is the model to whom the country girl of 1944 is assimilated when her destructive deed is characterized as one of 'pure love,' then clearly we

20. Sordello's death in Browning's poem may be read either as liberal disillusionment or as the outcome when reforming compromise is impossible. Certainly it represents Sordello's inability to combine art and politics. Pound's Cavalcanti, in the Italian cantos at least, cheerfully risks equating beauty with suffering and violence.

confront a core of ideas that is profoundly ambivalent. What sort of love is this?" (*Monument of Culture*, 217).

Obviously it is a "love" with its violence undisguised. Pound's celebration of this story is still more disturbing in light of Rainey's disclosure that Pound's source was a propaganda piece fabricated out of whole cloth, probably by the Italian newspaper where Pound read it. With Rainey, we must, in default of other evidence, believe that Pound assumed the authenticity of the story, but this assumption simply underscores the significance of violence in Pound's utopian vision. This creation of fascist propaganda, it would appear, seemed utterly convincing to him.[21]

A key question in the cultural and ethical reading of this story is why—for purposes of Italian propaganda and for Pound's purposes—the girl must be raped. Clearly, by being raped, she becomes a victim and martyr, a stance Pound himself adopts when he identifies with Cassandra and other victims in *The Pisan Cantos*. For propaganda purposes, the Canadians are shown to be wholly ruthless and to have perpetrated against innocent Italy a terrible crime. For Pound's purposes, the rape of the girl becomes a crime against nature which evokes a reciprocating—and thus justified—violence. Like usury and unlike the stories of divine rape in the cantos, this rape stands against natural order and increase. At one remove from its immediate political context, however, the story has a structure readily apparent to readers of nineteenth-century literature: the rescue of the victimized or prostituted woman whose purity is guaranteed by her violent death.[22]

This violence makes it possible for the poem to rescue the woman into heroism, into the cultural memory. In the process, the girl is transformed from a simple victim into a holy victim. The shepherdess—because she is violated and sacrificed—embodies the meaning of culture even amid its ruins. She can then be assimilated to the holy prostitute invoked in Pound's postscript to Remy de Gourmont; for she becomes like the "stray priestesses in the streets" and the "priestesses of the temple of Venus" who save the imperiled man from his own ignominious death. The girl becomes the savior of Italian masculinity, of Italian strength—which in September 1944 is threatened with im-

---

21. It was convenient, moreover, for Pound that the soldiers described in his source were Canadian, thus allowing violence to be deflected from U.S. soldiers. This is not to imply that the Allies were perfectly pure and the Fascists perfectly evil; it is such simple dichotomies that make propaganda successful.

22. Two striking examples are Browning's Pompilia in *The Ring and the Book* and Hardy's Tess Durbeyfield.

mediate defeat by the allies—and she does so precisely because she is violated by men who threaten Italy and is then revenged on these men with the help of her brother, with the help of the propagandist who invented this story, and with the help of the poet who chose to have his own alter ego, Cavalcanti, celebrate her. In regarding her as a heroine, the poet and Cavalcanti can both celebrate and diminish her. She is eroticized when Cavalcanti declares that despite his years she made him hunger for love, and she is diminished when, despite the violence of her death, she is lightly laid to rest with the diminutive "Che brava pupa! che brava pupetta!" (73.434).[23]

In Canto 73, the heroine is identified with Isotta and thus linked with the Tempio and with Malatesta. In the notes to further Italian cantos which become an important basis for *The Pisan Cantos*, she is implicitly connected to Cunizza. Pound returns there to the figure of Cunizza, who appears in Canto 72, and to goddesses he associates with her. The notes make clear a link between Cunizza and the Italian shepherdess. Cunizza defends Ezzelino, saying, "I call him a tyrant / but he never betrayed his own / my great brother" (Bacigalupo, "Annotated Translation," 23). The shepherdess and her brother become, metaphorically, the modern equivalents of Cunizza and Ezzelino, Cunizza who in old age freed her slaves and Ezzelino whose authority was based in his unusual cruelty. Violence and beauty are indissolubly linked.

Beauty and Violence in the Italian Notes

As Bacigalupo points out, in the notes to further Italian cantos Pound moves away "from the immediate political concerns of Cantos 72 and 73, to a sort of mythical-erotic-ecstatic stance prelusive to certain passages of the Pisan Cantos" ("Annotated Translation," 23). Yet even as Pound moves into the "erotic-ecstatic" stance in the notes, leaving explicit contemporary political reference behind, the contours of his idealization remain congruent with the more explicitly political

23. Bacigalupo translates this line, "A fine gal! A fine little gal!" ("Annotated Translation," 18). It is interesting to compare Yeats's analysis of political sacrifice in "September 1913" and "Easter 1916." In the first poem, the "wild geese" are not diminished but celebrated when Yeats writes, "They weighed so lightly what they gave." Pound works at something of this effect as well, but the effect is compromised—not only by an antifascist reader—but also by the eroticization of the heroine. Yeats views political sacrifice as more compromised and compromising of human capacities in "Easter 1916" even as he claims a "terrible beauty is born" (*Collected Poems*, 107, 178).

poetry that has preceded it. The female figures on whom the erotic-ecstatic vision turns curiously combine motherhood, purity, militancy, eros, and the naïve humility of the victim. The female figure, in short, becomes the locus of multiple projections. In these notes, which precede *The Pisan Cantos*, the female is the virgin mother, driven out by war from her sanctuaries (as in Canto 80), who has her little boy with her; she is the goddess Cytheraea, Venus, the "mother of Eros" who laments Adonis; she is Kannon and Kore; she is the presence of "eyes"—Cunizza's eyes—belonging to a woman in uniform; she is the guardian of cocoons and spinning; and she is Mary, the Star of the Sea. The figure of Mary is to be understood, Pound emphasized, as a European not an "oriental" presence. In his unpublished essay "European Paideuma" (1939) he argued, "The sea-board shrines of the Madonna delle Grazie are NOT oriental. They have most emphatically NOT come from Palestine. . . . The Madonna of the Italian peasant is to my knowledge a LOCAL (raumlich) divinity" (quoted in Bacigalupo, "Annotated Translation," 37 n. 140).

By identifying Mary with the spirit of Europe in this way, Pound can have the woman's voice in the Italian notes claim its identity with Io and with Europa. She thus claims she is both violated and pure, raped and somehow holy. At the same time she claims for the poet that art will again "be clean" with the Fascist axe that the gods will bring back to him (Bacigalupo, "Annotated Translation," 37). In these notes, as in *The Pisan Cantos* themselves, the implicit politics of the "erotic-ecstatic" vision are not far to seek. And as in *The Pisan Cantos* and other sequences of the poem, the female figure is dual, both positive and negative, loved and feared. The goddess may not be "oriental" or from "Palestine," but she inevitably brings forth her opposite:

> I am not Sophia, in fact I fear her
> hieratic / mosaic'd /
> Sophia Hecate I also don't know / never crowned,
>   in the high sphere
>   hieratic / distant state: harms, cuts: terror.
>   (38)

Mary/Io/Europa deny a connection to Sophia/Hecate. If Pound is answering Yeats's questioning in "Leda and the Swan" ("Did she put on his knowledge with his power?"), the answer would seem to be no. Even of Cunizza/Cytheraea we are told in these notes, "The more beautiful she is, the greater the peril," a feeling that leads directly to the thought of the "serpent, neschek; ruined paradise" and to an allusion to the donation of Constantine as the propagation of "poison" and "pandemonium."

The Italian notes, then, provide a crucial link between the explicit violence of the Italian cantos, 72 and 73, and the visionary evocations of beauty in *The Pisan Cantos*. The "erotic-ecstatic" vision requires its holy victims; its grandeur is predicated on the violence it can contain.

Both in the Italian cantos and in the notes that preceded the Pisan sequence, we see Pound grappling with the political and ethical implications of violence, the violence of war and the violence at the heart of his own erotic-ecstatic vision. The violence figured as feminine comes from the same dualism that is figured politically as purity versus impurity, order versus chaos in *The Pisan Cantos*. In Canto 80, Pound declares:

> the problem after any revolution is what to do with
> your gunmen
> as old Billyum found out in Oireland
>   in the Senate, Bedad! or before then
>   Your gunmen thread on moi drreams
>   O woman shapely as a swan,
> Your gunmen tread on my dreams
>
>   (80.510)

Erotic passion, political order, hieratic knowledge—how can they be one?

Balance and Conflict

The extraordinary tensions of *The Cantos* and of Pound's earlier poetry may be understood in terms of literary history, tropes, political and economic thought, gender and sexuality, or Pound's particular historical situation. Each of these analytic paths leads the critic to explicate contradictions and to describe a poetic practice constructed on a dualist understanding of history and of nature. Whether Pound's desired equipoise be guaranteed by poetic tradition made new, by an ecstatic-erotic vision of nature and the feminine, or by political authority bringing economic and natural law into their true harmony, such balance is achieved at a violent cost. Balance constantly threatens to give way to chaos.

Again and again, *The Cantos* themselves create metaphors that expose this precariousness, and again and again they invoke the balance that Pound's dualism requires but can seldom supply. In *The Pisan Cantos*, Pound looks for Aristotelian balance and finds it, as in other instances, in Chinese history. The great man, the fit subject for epic, is

> lord of his work and master of utterance
> > who turneth his word in its season and shapes it
> > Yaou chose Shun to longevity
> who seized the extremities and the opposites
> holding true course between them
> shielding men from their errors
> cleaving to the good they had found
> holding empire as if not in a mortar with it
> > nor dazzled thereby
> wd/ have put the old man, *son père* on his shoulders
> > and gone off to some barren seacoast
> > > > > (74.456)

Balance does not come from compromise but from seizing "the extremities and the opposites." In *The Pisan Cantos*, balance must be pushed back into antiquity, into a culture so remote as to make it seem possible, or it must arise out of memory—and risk the treacheries of the chaotic present.

So at the end of the Pisan sequence, Pound presents from personal and literary memory a series of vignettes that, unlike his political pronouncements, capture the precariousness of his dualism:

> Incense to Apollo
>
> > Carrara
> > > snow on the marble
> > snow-white
> > > against stone-white
> > on the mountain
> > and as who passed the gorges between sheer cliffs
> > as it might be by, is it the Garonne?
> > > where one walks into Spagna
> > that T'ao Ch'ien heard the old Dynasty's music
> > > as it might be at the Peach-blossom Fountain
> > where are smooth lawns with the clear stream
> > between them, silver, dividing,

and at Ho Ci'u destroyed the whole town
for hiding a woman, Κύθηρα δelvá
and as Carson the desert rat said
"when we came out we had
    80 thousand dollars' worth"
        ("of experience")
that was from mining

                  (84.552)

In the imagined utopia of the old dynasty, the peaceful land is ordered, divided by the clear stream; even this order can only be recalled by T'ao Ch'ien as the land of his lost youth. The modern poet
himself may discriminate whiteness—he may tell snow from marble—
but he may discriminate these purities only in a more dangerous and
precarious position. Threatened by dark Venus, by violence, by the
manipulation of money, he must pass through gorges, between the
sheer cliffs, in the landscape of the sublime. Actaeon and Vidal fore-
shadow this story from the beginning; betrayed by vision and by art
they are devoured by the dogs they themselves have brought to the
chase.

Chapter 7

Postromantic Epic in the
Bone Shop of History

Homer's Epos, it is remarked, is like a Bas-Relief sculpture: it does
not conclude, but merely ceases. Such, indeed, is the Epos of Universal History itself.
                —Thomas Carlyle, "Finis," *The French Revolution*

When we read even the visionary moments of *The Cantos* ethically
and politically, attending to their rhetorical claims, it becomes clear
that the poem arises from a radically dualist understanding of history
and of nature. Assertions of coherence struggle against an atomistic
multiplication of particulars. The metonymies of law bring with them
the chaos of the illicit; the metaphorical mappings from one domain
onto another devolve into the idiography of individual forms. Pound's
vision of nature and culture as a harmonious whole is threatened by
female fertility and by the course of history itself.

Even before the epic designs of *The Cantos* were apparent, Pound's
art was shaped by a pedagogic dedication to remaking the tradition
of poetry in English. The tremendous energy that later went into both
art and economic schemes was focused in his early years on an essentially hierarchical project of ordering a new poetic canon. This project, especially because it grew from and required his attention to his
own poetry, was itself conceived in terms of oppositions and contradictions. Like Wordsworth before him, Pound hoped to make poetry
new by redefining the relationships of prose and poetry, society and

art. In this effort, he took Robert Browning as his most significant poetic predecessor. To argue for a prose tradition in verse, he aligned Browning with Flaubert as the most important hinges between his own work and the past. Even so, Pound's taste was crucially shaped by the more pronounced aestheticism of the Pre-Raphaelites, Swinburne, and the Georgian poets. This double heritage formed the structure of his canonical arguments and shaped the practices of translation, imitation, and parody through which he made his own art. Especially in his early imitations, Pound practiced an aesthetic of contradiction, creating poems in markedly different voices, sometimes within the same text. As Louis Martz put it, his formation as an artist was an *oscillation* into the future.[1] This oscillation did not stop with the drafts of the early cantos but continued to characterize Pound's mature and more accomplished art.

Creating a canon, ordering the relationship of poetry and prose, was considerably easier than remaking the relationship of society and art; yet for Pound, as for his nineteenth-century predecessors, these concerns entailed each other. Like Browning's hero Sordello, Pound struggled to yoke "man and bard," to work out at once a poetic and political mission. This challenge was made all the more crucial by his epic ambitions. In taking on a genre that promised social as well as poetic coherence, one that promised to implicate itself in—if only by constructing it—some common ground of belief, Pound was forced to reckon with the legacies of historicism. His dedication to the possibility of epic itself led him toward an increasing concern with radical social transformation; the crisis of epic authorship became a crisis of authority.

Pound's contradictions are not an aberration—and we need to study him not because of a peculiar psyche, a kind of increasing paranoia and violence limited to his own personal situation. Nor is his significance limited to his important achievements in the technique of English free verse. If ever a person lived and breathed the contradictions of art as he inherited and fostered them, it was Pound. Less than many artists—less even than his friends William Carlos Williams and T. S. Eliot for example—did he have a life outside of and apart from his work as a writer. If Pound's career is not precisely a matter of life imitating art, it certainly displays a circular pattern of the exigencies of art shaping a life that in turn becomes the focus for art. The con-

---

1. Louis Martz uses the term *oscillation* in his introduction to Pound's *Collected Early Poems* (xvi).

tradictions implicit in his definition of poetry are writ large as his own lived contradictions. Pound's story—his poem and his life—presents a paradigm of one significant way of being an artist in the first half of our century. He had, for numerous reasons, the need to push cultural contradictions to their limits—in the process revealing their contours in less dramatic circumstances than his own.

Pound's fundamentally dualist view of history—coupled with his insistence on being, completely, the artist—made the compromises of liberal democracy impossible for him to imagine. His was a radical vision of social ills—from munitions manufacture to mass culture. Increasingly he viewed the poem not as the compromised and partially marginal comment on the world but as the privileged and possibly prophetic ordering of history. Order and chaos increasingly came to be figured in terms of the legitimate and heroic versus the illegitimate and filthy. As the efforts of heroes—and of the poem—faced continuing obstacles, the poem made stronger and stronger appeals to natural and social law. It made ever greater demands on the reader's belief even as it created its own.

Nietzsche observed of Thomas Carlyle that he confused the will to truth with the will to belief, and the same can be said of Pound. Repeatedly we see in *The Cantos* truth abandoned in the need for belief, belief presented as truth. The conflation is necessary if the poem is not to give up on the essentially romantic legacy of guaranteeing belief in the face of historical disaster—both the disasters of history and the disasters of historicism.

Romanticism, Modern Rootlessness, and the Necessities of Myth

This view of Pound's attempts to guarantee belief suggests that, despite his relative success in avoiding a family romance of precursors, I agree with those who maintain that romanticism and modernism are much more closely related than is sometimes implied in a differential periodization. Indeed the visionary moments of *The Cantos* invoke an idealism that is central to what Jerome McGann has called the romantic ideology. Romantic ideology in English poetry emerged in the epistemological crisis of historicism—and the historical crises of the French Revolution and Napoleonic Wars. In such crisis, McGann says, "Romantic Nature and Imagination" emerged as "touchstones of stability and order" (*Romantic Ideology*, 145). Poetry can make claims to reconnect human subjectivity and history and to restore meaning in social relationships by positing meaning in the natural world. As Wordsworth put it, poetry shows us the "love of nature" leading to the "love of man." Readers of *The Prelude*, however, have generally been compelled to admit that precisely this linkage between nature and society is the connection the poem cannot completely make. McGann shows how the romantic reliance on nature and imagination was an ideological claim (in the face of a compromised and compromising reality) from the first; this is so even for Byron, who most seems to resist romantic ideology. McGann's early temptation in reading Byron was precisely the temptation of Pound's early readers, who—influenced by the classicizing rhetoric of T. E. Hulme and Eliot and sometimes Pound himself—read only rejection of romantic ideology into the construction of modernism. McGann says of Byron what might equally be said of Pound: "What we can miss are Byron's Romantic illusions, the ideas and the ideologies which lead him to believe that they can be transcended in imaginative thought, 'our last and only place / Of refuge' " (*Childe Harold* 4.127). Finally, McGann concludes, Byron's poetry discovers what all romantic poems repeatedly discover: that there is "no place of refuge, not in desire, not in the mind, not in imagination" (145). Like Byron, Pound posits contradiction overcome in imagination; like Byron, he cannot give up his romantic illusions.

As *The Cantos* make visionary and prophetic claims, Pound attempts to posit an end to contradiction between order and chaos, beauty and power. Browning's version of Aeschylus's Helen invited the reader to "mark the suture" between beauty and violence; *The Cantos* attempt to erase the suture by means of imaginative integration. Order, finally, is claimed to be "now in the mind indestructible." In the visionary and explicitly Neoplatonic sequence in *Rock-Drill*, Pound calls, in the fashion of romantic ideology, on both nature and imagination, hoping that elegy (the poem when "there is no refuge") can be transformed into celebration:

> And there be who say there is no road to felicity
>   tho' swallows eat celandine
>   "before my eyes into the aether of Nature"
> The water-bug's mittens
>   petal the rock beneath,
> The natrix glides sapphire into the rock-pool.
>   NUTT overarching

"mand'io a la Pinella"
>   sd/ Guido
>   "a river",
"Ghosts dip in the crystal,
>   adorned"
That the tone change from elegy
>   "Et Jehanne"
>   (the Lorraine girl)
A lost kind of experience?
>   scarcely,
O Queen Cytherea,
>   che 'l terzo ciel movete.
>   (91.630–31)

Here and in the later cantos, Pound hopes that "the tone [can] change from elegy" to celebration, from lament to triumph.

But in their fragmentation—and in their truthfulness about fragmentation—*The Cantos* cannot fully enact such a movement. Fragmentation is figured formally in Pound's so-called ideogrammic method and ideologically, as in earlier romanticism, in the desire to heal what is posited as a division between word and thing. For Pound, much as for Emerson or Wordsworth, theories of language were as fully about the poet's historical situation as they were about language itself.

This linkage is clear in Pound's seizing on Fenollosa's work to further his own approach to language and culture. Fenollosa undoubtedly read Chinese in light of the nineteenth-century predisposition to regard the most primitive language as the most poetic, that is, to construct paradigms involving the decay or disease of language which only poetry can redeem. In Fenollosa's and Pound's view, Chinese represented a form of language closer to nature than modern English.[2] Chinese, Fenollosa claimed, carried with it visible etymology; it exhibited its history and culture, the true metaphors of its original force: "The very soil of Chinese life seems entangled in the roots of its speech." The ideogram brings together nature, memory, and history.

2. Fenollosa wished to show "how poetical is the Chinese form and how close to nature," and he claimed that neither nature nor the Chinese language have grammar— nor do the early roots of English. "All nations," he argued, "have written their strongest and most vivid literature before they invented a grammar" ("Chinese Written Character," 15). Chinese, he believed, was closer to action and further from abstraction than modern English.

It has in itself the quality that Wordsworth (among others) sought in poetry; it binds together humanity, nature, the vicissitudes of history. Fenollosa believed that, for writers of modern English, only poetic language had the same force as the ordinary Chinese character ("Chinese Written Character," 25).

Fenollosa's romantic program was acceptable to Pound not because it simply reiterated a romantic ideology of language but because it retained the earlier structure of feeling associated with the social dislocation of the poet and poetry while giving it a new language—both literally and figuratively. Chinese literature itself offered Pound a new and supposedly radically different language. Moreover, to describe Chinese, Fenollosa chose metaphors of action and objectivity that appealed to Pound's own need in this period to talk poetics in scientific and mechanical terminology. Fenollosa's vitalist metaphors were equally appealing—Chinese, he said in a suspiciously Poundian phrase, "retains the primitive sap, it is not cut and dried like a walking stick" ("Chinese Written Character," 25). Fenollosa was too close to English and American romanticism to celebrate a mechanical metaphor for itself, but his glorification of science, and his pseudoscience of Chinese etymology, appear to rescue science and poetry from the ravages of mere utility.

Chinese characters in this view then are close to nature, are vital, are an objective relation of particulars, and are capable of carrying their own etymology—cultural and historical memory—within themselves. They are valuable—like Wordsworth's poetic diction or Emerson's poetry—as an antidote, not to science but to what critics since at least 1790 had been calling an unpoetic age.

The divorce between word and thing, seen as a problem, is the effect of the bone shop of history; it is an expression of the poet's fear of self-alienation from his work, his fear of alienation from his audience, and his fear that his condition is a general one. These fears are born in the response to the commodification of writing and the cultural gendering of writing and reading. They are expressed directly in such prose pieces of Pound's as "Patria Mia" (1912, SP) and "Murder by Capital" (1933, SP) and indirectly in Fenollosa's metaphors for language. Fenollosa admired Chinese for something like organic form, and he saw the converse in modern English: "Our ancestors built the accumulations of metaphor into structures of language and into systems of thought. Languages today are thin and cold because we think less and less into them. We are forced, for the sake of quickness and sharpness, to file down each word to its narrowest edge of meaning.

Nature would seem to have become less like a paradise and more and more like a factory. . . . A late stage of decay is arrested and embalmed in the dictionary" ("Chinese Written Character," 24). Nature and language have become a knife factory; grammarians and philologists are the morbid anatomists of the knives' own makers.

Pound's emphasis on language clear and hard and his defense with Ford Madox Ford of the prose tradition in verse would seem to promote the very language Fenollosa distrusted. Yet Pound's emphasis on "presentation," on language making its referents and its resonance immediate, allowed him to find in the Chinese character both precision and connection with nature. Thus the Chinese character, he believed, carries with it (perhaps contradictorily) both nature and history.

It is in this context that we should read Pound's modernism as a postromanticism, with equal weight on both sides of that hybrid term. As we have seen with respect to Pater's "real illusions," the celebrated modernist mythical method partakes of the same problematic. Fenollosa described the universe conveyed in Chinese poetry and destroyed in the knife factory of modern Western languages as a universe "alive with myth." In this view, Chinese is a language in which word is peculiarly united to thing and things are united to each other (via nature) in mythological coherence. Through ideogram the arbitrary historical sign and the detached thing (the commodity produced for its utility or profitability) can be transformed into parts of an ordered whole. Fenollosa's Chinese character and Pound's "ideogram" serve the same function as Wordsworth's ordinary "language of men," Coleridge's "muthos," or Pater's "real illusions." Ideograms are myths in small compass.

In one of the most acute commentaries on the place of myth in modernism, Terry Eagleton describes modernist myth as both the symptom of a "reified social condition" and a "convenient instrument for making sense of it" (*Ideology of the Aesthetic*, 318). Myth furnishes the schemes that "elicit unity from chaos." As Eagleton succinctly puts it, the modernist defense of myth turns on the hope that

it is myth which can provide the missing mediations between the over-formalized on the one hand and the myopically particular on the other, between that which threatens to elude language in its abstract universality and that which slips through the net of discourse in its ineffable uniqueness. Myth would then figure as a return of the Romantic symbol, a reinvention of the Hegelian "concrete universal" in which every phenomenon is secretly inscribed by a universal law, and any time, place or identity pregnant with the burden of the cosmic whole. If this can be achieved, then a history in crisis might once more be rendered stable and significant, reconstituted as a set of hierarchical planes and correspondences. (319)

This nice symmetry, as Eagleton shows, is easier to posit than to achieve. As he goes on to imply, modernisms may be discriminated on the basis of the claims they make for myth. T. S. Eliot may be confident of disclosing through myth a pattern in reality; Joyce ironizes his own myth making and thus reveals modernist myth itself as essentially arbitrary artifice. The "hermeneutical violence" of yoking Bloom to Ulysses is readily apparent. For Eagleton this symbolic system yoking myth to daily particulars operates on the same logic as that of the "commodity form which is partly responsible for the chaos it hopes to transcend" (319–20).

Building on Eagleton's analysis, I posit that the demands myths make on readers' beliefs also allow us to discriminate among modernisms. Both Joyce's and Pound's myths show the essential artifice of their construction; both are bulwarks against being overwhelmed by atomized particulars—be they commodities per se or historical data. But "hermeneutical violence" (not to mention rhetorical violence) seems to me a more precise description of Pound's mythical method than of Joyce's; for Pound's hermeneutic is driven by a will to believe, Joyce's by a will to play. Joyce's mythological ironies, like Browning's historical ones, keep the text's meanings in motion.[3] Browning's historicized myths derive belief from skepticism (as in the Pope's monologue) or sometimes skepticism from belief (as in "Bishop Blougram's Apology"). Browning has the liberal's tendency, moreover, to avoid postulating new sources of social coherence. Joyce's mythicized history of Dublin also refuses coherence as a virtue, particularly as any posited social coherence must come out of the oppositions of British colonialism. For Pound, however, myth entails not play and skepticism but coherence and belief. It is an answer to historicist tendencies toward aestheticism and empiricism and to the destabilizing potential of irony. Historicist skepticism cannot, in itself, ground Pound's claims to epic coherence.

Pound's myth goes to great lengths to disclaim its own arbitrariness even as it reveals it. His rhetorical and political violence are generated

3. The best study of nineteenth-century mythical method in literature is Shaffer, "*Kubla Khan.*"

in the essentially ideological effort of concealing the relentlessly de-mythologizing force of history. The obvious *bricolage* of his myths, the patently willed belief in the poem's visions, can only claim cultural centrality by means of an equally strong will to power. For Pound, a new mythological, linguistic, and cultural unity can be forged despite atomistic particularity and historical flux; but such unity requires a hero as artist.

The poem's effort is to claim the inevitability of the very particulars it shows to be arbitrary. This contradictory situation obtains not only with historical particulars and with myth but also with the poem's Chinese characters. Though the poem, following Fenollosa, claims for Chinese characters the status of right naming and pictographic con-nections to things, for the vast majority of Pound's readers, Chinese characters serve simply as an additional source of estrangement.[4]

As both Eagleton and Raymond Williams have indicated, the es-sential arbitrariness of the modern mythical method—and the gap that makes Joyce's irony and Pound's ragpicking possible—is also founded in the deracination of modern artists. Although Wordsworth could praise the healing possibilities of local particularities and though Wil-liam Carlos Williams made a similar move, even this localism was not possible for Pound.[5] Instead of celebrating the local, Pound trans-formed nostalgic desire that arose through deracination by replacing the local with a variety of exotica—Chinese characters, Neoplatonic and occult lore, Gourmont's peculiar physiology of love, even Italy itself.[6]

4. A similar ideological structure lies in the persistence of those Pound critics who insist that Chinese is primarily pictographic rather than logographic, despite the great pre-ponderance of linguistic evidence to the contrary. Pound himself in some measure persisted similarly, though during the middle part of his career when the controversy was important in Sinological circles, he was as interested in larger problems of trans-lation as in the structure of characters. For the controversy that refuses to die see Gordon, "Pound's Chinese." Gordon is responding to Chang Yao-Xin's article of 1988; clearly he thinks that Pound's visionary claims and the pictographic nature of Chi-nese characters are mutually dependent. He laments that the phonetic explanation of characters "obliterates the 'entire' green world" from Chinese and "reduces it to a wasteland of abstractions and meaningless phonetics" (199). For an earlier version of the controversy among Sinologists see the arguments between Herlee Creel and Peter A. Boodberg, for example, in Boodberg, " 'Ideography' or Iconolatry."
5. Responding to a similar situation, William Carlos Williams took a different tack, defending the local and particular and criticizing Eliot and Pound as the "dogs" who ran out after the rabbits—in their European exile. Not surprisingly, in *Paterson*, Wil-liams came to defend both local particularity and the force of memory; and from the first he was less troubled than Pound by the possibilities of disorder.
6. Of course Italy has served English-speaking writers for years as the canvas on which

Pound shared both the deracination of many modern artists and the linguistic specificity of that situation. As Raymond Williams puts it, not only were many modernist and avant-garde movements "located in the great metropolitan centres" but many of their members

> were immigrants into these centres, where in some new ways all were strangers. Language, in such situations, could appear as a new kind of fact: either simply as "medium," aesthetic or instrumental, since its naturalized continuity with a persistent social settlement was unavailable; or, of course, as system: the distanced, even the alien fact. . . . The old hegemony of capital over its provinces was extended over a new range of disparate, often wholly alien and exotic, cultures and languages. (*Politics of Modernism*, 78)

When language itself is perceived not as natural but as an alien system, it is not a language of "a people" but

> the material of groups, agencies, fractions, specific works, its actual society and complex of writers and game-players, translators and sign-writers, interpreters and makers of paradoxes, cross-cultural innovators and jokers. The actual social processes, that is to say, involved not only an Apollinaire, a Joyce, an Ionesco, a Beckett, but also, as Joyce recognized in Bloom, many thousands of extempore dealers and negotiators and persuaders: moreover not even, reliably, these as distinct and separate groups. (78)

If language is not natural but an alien system and if the artist is to some extent also an alien, then jokers, persuaders, and cross-cultural innovators are called for.

We can understand the deracinated situation of modern writers as an intensification of the situation of nineteenth-century English poets. George Bornstein has shown (in *Postromantic Consciousness*) that Pound to some extent identified with Byron, Shelley, Keats, and Browning as exiles (22–23). The situation of exile and linguistic entrepreneurship obviously sums up salient aspects of Pound's career—his generosity in maneuvering as an impresario of modernism, creating "imagism," cocreating *The Waste Land*, fostering publication and patronage for Joyce. Pound is at once a dealer and a persuader, an

---

to paint their own fantasies and to imagine both a new world and the corruption of an old. See, for example, Helsinger, *Ruskin and the Art of the Beholder*, not to mention the figuration of Italy in American novels from Hawthorne's *Marble Faun* to James's *Daisy Miller*.

interpreter and a cross-cultural innovator. But rather than using cross-cultural jokes to turn "political oppression to artistic advantage" and making up culture as he goes along, as Eagleton says Joyce does, Pound embraces the exotica of *The Cantos* in a progressively deracinated attempt to educe a system from a phalanx of particulars.[7] And Pound's serial deracination—from Philadelphia, to Italy, to London, to Paris, to Italy, to St. Elizabeth's, to Italy again—is matched only by the proliferation of his mythological, legal, economic, and monetary systems.

These systems projected onto particulars are claimed by the non-discursive structure of the poem to have emerged from the particulars. Order or law is, implicitly, inherent in particulars—at least it should be. Violence, to reiterate, lies in the difficulty of making such a claim against the evidence of the poem and the world. Palpable elysium, Pound wrote, is found in the halls of hell (81.535). Yet the poem elides the contradiction between this claim and its own advice that one might "learn of the green world what can be thy place / In scaled invention or true artistry" (535).

Pound's True Heritage: The Hero as Poet

The Cantos are built on the hope that disparate and isolated particulars, disparate and isolated words can be ordered in a fashion transcending the merely personal order of autobiography or elegy. They are built on the hope that this aesthetic order is founded in nature. Such aestheticism, as we have seen, is intimately connected to the possibilities of existential historicism as variously developed by Browning, Burckhardt, and Pater, but it goes beyond Pater's indirections to level an aesthetic critique at the very conditions that make aestheticism possible. In attempting to make "cosmos" from "chaos," Pound seeks not aestheticist appreciations but the yoking of power and beauty (as in *Jefferson and/or Mussolini*, for example). Pound's search for order and for epic coherence, moreover, makes historicist irony and patterning insufficient.

In his complex relation to and partial rejection of existential historicism, we can place Pound both in what Eagleton has characterized as the "left-aesthetic tradition" and in a right-wing appropriation of that tradition. Eagleton believes that

7. On Joyce, deracination, and made-up culture, see Eagleton, *Ideology of the Aesthetic*, 321.

the left-aesthetic tradition, from Schiller and Marx to Morris and Marcuse has much to be said for it: art as critique of alienation, as an exemplary realization of creative powers, as the ideal reconciliation of subject and object, universal and particular, freedom and necessity, theory and practice, individual and society. All of these notions could be equally deployed by the political right; but while the bourgeoisie is still in its progressive phase, this style of thinking comes through as a powerfully positive utopianism. From the end of the nineteenth century, however, this heritage begins to turn sour, and this is the moment of modernism. Modernism is one of the inheritors of the radical aestheticizing, but in the negative mode. (*Ideology of the Aesthetic*, 369)

In Pound's work we find both the powerful utopianism and the critique of alienation characteristic of the left-aesthetic tradition, and we find the deployment of these notions in the name of authoritarian order. Such possibilities were implicit in at least the English development of these positions from the beginning. Though the authoritarian possibilities of aestheticism were stoutly resisted by Morris, the aesthetic as critique of alienation presented its double face in the "Tory socialism" of Morris's predecessor Ruskin and still more obviously in the work of Ruskin's mentor, Thomas Carlyle.

Carlyle's historicism, as I have argued, gave way in the face of intractable social circumstance to a radical individualism deeply akin to Pound's; indeed Carlyle's end is remarkably similar to Pound's, so much so that a comparison of the two indicates the persistent tension between historicist detachment and utopian vision. Although there is no evidence that Pound was directly influenced by Carlyle's work, it is certain that the Carlylean streak was not to be missed in Ruskin's work as Pound read it and in the circles involving the Fabians and A. R. Orage, whom Pound encountered in London (see Coyle, " 'Profounder Didacticism' "). Considering the political aesthetic of Carlyle and Pound together allows us to see how both writers' lives and works were riven with similar contradictions and to appreciate how deeply Pound's dualisms were rooted in his social formation.

Carlyle's own invention of the term *cash nexus* and his analysis of deracination and alienation in "Signs of the Times," "Chartism," and other essays formed the outstanding critique of finance capital and consumption in his time. In Carlyle's discussion of the cash nexus and his emblematic uses of money, however, we have a foretaste of Pound's fixation on the monetary aspects of economics. Though Ruskin, Marx, and Morris followed much of Carlyle's argument, they focused primarily on production and work. Carlyle, for his part, exhorted his audiences to work; yet except for his criticism of the waste of the workhouse and his proposal to organize poor laborers on the model of a draft army, he did not often discuss work in detail. Instead he came increasingly to take the cash nexus as an emblem— not of the alienation of labor only—but of all social evils and hypocrisies. Pound ascribed a similar role to usury.

Like Pound, Carlyle lamented the corruption of speech or writing into cash and into an inflated currency not founded in nature. The relationships of word and thing or words and truth are corrupted as words themselves become part of the cash nexus. So in his criticism of British politics in the "Stump-Orators" essay, Carlyle exclaims,

> If speech is the bank-note for an inward capital of culture, of insight and noble human worth, then speech is precious, and the art of speech shall be honoured. But if there *is* no inward capital; if speech represent no real culture of the mind but an imaginary culture; no bullion, but the fatal and almost hopeless deficit of such? Alas, alas, said bank-note is then a *forged* one; passing freely current in the market; but bringing damages to the receiver, to the payer, and to all the world . . . eloquent talk, disunited from Nature; but . . . nature . . . will reject your forged note one day, with huge costs. (*Latter-Day Pamphlets*, in *Works*, 20:179)

Speech itself has become forgery, and the writer's task is to rescue it from "sham." Speech has become a free-floating signifier of status, wealth, "imaginary culture." Nature, Carlyle hopes and prophesies, will one day put things right; a possibly violent rectification will reunite word and thing. In a similar vein, Pound praises Valla's detection of the forgery of the donation of Constantine; he makes a slogan of right naming; and he castigates those who refuse to found credit on the abundance of nature. Usury is essentially a forgery and a lie; it is against nature.

More striking than connections of this kind—and there are many more—is the general pattern of Carlyle's and Pound's lives. Like Pound, Carlyle exploited and chafed against the role of the outsider. As a Scotsman and cultural critic he felt himself to be alienated from his culture even when he was being acclaimed as a prophet or sage and when wholeheartedly supporting Britain's imperial conquests. Pound for his part lived with a similar contradiction, though he was never so central a cultural figure as Carlyle. Both writers increasingly took on the role of prophet, seeking centrality even as they defined

the prophet as one without honor in his own country. The urgency of
the prophet's task and the frequent obligation of the prophet to separate the good from the evil are rooted for Carlyle and for Pound in
their youthful Calvinism—a belief system both men rejected even as
it shaped their intellectual lives.

As they aged, both Carlyle and Pound felt an increasing urgency of
social mission. What in Carlyle's early historicism was seriously play-
ful irony became a mordant series of ironic judgments coupled with
an ever greater admiration for authority; similarly for Pound the necessary ignorances and possibly ironic gaps of an existential historicist
understanding of history gave way to a growing compulsion to
wrench order from chaos and to blame chaos itself on scapegoats—
Jews, politicians, and financiers. The answer to chaos for both men
was not only a change in economic system but a proper restoration
of hierarchy and authority, founded in some less than clear fashion
on nature.

The "left-aestheticism" of Morris and, to an extent, Ruskin focused
on restoring aesthetic pleasure to production and work. Both Carlyle
and Pound shared—and for Carlyle's part helped found—this left-
aesthetic critique of production; yet both ended by aestheticizing order
itself and, consequently, by aestheticizing power. Thus Pound attempted to see Mussolini as a figure for the artist; and Carlyle could
imagine a society organized in a hierarchical harmony in which the
lower persons intuitively recognized the superiority of the higher.
When order and, hence, power were aestheticized and functioned
with their own self-grounded teleology the way "the beautiful" does,
disorder could be characterized in terms of ugliness, filth, and the
transgression of hierarchical relationships. So for Carlyle and for
Pound, scatology had a salient role. Both discussed social issues in
metaphors of filth, swamp, and disease. In "The New Downing
Street," for instance, Carlyle asked: "The Idle Workhouse, now about
to burst of overfilling, what is it but the scandalous poison-tank of
drainage from the universal Stygian quagmire of our affairs?" (*Latter-
Day Pamphlets*, in *Works*, 20:159).[8] This is not far from the Stygian quag-

---

8. Of course for Carlyle, these were issues in themselves—given the conditions of public
   health in England—even as the drainage of swamps was a public health and agricultural issue for Mussolini and for Pound. But both Carlyle and Pound rely on filth,
   disease, and the swamp as tropes for larger social conditions. The two most interesting studies of Carlyle's radicalism and of the political dimension of his changing
   career are Rosenberg, *Seventh Hero*; and Vanden Bossche, *Carlyle and the Search for
   Authority*.

mire of Pound's hell cantos and their later incarnations. And so for both men equally, the scatological lamentation works two ways: it may be used to criticize those who have created the swamp, and it may pollute those who speak it. Carlyle's notorious racism and defense of slavery and Pound's anti-Semitism arise in this ambiguous power of filth. Both men's racism and anti-Semitism are made possible by aestheticizing power and hierarchy.

For Carlyle and Pound, alienation and the cash nexus could only be combated by a heroic individualism. As in the "Tory" part of Ruskin's "Tory socialism," both Carlyle and Pound favored a paternalist ethos, but their paters were not as benevolent as Ruskin's model, self-sacrificing leaders. Rather, heroic individuals could be characterized as lawgivers, artist-makers, and scourges of a corrupt society. Only in the most fortunate circumstances (say, for Pound, America before the Civil War or Italy under Leopold) could the hero practice art and politics in a seamless unity. The unity Carlyle believed he found in the Middle Ages of *Past and Present*, Pound found in an idealized neo-Confucian reading of Chinese history and in the United States before the rise of finance capital on a large scale. The poet's real situation—the treacheries of historiography and of history itself—made such unity unlikely in either Carlyle's or Pound's own time. Indeed aestheticizing political order requires that such order be located in a time now gone and inaccessible or in a projected future.

Thus Carlyle could assert at once that history is the "true Epic poem" and that his own age was unpoetic; he could argue that no age is heroic to itself and that his countrymen must look to history for heroes, as their own time presented only sham heroes to view; that history itself represents a spiritual and natural order even though his own historical moment is one of sham order and sham speech for which nature will exact a heavy price. The true epic poem—or history—then can be written only when history cooperates. The disappointments of history, and the despair of a disappointed prophet, leave Carlyle in his old age first with memoir (in part restitution to Jane) and then with a depressed and despondent silence.

Pound, likewise, attempted to bring a cosmos from chaos, to write paradise when to *write* paradise was also to make it. For him, as much as for Carlyle, true history was the only possible epic. But for Pound, as for Carlyle, such history was far to seek. Pound too came to memoir, to the oblique self-reflection of the last cantos and fragments, and ultimately to despondent silence.

"Oh a poet's ending"

It was a silence befitting an unpoetic age, not a Carlylean or Poundian despondent silence, that Carlyle had urged on his younger friend Robert Browning. Though not he did not suggest that Browning "sulk and leave the world to novelists," as Pound later threatened to do, Carlyle did insist that history and topical prose were the preferred antidotes to an unpoetic age. Clinging to and struggling within his own existential historicist and limited claims for history, Browning did not take Carlyle's and Pound's more radical course; neither did he find it necessary, as Morris did, to move toward a socialist understanding of art. Browning persisted; championing indirection and working within the historicist constraints Carlyle rejected, he continued to question power and to seek, despite his historicist skepticism, for a usable faith. Browning's skepticism usually ensured him against the possibility of taking the hero as poet (or the poet as hero), possibilities he investigated early on in Sordello's dilemmas.

In his old age, with the luck of health, prosperity, and Britain's relative political stability in congruity with his own liberal ideology, Browning continued to write, to joke, to ironize, to proclaim his own rather unorthodox hope of heaven. Browning's beginning, though it was attentive to and critical of Victorian social conditions, was characterized by a general faith in democracy and a general distrust of despotism. His end was strikingly different from Carlyle's and Pound's; for he retained this distrust of absolutisms of all kinds. For Browning there was no despondent silence.

Browning's last book, *Asolando*, appeared on the day of his death. Its last long poem, "Reverie," questioned, one last time, the connections between love and power. Proclaiming that the role of faith is to imagine the possibility of a providential history, the poet concedes that knowledge itself reveals the "ever resistless fact" that power, good, and providence are irreconcilable on earth. Although he declares his faith that power and love (history and providence) will be united "yonder, worlds away" (line 218), Browning admits:

> Even as the world its life,
>   So I have lived my own—
> Power seen with Love at strife,
>   That sure, this dimly shown,
> —Good rare and evil rife.
>
>   (lines 171–75)

So situated, the poet does not unite diagnosis and pattern as Pound wished to do in his epic; rather, the poet can achieve diagnosis more readily than pattern. To write paradise is impossible; to imagine it is possible only when the paradise is projected "worlds away."

Meanwhile, the poet struggles with "knowledge" to construct a teleology without telos and poetic forms adequate to it. Epic and poetic heroism are seriously compromised. Of Sordello's art, all that remained was a snatch of song sung by a child at Goito; of *Sordello*, what remains most powerful is its examination of the obstacles to uniting poetry and power, social vision and the renovation of language.[9] At the last, in *Asolando*, Browning deferred telos to an unorthodox heaven of becoming. His was a heaven eminently suited to historicist incompletion and to Victorian liberal individualism. Its coherence could only be proved by the last experiment, death.

Unlike his poetic father's last volume, Pound's final cantos do not relinquish the desire to make coherence in the very bone shop of history. Neither chaos nor the need for order can be projected into another world. The poet's situation—historical, personal, and poetic—is altogether more stark. In Canto 116, Pound says that the young are still burdened with the records of history, with a tangle of laws, with a literature that heals nothing. The poem's effort, like Mussolini's effort as Pound saw it, is still "To make Cosmos— / To achieve the possible."

The poignancy of *The Cantos*, for readers who find poignancy in a poem so violent, is in their never giving up on their desire to make the world better, a desire Pound understood as the effort to "make Cosmos." Yet the very terms of the dream, the dream of benevolent and natural hierarchy in a modern industrial world, contained its own undoing. The poet was left, in the words of the last fragments, with a question: "Where is what I loved?" This question surely answers the poem's earlier one, "And as to why they go wrong, / thinking of rightness" (116.811).

Where is what I loved? In great measure it is violently destroyed in the contradictions of its own dreaming; if anything is left, it is in the valediction to Olga Rudge now placed at the end of the Faber edition of *The Cantos*. But as to "why they go wrong," the fragments answer:

9. Even at the end of his life Browning persisted in diagnosing love and power; in "Imperante Augusto Natus Est—" and "Development" (published in *Asolando*) he subjects epic seriousness to historical or affectionate ironies.

That I lost my center
                    fighting the world.
The dreams clash
                    and are shattered—
and that I tried to make a paradiso
                                        terrestre.
              (Notes for Canto 117 et. seq., 816).

Ironically, the clashing dreams, the oscillations and contradictions of *The Cantos* come back, in Canto 116, to late-nineteenth-century irony, the ironies *The Cantos* have gone so far to escape. Pound returned, in part and in fragments, to the mental landscape of Jules Laforgue, to the "deeps in him," and to the terrible ironies of a paradiso terrestre that could only be "a nice quiet paradise / over the shambles."

Appendix

The following passages of prose and verse are the text of a seven-page typescript, with pencil emendations found in the folder of Pound's college verse at the Beinecke Rare Book and Manuscript Library at Yale University. I have regularized spelling, punctuation, and paragraphing, except where such emendations would not reflect the sense or tone of the original. Pound's title appears after a prose exordium and applies most directly to the dramatic monologue that follows it. The monologue in turn is followed by a prose passage that gradually modulates toward a poetic line and back to ordinary prose. I have attempted to replicate these shifts.

Oh yes, I have studied Browning, but one does not imitate by using a sonnet of Dantesque form. I had been reading Shelley within the week, but so far as I know Shelley has written no poem for painting. Though you may find my opening line form at the beginning of "Queen Mab."

Nor do I remember a single line for the masters (of Italy or elsewhere). The cor cordium was attuned to the winds and the sunlight, and his [Shelley's] kin art was music, as Browning's is that of the brush.

C'est la vie.

In Praise of the Masters

No I don't cotton to your squirks and spirals.
Beauty be dagged sir. My work-(life).
My own mug sir, so please you, yes sir,
three on one wall here. Vain?

Bless your simplicity, were I a vain man
would I tell all time coming that my nose was
blunt as a sack stein? Vain sir, God please you,
is this a phiz o large vanity?
But tis truth sir. So please you, tis truth sir.
 Yes I know your thin Botticellis, your vainly cute
   sunspangles
and tumble down roses. Thin as a web sir.
 But we're a cold land sir, none o that ruction.

Saskia a beauty? Oh that one!
Well, she passes, passes sir, passes.
 But here with the flower—both o my moonshine—
here she is really. She, me and the beaker,
gaydogs together. Kermess? No, bless you,
just our day's toggery, any old day sir.
Life's no fine fluffery, wish-waddled delicacy.
Give me a wench as can go with her hearth-mate
up, down and long ways, no fear o her petticoats.

This like Mona Lisa? Drat your Elizas.
 I knew not who tis like, but she
   was such or some suchly. And caught me out prettily—
a clipping good armful Sasky old girl is.

 But beauty? What in hell's eggs are you
grumbling and mumbling o beauty for?
I paint what I see sir. Damme. Lights and no lights,
folk as they come to me. Your spindle shanked
goddesses, where do you find em?
I see no such a running o our ways.

Paint what I see sir. Tain't such as'll
be pleasin to your finicky lordship. Small beans to me sir.
No stick in my craw, take what I find.
But tis truth sir.
Egad tis the truth sir. An't sticks.

                    Rembrandt.
Being a blunt man, he hath small care o metrics and luted
   enwebments.

No, we artists are a silent crew
   save in our words, sir.
                    Save in our words.

 I know this note is going to be rather preposterous, but I have not taken
my go to . . . slips, and hacked a small magazine and had my best stuff con-

tinually fired for nothing. Neither have I had any shreds of genius and temperament that I may possess whanged black and blue in order that I may come whining or trying to sell a "second rate thing on a hard luck story."

I know have hit a real thing, and all I ask is that you really think about the stuff before you call the ambulance.

That I being a nameless noise should demand ten illustrations for two pages of verse is "preposterous"?

But ten old masters just for once would do the magazine no harm and might make a star make-up. Now unless you either knew Rembrandt and Raphael and Leonardo and Fra Angelico or unless you have patience to study the prints enclosed and then read the verses and then go back to the prints, you may as well send the thing back at once.

As for the old masters, I am no crank on antiquities, but I continually hear the philistine hiccuping, "What is there in the old masters," and I continually hear the modern disciple of Monet sneer that the old fellows are very much overestimated. And on the whole a little interpretation can do very little harm. I am sorry I have no decent copy of "The Annunciation" at hand. (I suppose Gowans and Gray might lend you the plates of most of the pictures. They ought to be full page.) I think the thing is of enough weight to ask at least consideration.

I know poetry is used to fill in page tails where the prose don't run, but I am not calling the public nor the editorial staff together that they may witness my skill in versification (you are perfectly welcome to continue to fire my sonnets till crack of doom). I know quite a little about fancy metric also, but that is not the matter under the hammer.

Most anyone who knows Rembrandt at all will be able to fathom the first of these poems. Wherein he speaketh. The second is a deeper thing.

I have read my Rembrandt, I have pondered on the Mona Lisa as men have and will till canvas be a name and paint is forgotten. But most of all "The Annunciation" had come as a new thing to me. (Also I have watched these old masters make pale some very beautiful modern things. Notably "Morphine" by Matignon and a Carrière. Both of which are wonderfully beautiful. Had I been thinking Velasquez I should have written, "Art's mother, Skill.")

I had said Rembrandt is the Shaxpeare of paint. But the Mona Lisa tainted the Third of Saskia; twas as if one should compare Anne Hathaway and Beatrice, the earthly Beatrice. And then faint and above them all wonderfully like one that should be nameless, Angelico's maiden.

> And as a faint wind in the darkness.
> Hail. Thou art highly favoured.
>
> (And the angel, seeing that she trembled,
> "Ne tiemas!")
>
> And later if you shut your eyes, or gaze into the hollow of
> heaven where the stars are dim, you may hear
> no ponderous organing or swell of chorus, but that faint

maid-whisper, slowly, slowly gaining in its boldness.
> Ecce ancilla domine.

And then,
> Magnificat anima mea.

My spirit hath rejoiced, deo salvatore meo
> redentore.

For he hath regarded the low estate of his hand-maiden,

> he hath put down the mighty from their seats

and
> exalted them of low degree

hath

And if after these things you burst not into PAEAN for the wonder that men have done such things, such things as these old paintings, mortescent as their canvases and eternal, then I know you not.

Twas after I had seen these things and had gone into the night and come back to Jeanne of Aragon, done of Raphael, that painter whose pictures are as lutany and sound of viol played afar off, that thinking on the marvel how not one great painter had been sent to us. . . . But so many that I had been rapt into ecstasy by four in scarce so many hours.

Oh look, but look at the ten old wonders that I send you here. (I had forgotten Titian, and Blake and Velasquez. Murillo I had lost since boyhood. Van Dyke as faded in Rembrandt, and Van Dyke I love. Michelangelo, I thought not of. And Guido Reni I remember only now because a corner of St. Michael is before me.)

Turner and Whistler and the wizards of color and all the moderns were absent in my vision. Cimabue, Jordaens, the host we half know. Botticelli, Ribera—oh, I had not counted the multitude.

Only the four great lights gleamed out, and of their light I made it.

Inarticulate, mayhap, but oh I would have you understand it. I speak not for myself. There is too much, too much in the old mystery that you should pass it hastily, that you should glance and turn aside because its meaning is not of veneer and gloss that you may have in the twinkling.

That I send you only ten of the signets is my weakness, but oh, you have memories. You must have understood and borne with you some of the spell and lure that dwelleth in the shadows of their limning. And the lost lyrics of their tone, the strange faint shades that dwelt there ere time half hid them in forgetfulness. And left their whispers for only him that will watch the lights change upon their surfaces till the guards of the Prado and the Louvre know him. And come gently at the closing time, "Señor 'va 'sta tarde" and "Il faut, M'sieu. . . ."

Bibliography

Abrams, M. H. *The Mirror and the Lamp*. New York: Oxford University Press, 1953.

Arendt, Hannah. Introduction to *Illuminations*, by Walter Benjamin. Translated by Harry Zohn. New York: Schocken, 1969.

Arnold, Matthew. *The Letters of Matthew Arnold to Arthur Hugh Clough*. Edited by Howard Foster Lowry. London: Oxford University Press, 1932.

Bacigalupo, Massimo. "Ezra Pound's Cantos 72 and 73: An Annotated Translation." *Paideuma* 20 (1991): 9–41.

———. *The Formed Trace: The Later Poetry of Ezra Pound*. New York: Columbia University Press, 1980.

Baudelaire, Charles. *The Painter of Modern Life and Other Essays*. Translated and edited by Jonathan Mayne. Greenwich, Conn.: Phaidon, 1964.

———. *The Parisian Prowler*. Translated by Edward K. Kaplan. Athens: University of Georgia Press, 1989.

Beach, Christopher. *ABC of Influence: Ezra Pound and the Remaking of American Poetic Tradition*. Berkeley and Los Angeles: University of California Press, 1992.

———. "Ezra Pound and Harold Bloom: Influences, Canons, Traditions and the Making of Modern Poetry." *ELH* 56 (1989): 463–83.

Beale, Walter. *A Pragmatic Theory of Rhetoric*. Carbondale: Southern Illinois University Press, 1987.

Bell, Ian F. A. *Ezra Pound: Tactics for Reading*. London: Vision, 1982.

Bellamy, Elizabeth J. *Translations of Power: Narcissism and the Unconscious in Epic History*. Ithaca: Cornell University Press, 1992.

Benjamin, Walter. *Illuminations*. Edited by Hannah Arendt. Translated by Harry Zohn. New York: Schocken, 1969.

Bernstein, Michael André. *The Tale of the Tribe: Ezra Pound and the Modern Verse Epic*. Princeton: Princeton University Press, 1980.

Birnbaum, Lucia Chiavola. *Liberazione della Donna: Feminism in Italy*. Middletown, Conn.: Wesleyan University Press, 1986.

Bloom, Harold. *The Anxiety of Influence: A Theory of Poetry*. New York: Oxford University Press, 1973.

Boodberg, Peter A. " 'Ideography' or Iconolatry." In *Selected Works of Peter A. Boodberg*, compiled by Alvin P. Cohen. Berkeley and Los Angeles: University of California Press, 1979. Reprinted from *T'oung Pao* 35 (1940): 266–88.

Bornstein, George. *Poetic Remaking: The Art of Browning, Yeats, and Pound.* University Park: Pennsylvania State University Press, 1988.

——. *The Postromantic Consciousness of Ezra Pound.* Victoria, B.C., Canada: University of Victoria, English Literary Studies, 1977.

——. " 'What Porridge Had John Keats?': Pound's 'L'Art' and Browning's 'Popularity.' " *Paideuma* 10 (1981): 303–6.

——, ed. *Ezra Pound among the Poets.* Chicago: University of Chicago Press, 1985.

Bridenthal, Renate, Atina Grossmann, and Marion Kaplan. *When Biology Became Destiny: Women in Weimar and Nazi Germany.* New York: Monthly Review Press, 1984.

Browning, Robert. *The Poems of Robert Browning.* 2 vols. Edited by John Pettigrew and Thomas J. Collins. New Haven: Yale University Press, 1981.

——. *The Ring and the Book.* Edited by Richard D. Altick. New Haven: Yale University Press, 1981.

Burckhardt, Jacob. *The Civilization of the Renaissance in Italy.* 2 vols. Edited by S. G. C. Middlemore. Translated by Ludwig Geiger and Walter Gotz. New York: Harper and Row, 1958.

——. *Force and Freedom: Reflections on History.* Edited by James Hastings Nichols. New York: Pantheon, 1943.

Burke, Kenneth. *A Grammar of Motives.* New York: Prentice-Hall, 1945.

Bush, Ronald. *The Genesis of Ezra Pound's Cantos.* Princeton: Princeton University Press, 1976.

Byron, George Gordon, Lord. *Don Juan.* Edited by Leslie A. Marchand. Boston: Houghton Mifflin, 1958.

Carlyle, Thomas. *Letters of Thomas Carlyle to John Stuart Mill, John Sterling, and Robert Browning.* Edited by Alexander Carlyle. 1923. Reprint, New York: Haskell House, 1970.

——. *The Works of Thomas Carlyle.* Centenary Ed. Edited by H. D. Traill. 30 vols. London: Chapman and Hall, 1896–99.

Carlyle, Thomas, and John Ruskin. *The Correspondence of Thomas Carlyle and John Ruskin.* Edited by George Allan Cate. Stanford: Stanford University Press, 1982.

Carpenter, Humphrey. *A Serious Character: The Life of Ezra Pound.* Boston: Houghton Mifflin, 1988.

Casillo, Robert. *The Genealogy of Demons: Anti-Semitism, Fascism, and the Myths of Ezra Pound.* Evanston: Northwestern University Press, 1988.

——. "The Italian Renaissance: Pound's Problematic Debt to Burckhardt." *Mosaic,* 22 (1989): 13–29.

——. "The Meaning of Venetian History in Ruskin and Pound." *University of Toronto Quarterly* 55 (1986): 235–60.

Chace, William M. *The Political Identities of Ezra Pound and T. S. Eliot.* Stanford: Stanford University Press, 1973.

Chai, Leon. *Aestheticism.* New York: Columbia University Press, 1990.

Christ, Carol. *Victorian and Modern Poetics.* Chicago: University of Chicago Press, 1984.

Clark, Donald Lemen. "Imitation: Theory and Practice in Roman Rhetoric." *Quarterly Journal of Speech* 37 (1951): 11–22.

Clément, Catherine. *The Lives and Legends of Jacques Lacan.* Translated by Arthur Goldhammer. New York: Columbia University Press, 1983.

Corbett, Edward P. J. "The Theory and Practice of Imitation in Classical Rhetoric." *College Communication and Composition* 22 (1971): 243–50.

Coyle, Michael. " 'A Profounder Didactism': Ruskin, Orage, and Pound's Reception of Social Credit." *Paideuma* 17 (1988): 7–28.

Dasenbrock, Reed Way. *Imitating the Italians: Wyatt, Spenser, Synge, Pound, Joyce.* Baltimore: Johns Hopkins University Press, 1991.

De Grazia, Victoria. *The Culture of Consent: Mass Organization of Leisure in Fascist Italy.* Cambridge: Cambridge University Press, 1981.

De Man, Paul. *Allegories of Reading.* New Haven: Yale University Press, 1979.

——. *Blindness and Insight: Essays in the Rhetoric of Contemporary Criticism.* 2d rev. ed. Minneapolis: University of Minnesota Press, 1983.

Desan, Philippe, Priscilla Parkhurst Ferguson, and Wendy Griswold, eds. *Literature and Social Practice.* Chicago: University of Chicago Press, 1989.

Dilthey, Wilhelm. *Pattern and Meaning in History: Thoughts on History and Society.* Edited by H. P. Rickman. New York: Harper, 1962.

Donner, Henry Wolfgang, ed. *The Browning Box: Or the Life and Work of Thomas Lovell Beddoes as Reflected in Letters.* London: Oxford University Press, 1935.

Dowling, Linda. *Aestheticism and Decadence: A Selective Annotated Bibliography.* New York: Garland, 1978.

——. *Language and Decadence in the Victorian Fin de Siècle.* Princeton: Princeton University Press, 1986.

Durant, Alan. "The Language of History in *The Cantos.*" In *Ezra Pound and History,* edited by Marianne Korn. Orono, Maine: National Poetry Foundation, 1985.

Eagleton, Terry. *Criticism and Ideology: A Study in Marxist Literary Theory.* London: New Left Books, 1976.

——. *The Ideology of the Aesthetic.* Cambridge: Blackwell, 1990.

Eliot, T. S. "Tradition and the Individual Talent." In *Selected Essays, 1917–1932.* New York: Harcourt, Brace, 1932.

Espey, John. *Ezra Pound's "Mauberley": A Study in Composition.* Berkeley and Los Angeles: University of California Press, 1974.

Fang, Achilles. "Fenollosa and Pound." *Harvard Journal of Asian Studies* 20 (1957): 213–38.

Faulkner, Peter. "Pound and the Pre-Raphaelites." *Paideuma* 13 (1984): 229–44.

Fenollosa, Ernest. "Chinese Written Character as a Medium for Poetry." In *Instigations of Ezra Pound.* New York: Boni and Liveright, 1920.

Ford, Ford Madox [Ford Hermann Hueffer]. *Collected Poems.* New York: Oxford University Press, 1936.

——. *Critical Writings of Ford Madox Ford.* Edited by Frank MacShane. Lincoln: University of Nebraska Press, 1964.

——. *The March of Literature.* New York: Dial, 1938.

——. *Thus to Revisit.* New York: Dutton, 1921.

——. *Women and Men.* Paris: Three Mountains, 1923.

Froula, Christine. "Browning's *Sordello* and the Parables of Modernist Poetics." *ELH* 52 (1985): 956–92.

Gallup, Donald. *Ezra Pound: A Bibliography.* Charlottesville: University Press of Virginia, for the Bibliographical Society of the University of Virginia and St. Paul's Bibliographies, 1983.

Gibson, Mary Ellis. *History and the Prism of Art: Browning's Poetic Experiments*. Columbus: Ohio State University Press, 1987.
——, ed. *Critical Essays on Robert Browning*. New York: G. K. Hall, 1992.
Girard, René. *The Scapegoat*. Translated by Yvonne Freccero. Baltimore: Johns Hopkins University Press, 1986.
Gordon, David. "Pound's Chinese: A Dead Language?" *Paideuma* 18 (1989): 197–201.
Gourmont, Remy de. *The Natural Philosophy of Love*. Translated with a postscript by Ezra Pound. New York: Boni and Liveright, 1922.
Gregor, A. James. *Italian Fascism and Developmental Dictatorship*. Princeton: Princeton University Press, 1979.
Hall, Donald. *Remembering Poets: Reminiscences and Opinions*. New York: Harper and Row, 1979.
Harris, Kenneth Marc. *Carlyle and Emerson: Their Long Debate*. Cambridge: Harvard University Press, 1978.
Helsinger, Elizabeth. *Ruskin and the Art of the Beholder*. Cambridge: Harvard University Press, 1982.
Hempel, Carl G. *Aspects of Scientific Explanation*. New York: Free Press, 1965.
Irigaray, Luce. *This Sex Which Is Not One*. Translated by Catherine Porter with Carolyn Burke. Ithaca: Cornell University Press, 1985.
Isaak, Jo-Anna. "The Revolution of a Poetics?" In *Modernism: Challenges and Perspectives*, edited by Monique Chefdor, Ricardo Quinones, and Albert Wachtel. Champaign: University of Illinois Press, 1986.
Jakobson, Roman. *Essais de linguistique generale*. Paris: Minuit, 1963.
——. *Main Trends in the Science of Language*. New York: Harper and Row, 1974.
——. *On Language*. Edited by Linda R. Waugh and Monique Monville-Burston. Cambridge: Harvard University Press, 1990.
——. *Studies on Child Language and Aphasia*. The Hague: Mouton, 1971.
——. "Two Aspects of Language and Two Types of Aphasic Disturbances." In *Language in Literature*, edited by Krystyna Pomorska and Stephen Rudy. Cambridge: Harvard University Press, Belknap, 1987.
Jakobson, Roman, C. Gunnar, M. Fant, and Morris Halle. *Preliminaries to Speech Analysis*. Cambridge: M.I.T. Press, 1961.
Jakobson, Roman, and Morris Halle. *Fundamentals of Language*. Gravenhague: Mouton, 1956.
James, Henry. *Notes on Novelists*. 1914. Reprint, New York: Biblo and Tannen, 1969.
Jameson, Fredric. *Fables of Aggression: Wyndham Lewis, the Modernist as Fascist*. Berkeley and Los Angeles: University of California Press, 1979.
——. "Marxism and Historicism." In *The Ideologies of Theory: Essays 1971–1986*. Vol. 2. Minneapolis: University of Minnesota Press, 1988.
Jullian, Philippe. *Dreamers of Decadence: Symbolist Painters of the 1890s*. Translated by Robert Baldick. New York: Praeger, 1971.
Kazin, Alfred. "Language vs. History: Ezra Pound's Search for Authority in America." In *The Problem of Authority in America*, edited by John P. Diggins and Mark E. Kain. Philadelphia: Temple University Press, 1981.
Kellner, Hans. *Language and Historical Representation: Getting the Story Crooked*. Madison: University of Wisconsin Press, 1989.
Kenner, Hugh. *The Poetry of Ezra Pound*. New York: Kraus Reprint, 1968.

——. *The Pound Era*. Berkeley and Los Angeles: University of California Press, 1971.

Koestenbaum, Wayne. "*The Waste Land*: T. S. Eliot's and Ezra Pound's Collaboration on Hysteria." *Twentieth Century Literature* 34 (1988): 113–39.

Korn, Marianne. "Truth Near Perigord." *Paideuma* 10 (1981): 571–79.

——, ed. *Ezra Pound and History*. Orono, Maine: National Poetry Foundation, 1985.

Krieger, Leonard. *Ranke: The Meaning of History*. Chicago: University of Chicago Press, 1977.

Lacan, Jacques. *Feminine Sexuality: Jacques Lacan and the École Freudienne*. Edited by Juliet Mitchell and Jacqueline Rose. Translated by Jacqueline Rose. New York: Norton, 1982.

Lakoff, George. *Women, Fire, and Dangerous Things: What Categories Reveal about the Mind*. Chicago: University of Chicago Press, 1987.

Lakoff, George, and Mark Johnson. *Metaphors We Live By*. Chicago: University of Chicago Press, 1980.

Lanham, Richard A. *A Handlist of Rhetorical Terms*. Berkeley and Los Angeles: University of California Press, 1968.

Lauber, John. "Pound's *Cantos*: A Fascist Epic." *Journal of American Studies* 12 (1978): 3–21.

Le Goff, Jacques. *Your Money or Your Life: Economy and Religion in the Middle Ages*. Translated by Patricia Ranum. New York: Zone Books, 1988.

Lipking, Lawrence. *The Life of the Poet: Beginning and Ending Poetic Careers*. Chicago: University of Chicago Press, 1981.

Litz, A. Walton. *Eliot in His Time: Essays on the Occasion of the Fiftieth Anniversary of "The Waste Land."* Princeton: Princeton University Press, 1973.

Lodge, David. *Language of Fiction: Essays in Criticism and Verbal Analysis of the English Novel*. London: Routledge and Kegan Paul, 1966.

——. *The Modes of Modern Writing: Metaphor, Metonymy, and the Typology of Modern Literature*. Ithaca: Cornell University Press, 1977.

Longenbach, James. "Ezra Pound's *Canzoni*: Toward a Poem Including History." *Paideuma* 13 (1984): 389–405.

——. *Modernist Poetics of History: Pound, Eliot, and the Sense of the Past*. Princeton: Princeton University Press, 1987.

——. *Stone Cottage: Pound, Yeats, and Modernism*. New York: Oxford University Press, 1988.

McDonald, Gail. *Learning to Be Modern: Pound, Eliot, and the American University*. Oxford: Oxford University Press, Clarendon, 1993.

McGann, Jerome J. "The *Cantos* of Ezra Pound, the Truth in Contradiction." *Critical Inquiry* 15 (1988): 1–23.

——. *The Romantic Ideology: A Critical Investigation*. Chicago: University of Chicago Press, 1983.

——. *The Textual Condition*. Princeton: Princeton University Press, 1991.

——. *Towards a Literature of Knowledge*. Chicago: University of Chicago Press, 1983.

Makkreel, Rudolf A. *Dilthey: Philosopher of the Human Sciences*. Princeton: Princeton University Press, 1975.

Mandelbaum, Maurice. *The Anatomy of Historical Knowledge*. Baltimore: Johns Hopkins University Press, 1977.

Marcus, Penelope, ed. *Burne-Jones: The Paintings, Graphic and Decorative Work of Sir Edward Burne-Jones, 1833–1898*. London: Arts Council of Great Britain, 1975.

Martz, Louis. Introduction to *The Collected Early Poems of Ezra Pound*. New York: New Directions, 1982.

Michelet, Jules. *History of the French Revolution*. Translated by Charles Cooks. Chicago: University of Chicago Press, 1967.

Miller, J. Hillis. *The Disappearance of God: Five Nineteenth-Century Writers*. Cambridge: Harvard University Press, Belknap, 1963.

Moers, Ellen. *The Dandy: Brummel to Beerbohm*. Lincoln: University of Nebraska Press, 1978.

Nagy, Niclas Christoph de. *The Poetry of Ezra Pound: The Pre-Imagist Stage*. Bern: Francke, 1960.

Nänny, Max. "Context, Contiguity, and Contact in Ezra Pound's *Personae*." *ELH* 47 (1980): 368–98.

———. "More Menippius than Calliope: A Reply." *Paideuma* 13 (1984): 263–68.

Nietzsche, Friedrich. *The Use and Abuse of History*. Translated by Adrian Collins. New York: Bobbs-Merrill, 1957.

North, Michael. *The Political Aesthetic of Yeats, Eliot, and Pound*. New York: Cambridge University Press, 1991.

Parker, Andrew. "Ezra Pound and the 'Economy' of Anti-Semitism." *Boundary* 9 (1982–83): 103–28.

Pater, Walter. *Greek Studies*. 1895. Reprint, New York: Macmillan, 1908.

———. *Plato and Platonism*. 1893. Reprint, London: Macmillan, 1910.

———. *The Renaissance*. Edited by Donald H. Hill. Berkeley and Los Angeles: University of California Press, 1980.

Perl, Jeffrey M. *The Tradition of Return: The Implicit History of Modern Literature*. Princeton: Princeton University Press, 1984.

Pound, Ezra. *ABC of Reading*. New York: New Directions, 1960.

———. "Canto 72." Edited by James Laughlin. *Paris Review* 35 (1993): 308–17.

———. *The Cantos of Ezra Pound*. New York: New Directions, 1991.

———. *Collected Early Poems of Ezra Pound*. Edited by Michael John King. New York: New Directions, 1976.

———. *Ezra Pound and Japan: Letters and Essays*. Edited by Sanehide Hodama. Redding Ridge, Conn.: Black Swan, 1987.

———. *"Ezra Pound Speaking": Radio Speeches of World War II*. Edited by Leonard W. Doob. Westport, Conn.: Greenwood, 1978.

———. *Ezra Pound's Poetry and Prose Contributions to Periodicals*. 10 vols. Edited by Lea Baechler, A. Walton Litz, and James Longenbach. New York: Garland, 1991.

———. *Gaudier-Brzeska: A Memoir*. New York: New Directions, 1961.

———. *Guide to Kulchur*. New York: New Directions, 1952.

———. *Instigations of Ezra Pound, Together with an Essay on the Chinese Written Character by Ernest Fenollosa*. New York: Boni and Liveright, 1920.

———. *Jefferson and/or Mussolini*. New York: New Directions, 1936.

———. *Literary Essays of Ezra Pound*. New York: New Directions, 1954.

———. Manuscript materials in the Pound archive, Beinecke Rare Book and Manuscript Library, Yale University and in the Poetry Magazine Collection, University of Chicago.

———. *Pavannes and Divagations*. New York: New Directions, 1975.

———. *Personae: The Shorter Poems of Ezra Pound*. Rev. ed. Edited by Lea Baechler and A. Walton Litz. New York: New Directions, 1990.

——. *Pound/Ford: The Story of a Literary Friendship.* Edited by Brita Lindberg-Seyersted. New York: New Directions, 1982.

——. *Pound/Joyce: The Letters of Ezra Pound to James Joyce.* Edited by Forrest Read. New York: New Directions, 1967.

——. *Pound/Lewis: The Letters of Ezra Pound and Wyndham Lewis. The Correspondence of Ezra Pound.* Edited by Timothy Materer. New York: New Directions, 1985.

——. *Selected Letters of Ezra Pound, 1907–1941.* Edited by D. D. Paige. New York: New Directions, 1971.

——. *Selected Prose, 1909–1965.* Edited by William Cookson. New York: New Directions, 1973.

——. *The Spirit of Romance.* New York: New Directions, 1968.

——. *Translations.* New York: New Directions, 1964.

Ezra Pound and Dorothy Shakespear: Their Letters 1909–1914. Edited by Omar Pound and A. Walton Litz. New York: New Directions, 1984.

Pratt, Mary Louise. *Toward a Speech Act Theory of Literary Discourse.* Bloomington: Indiana University Press, 1980.

Quint, David. "Epic and Empire." *Comparative Literature* 41 (1989): 1–32.

Rabaté, Jean-Michel. *Language, Sexuality, and Ideology in Ezra Pound's Cantos.* Albany: State University of New York Press, 1986.

Rainey, Lawrence. *Ezra Pound and the Monument of Culture: Text, History, and the Malatesta Cantos.* Chicago: University of Chicago Press, 1991.

Redman, Tim. *Ezra Pound and Italian Fascism.* Cambridge: Cambridge University Press, 1991.

Ricoeur, Paul. *The Rule of Metaphor: Multi-Disciplinary Studies of the Creation of Meaning in Language.* Translated by Robert Czerny et al. Toronto: University of Toronto Press, 1981.

Riede, David. "Painting, 1859–1882." In *Dante Gabriel Rossetti and the Limits of Victorian Vision.* Ithaca: Cornell University Press, 1983.

Rose, Jacqueline. Introduction to *Feminine Sexuality: Jacques Lacan and the École Freudienne.* New York: Norton, 1982.

Rosenberg, Philip. *The Seventh Hero: Thomas Carlyle and the Theory of Radical Activism.* Cambridge: Harvard University Press, 1974.

Rossetti, Christina. *The Complete Poems of Christina Rossetti.* 3 vols. Edited by R. W. Crump. Baton Rouge: Louisiana State University Press, 1979.

Ruskin, John. *The Works of John Ruskin.* Edited by E. T. Cook and Alexander Wedderburn. Library ed. 39 vols. London: George Allen, 1903–1912.

Sanders, George. "The Carlyle-Browning Correspondence and Relationship: I and II." *Bulletin of the John Rylands Library* 57 (1975): 213–46.

Schneidau, Herbert N. *Ezra Pound: The Image and the Real.* Baton Rouge: Louisiana State University Press, 1969.

——. "Wisdom Past Metaphor: Another View of Pound, Fenollosa, and Objective Verse." *Paideuma* 5 (1976): 15–29.

Shaffer, Elinor S. *"Kubla Khan" and "The Fall of Jerusalem": The Mythological School in Biblical Criticism and Secular Literature, 1770–1880.* London: Cambridge University Press, 1975.

Showalter, Elaine. *Sexual Anarchy: Gender and Culture at the Fin de Siècle.* New York: Viking, 1990.

Sicari, Stephen. *Pound's Epic Ambition: Dante and the Modern World.* Albany: State University of New York Press, 1991.

——. "Reading Pound's Politics: Ulysses as Fascist Hero." *Paideuma* 17 (1988): 145–68.

Slatin, Miles. "A History of Cantos I-XVI, 1915–1925." *American Literature* 35 (1963–64): 183–95.

Smith, P. H., and A. E. Durant. "Pound's Metonymy: Revisiting Canto 47." *Paideuma* 8 (1979): 327–33.

Smith, Stan. "Neither Calliope nor Apollo: Pound's Propertius and the Refusal of Epic." *English* 34 (1985): 212–31.

Sonstroem, David. *Rossetti and the Fair Lady*. Middletown, Conn.: Wesleyan University Press, 1970.

Stern, Fritz, ed. *The Varieties of History from Voltaire to the Present*. New York: Meridian, 1956.

Surette, Leon. "Ezra Pound and British Radicalism." *English Studies in Canada* 9 (1983): 435–51.

Surtees, Virginia. *The Paintings and Drawings of Dante Gabriel Rossetti*. Oxford: Oxford University Press, Clarendon, 1971.

Swansea, Charleen Whisnant. Charleen Whisnant Swansea Papers, #4027, Ezra Pound Sub-group. In the Southern Historical Collection, Wilson Library of the University of North Carolina at Chapel Hill.

Swinburne, Algernon Charles. "The Chaotic School." In *New Writings by Swinburne*, edited by Cecil Y. Lang. Syracuse: Syracuse University Press, 1964.

Taylor, Christiana J. *Futurism: Politics, Painting, and Performance*. Ann Arbor: University Microfilms International, UMI Research Press, 1979.

Terrell, Carroll F. *A Companion to the Cantos of Ezra Pound*. 2 vols. Berkeley and Los Angeles: University of California Press, 1980.

Tisdall, Caroline, and Angelo Bozzola. *Futurism*. London: Thames and Hudson, 1977.

Tucker, Herbert F. *Tennyson and the Doom of Romanticism*. Cambridge: Harvard University Press, 1988.

Turner, Mark. *Death Is the Mother of Beauty: Mind, Metaphor, Criticism*. Chicago: University of Chicago Press, 1987.

Vanden Bossche, Chris R. *Carlyle and the Search for Authority*. Columbus: Ohio State University Press, 1991.

White, Hayden. *Metahistory: The Historical Imagination in Nineteenth-Century Europe*. Baltimore: Johns Hopkins University Press, 1973.

——. *Tropics of Discourse*. Baltimore: Johns Hopkins University Press, 1978.

Wilhelm, James J. *Dante and Pound: The Epic of Judgement*. Orono: University of Maine Press, 1974.

——. *Ezra Pound in London and Paris, 1908–1925*. University Park: Pennsylvania State University Press, 1990.

Williams, Carolyn. *Transfigured World: Walter Pater's Aesthetic Historicism*. Ithaca: Cornell University Press, 1989.

Williams, Raymond. *Marxism and Literature*. Oxford: Oxford University Press, 1977.

——. *The Politics of Modernism: Against the New Conformists*. Edited by Tony Pinkney. London: Verso, 1989.

——. *Resources of Hope: Culture, Democracy, Socialism*. Edited by Robin Gable. London: Verso, 1989.

Williams, William Carlos. *Paterson*. New York: New Directions, 1992.

Witemeyer, Hugh. " 'Of Kings' Treasuries': Pound's Allusion to Ruskin in *Hugh Selwyn Mauberley.*" *Paideuma* 18 (1986): 24–31.
———. *The Poetry of Ezra Pound: Forms and Renewal, 1908–1920.* Berkeley and Los Angeles: University of California Press, 1969.
Woolf, Virginia. *Mrs. Dalloway.* New York: Harcourt, Brace, 1925.
Yeats, William Butler. *Collected Poems.* New York: Macmillan, 1956.
———. Introduction to *Oxford Book of Modern Verse, 1892–1935.* New York: Oxford University Press, 1936.

Index